THE OAKWOOD PRESS

BOGIE CARRI.

OF THE

LONDON, BRIGHTON

&

SOUTH COAST RAILWAY

by
David Gould

With Drawings by P.J. Newbury

THE OAKWOOD PRESS

© Oakwood Press and David Gould 1995

British Library Cataloguing-in-Publication Data
A record for this book is available from the British Library
ISBN 0 85361 470 9

Typeset by Oakwood Graphics.
Printed by Alpha Print (Oxford) Ltd, Witney, Oxon

Front Cover Top: Seven-coach bogie block set built by Birmingham Railway Carriage and Wagon Co. in 1901, posed when new with class 'E4' 0-6-2 tank locomotive No. 514 Barcombe. Third Brake No. 1303 behind engine. *Official photo*

Front Cover Bottom: Bogie on one of the 'Balloon' trailer Third Brakes at Cranleigh, June 1938. *E.R. Lacey*

Rear Cover: Stroudley six-compartment bogie First No. 74 of 1889, here shown in about 1905 at Brighton with all the doors open and formed in the 'City Limited', which had probably just arrived. *G.B. Spencer Johnstone*

Other Oakwood Press books by the same author:
Bogie Carriages of the South Eastern & Chatham Railway
Bulleid's SR Steam Passenger Stock
Maunsell's Steam Carriage Stock
SE&CR in the 1914-18 War
Southern Railway Passenger Vans

Published by
The OAKWOOD PRESS
P.O. Box 122, Headington, Oxford.

Contents

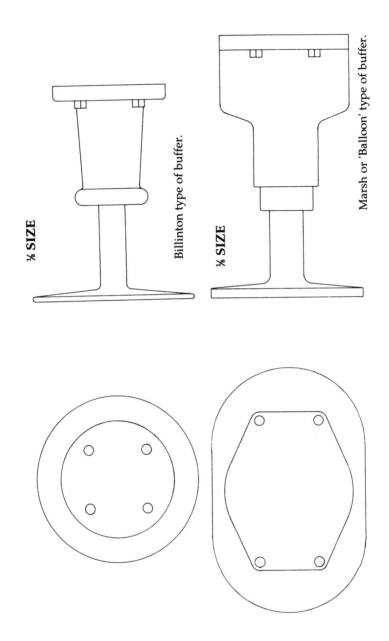

⅛ SIZE

Billinton type of buffer.

⅛ SIZE

Marsh or 'Balloon' type of buffer.

Introduction

On the London, Brighton & South Coast Railway the construction of bogie carriage stock, after the appearance of William Stroudley's few specimens, fell neatly into three distinct periods. Between 1894 and 1905 was the Billinton Era, during which new construction comprised mainly 48 ft carriages, all with arc roofs. Next, between 1905 and 1907, came the Marsh Era with construction concentrated on higher and wider elliptical-roofed vehicles. This was followed by the Panter Era, from 1907 to 1924, during which large numbers of Billinton six-wheelers were converted to bogie stock and even new construction reverted to the style of Marsh's predecessor, except that most carriages were now 54 ft in length. In the present work, which incorporates parts of P.J. Newbury's *Carriage Stock of the LB&SCR*, published by Oakwood Press in 1976, the carriages are described in the sequence noted above. For each of the 'eras' third-class vehicles are dealt with first, then second-class, Composites, first-class and Saloons. It is hoped that this arrangement will assist the reader in locating particular types of carriage, which in the original book were rather jumbled up.

LB&SC carriage numbering employed the then normal system whereby each class (including any Saloons and brake-fitted vehicles within that class) had its own series of numbers. Firsts were numbered from 1 to 566, Seconds from 1 to 540, Composites (including 1st/2nd, 1st/3rd and 2nd/3rd) from 1 to 658, and Thirds from 1 to 1410. The system also followed the deplorable practice of new vehicles (when they were 'renewals' for accountancy purposes) taking the numbers of old ones recently withdrawn with the result that there were few consecutive runs of numbers for each new design. Carriages built on 'capital' account, being additions to the fleet, *were* numbered consecutively. Electric stock had an entirely different number series starting at 3201, initially for all vehicles but later for motor cars only, and at 4001 for trailers.

On the abolition of second-class bookings (in the suburban area in June 1911 and elsewhere, except for Continental services, in June 1912) almost all the LB&SC's Seconds and Second/Third Composites were renumbered as third-class from 1501 to 1785, no attempt being made to group types of carriage together. In 1923, when the LB&SC became a constituent of the new Southern Railway, a scheme for carriage renumbering was drawn up. The following sequences were employed for ex-LB&SC bogie vehicles :

Thirds	1960-2338	First Brakes	7766-7775
Third Brakes	3760-4042	Saloons	7969-7973
Second Brakes	4493-4494	Motor Third Brakes	8567-8616
Seconds	4495	Trailer Thirds	9169-9208
Composites	5868-6286	Trailer Composites	9655-9674
Composite Brakes	6923-6938	Driving Tlr. Compos	9811-9914
Firsts	7543-7651	Brake Vans	909-929

Some vehicles were withdrawn or converted to D.C. electric carriages without ever carrying their allotted SR numbers, but the great majority of LB&SC bogie coaches appeared in SR colours with new numbers painted on. A Diagram Number was issued by the LB&SC for each type of carriage, together with a simplified drawing showing main dimensions and, of particular importance to the carriage department, seating capacity. Any carriage that had its seating altered, or was re-classed, would receive a new diagram number, with the result that there were more diagrams than there were basic types of coach. The original series of diagram numbers was allocated in sequence as new designs appeared, but in 1911 this was abandoned and new diagrams were organised by class. Only the post-1911 diagram numbers, together with their SR equivalents issued in 1924, are quoted in the carriage descriptions that follow. The drawings are reprinted from Newbury, and in addition there are seating layout plans of vehicles whose internal layout cannot be determined from photographs or drawings of the exterior. These plans are based on those in the SR Diagram Book. I am indebted to R.W. Kidner and Mike King for sending me many notes on LB&SCR carriages over the years, and to Denis Cullum and R.C. Riley for loaning their copies of carriage working books of various periods. The drawings of brake vans by M.S. King are reproduced with his permission, and other drawings of LB&SCR carriages are available from him at 16 Barricane, St Johns Hill Road, Woking GU21 1RB.

David Gould
East Grinstead,
1994

L

O

V

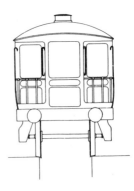

Chapter One

William Stroudley's Bogie Carriages

Born in Oxfordshire on 6th March, 1833, William Stroudley began his railway career at the age of 21 as a fitter on the Great Western Railway and later held the same position on the Great Northern Railway. In October 1861 he moved to Scotland, first as works manager at Cowlairs, Edinburgh & Glasgow Railway, then in July 1865 as locomotive and carriage superintendent of the Highland Railway. Stroudley was offered the post of locomotive and carriage superintendent of the London, Brighton & South Coast Railway and he took up his duties at Brighton on 1st February, 1870.

His first actions were to reorganise Brighton Works and to introduce his policy of standardisation both in locomotives and carriages. Large numbers of four- and six-wheeled carriages were constructed between 1872 and 1891; most of these four-wheelers were 26 ft long over body and all were arc-roofed, the radius of the roof being 10 ft 4½ in. Bogie carriages first appeared in 1879 when Stroudley ordered six from Cravens Ltd and six from Cleminsons. These were Firsts, as were a further six constructed during 1889; no bogie Seconds or Thirds were built during Stroudley's time. The only other bogie carriage was an inspection saloon, also built in 1889.

After 1875 all carriage stock was fitted with the Westinghouse air brake, which remained standard on the LB&SCR until 1924. After experiments with electric lighting using Fauré cells, Stroudley and the LB&SCR's electrician, Houghton, introduced electrically-lit trains in which an accumulator in the guard's van supplied the current, together with a large dynamo, also in the van, axle-driven by a large belt that came through a hole in the floor. Because one van supplied the current for lighting the entire train, the system was practicable only for semi-permanently coupled trains. Most carriages were gas-lit, with the gas cylinders fixed to the frame of each vehicle, together with a pressure-gauge fitted beneath the footboards to inform the carriage examiners on the quantity of gas in each cylinder.

A system of on-train communication was patented by Stroudley and Rusbridge (who was a coachbuilder at Brighton Works). It was electric, using a single wire, and was operated by a knob mounted on the compartment partitions of the carriages. It actuated bells on both the locomotive and the guard's van, but did not itself cause the brakes to be applied. It became standard equipment on the LB&SCR in 1887 and was in use right up to the end of the Company's existence, by which time a piped communication chain was replacing the original knob release.

Livery was varnished mahogany with gilt lining and white roofs. Lettering was in gold, shaded red. Upholstery in the 1st-class compartments was blue plush or, for smoking compartments, buffalo hide.

Stroudley died in office on 20th December, 1889. His influence on LB&SCR methods and practice had been substantial; he had improved the locomotive and carriage stock out of all recognition; he had made the passenger's journey as safe as possible by the early introduction of the air brake and the communication cord. He had imbued an *esprit de corps* at Brighton, and his sudden death at the early age of 56 was a shock to the Directors and staff of the LB&SCR, for he was very highly regarded by all.

EIGHT-WHEEL FIRSTS

Nos. 761-772

Body length: 49 ft 4½ in. Body width: 8 ft.
Compartments: Seven (6 ft 11 in. between partitions). Seats: 42.
Tare weight: 21 tons. Built 1880.

Very little is known about these 12 pioneer eight-wheel Firsts. Six were ordered from Cravens Ltd, Nos. 761-766, and six from Cleminson, Nos. 767-772, both batches being delivered in 1880. They were radially-trucked, the Cleminson vehicles having what was described as a 'flexible wheelbase', and so strictly speaking they were not true bogie carriages. They may have been built for working in the fast City trains, which always commanded the best rolling stock. The Cravens series were withdrawn between 1909 and 1911 and the Cleminsons between 1911 and 1916; No. 771 of the latter batch was converted into a Mess Room at Lancing in August 1916.

BOGIE FIRSTS

Nos. 73-78

Body length: 48 ft. Body width: 8 ft.
Compartments: Six (7 ft 9¼ in. between partitions). Seats: 36.
Tare weight : 20 tons 10 cwt. Diagram No. 43. Built 1889.

Built at Brighton during the half-year ending December 1889, these six bogie Firsts were intended for and ran in the fast City trains and were electrically lit on Stroudley's system, current being supplied from four-wheel vans. The bogies had no headstocks but included laminated bolster springs and helical side springs. The iron-spoked wheels ran noisily. Nos. 73-78 were the first LB&SC carriages to feature a higher roof than Stroudley's standard 10 ft 4½ in. - radius one, whose height above rail level was 11 ft 2½ in.; these bogie Firsts were about 11 ft 9½ in. from rail level to rooftop, and the roof radius was about 7 ft.

On 1st May, 1891, the 8.45 am Brighton to London Bridge was in charge of 'Gladstone' class 0-4-2 locomotive No. 175 *Hayling*, the train including all six bogie Firsts; the formation was a four-wheel brake van, four six-wheel Firsts, two bogie Firsts, Pullman car *Jupiter*, three bogie Firsts and a four-wheel brake van for London Bridge; and a four-wheel brake, a bogie First and a six-wheel First for Victoria, slipped at East Croydon. The London Bridge portion had just passed through Norwood Junction when it became derailed north of the station; the cause was a fracture of a weak cast-iron bridge. The whole train came off the road, but damage was slight and injuries few. After repairs all the bogie

Firsts were returned into traffic.

Following the introduction of new stock for the 'City Limited' services in 1907, the Stroudley Firsts achieved 'second-rank' status. It is not known if any were formed into numbered sets, but certainly none was so-formed by 1917. Withdrawal of all six was effected in 1919: Nos. 73 and 78 in September, Nos. 74 and 75 in October, and Nos. 76 and 77 in December.

BOGIE INSPECTION SALOON

No. 72 (SR No. 7969)

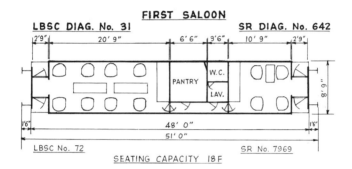

FIRST SALOON

LBSC DIAG. No. 31   SR DIAG. No. 642

SEATING CAPACITY 18 F

Body length: 48 ft. Body width: 8 ft 9 in. Bogie centres: 29 ft.
Compartments: Two saloons, plus pantry, lavatory and WC compartments.
Seats: 18 (11 in one saloon, 7 in the other).
Tare weight: 24 tons. Diagram No. 31 (SR No. 642). Built 1889.

In 1889 a very fine Directors' Inspection bogie Saloon was built to the designs of Mr Stroudley. It had a somewhat 'Wild West' air about it, for it featured open end verandahs with steps to facilitate boarding and alighting at track level. The two main saloon compartments were connected by a short side corridor which ran past a centrally-placed pantry and separate lavatory and WC compartments. Most of the seating was in individual armchairs, and there were fixed tables.

R.J. Billinton rebuilt the saloon with partly-enclosed end vestibules in 1900, at the same time replacing the bogies with a set taken from the Pullman car *Maud*, which had been wrecked in a collision at Wivelsfield on 23rd December, 1899. The end doors were very deeply inset, which meant that the verandah was still partly open, although roofed. Later still, the saloon was given steam heating equipment. Lighting was by gas.

After a new Directors' Inspection Saloon had been built in 1914, there was less use for No. 72, and so when it was taken into SR stock in 1923 it was reclassified as First Saloon and numbered into the SR's saloon series as No. 7969, the number being applied at Lancing in May 1925. Vacuum brakes were added in November 1925, but there was no future for such a non-standard vehicle and so withdrawal was effected at the end of 1930.

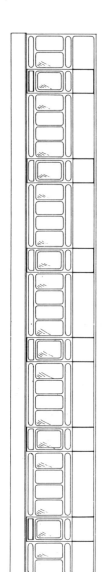

Stroudley First of 1889,
Diagram 43.

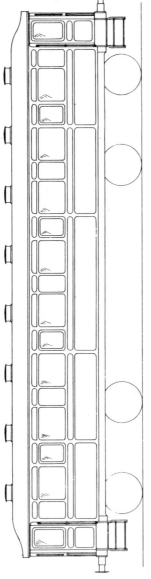

Stroudley Inspection Saloon,
Diagram 31, shown here as
modified by Billinton with
vestibules. Pullman bogies
after rebuilding. (Note : end
elevation on p. 6)

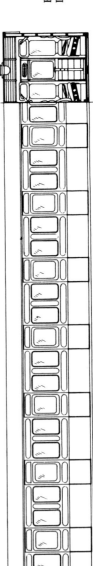

Billinton Third,
Diagram 161.

Chapter Two

Robert Billinton's Bogie Carriages

Robert John Billinton was born at Wakefield, Yorkshire, on 5th April, 1845. His senior railway positions before he became locomotive, carriage, wagon and marine superintendent on the LB&SCR in February 1890 were as Brighton Works manager under Stroudley, and as chief draughtsman at Derby under S.W. Johnson.

Stroudley-design carriages continued to appear for a few years, but from 1894 Billinton's bogie vehicles were put into traffic. Stylistically they, and the six-wheeled carriages, were similar to Stroudley's, but the major change was in the roof which, although a plain arc, was higher in centre, with a radius of 7 ft 0⅛ in. Some other small changes were made, the most obvious being the use of bolection mouldings for the sidelight glass, and the introduction of incandescent gas mantles, with their distinctive tops. Billinton continued and expanded the standardisation policy inherited from his predecessor, and such things as upholstery and interior fittings continued unchanged in style until Grouping. In the first-class compartments the seats were upholstered in blue plush, with blue hide in the smoking compartments. The underside of the seat cushions, the arm rests and the inside of the doors below the droplights were covered in American buffalo hide. Roofs and ends were decorated in lincrusta, the mouldings being in American walnut. The floor covering was 'Kork' matting and a blue Axminster rug; also blue were the window blinds and paintwork. Second-class compartments were upholstered in brown figured velvet or Vulcan leather; the roof and ends were again lincrusta but with mahogany mouldings. The floor covering was 'Kork' matting and a brown rug. Both first- and second-class compartments were fitted with cigar-ash trays, match striking plates and double luggage racks, and the seat-backs had lace antimacassars. The third-class passenger could study the figured rep upholstery, the linoleum on the floor, the varnished woodwork and the single luggage rack above each seat, and he might have noted the absence of ash trays. Enamelled iron advertisements were fixed to the insides of all doors in third-class compartments. Every compartment, irrespective of class, had a mirror, a frame with a map of the LB&SCR system, and two frames showing six photographs each, all these being views of places served by the LB&SC. Five thousand of these pictures were supplied by Curzon, Robey & Co. in January 1900 at three shillings and sixpence each. On the inside of all carriage doors were painted the number of the vehicle and the class. The first of Billinton's carriage designs to appear were six-wheelers, with gas lighting; many were converted to bogie stock, still retaining their original lighting system, in 1907-10. From about 1898 Stone's electric lighting began to be used, and in May 1902 a decision was made to install electric lighting in all new construction. The dimensions of Billinton's bogie carriages were standardised at 48 ft for length of body, 8 ft for the width, 11 ft 9½ in. for height from rail to top of roof, and the bogies had a wheelbase of 8 ft. Lavatories were very sparingly provided.

In April 1898 a decision was made to build only bogie carriages for main line services (the last non-bogie vehicles appeared in 1904 for suburban services). In July 1898 a fully-vestibuled corridor train was authorised to be built, but apparently the Brighton Board had second thoughts about the expense and the probable reduction in seating capacity per carriage, and cancelled the order, at the same time authorising a batch of non-corridor lavatory Composites. On 5th October, 1898, Albert Harry Panter, the son of W. Panter (carriage superintendent of the London & South Western Railway since 1885), was appointed general foreman of the LB&SC carriage department. He was later to become carriage and wagon superintendent.

Carriage livery was originally varnished 'mahogany red', with gold lining on the mouldings. The colour is assumed to have been the reddish-brown of Honduras mahogany. Later, mahogany-coloured paint was used. Brake-ends were usually vermilion red, and roofs white. Lettering was in gold, shaded red.

When Billinton died at Brighton on 7th November, 1904, he left a carriage stock that was largely six-wheeled and without lavatories, but there was a fair proportion of bogie stock, and many examples of this were lavatory-fitted. Electric lighting was on the increase. The general standard of comfort enjoyed by the passenger was good, and even the suburban 'Block' sets were better than most other local trains of the period.

A few standard dimensions of Billinton carriages are set out below.

Door width: 2 ft 2 in. Door droplight: 1 ft 6 in. x 2 ft 0½ in.
Quarterlights: 1 ft 4 in. x 2 ft 5 in.
Waist panels: 6 in. Centre panels: 2 ft 6 in. high. Upper panels: 5½ in.
Lower panels: 1 ft 11½ in.
Mouldings: 2 in. wide. Commode handles: 2 ft long.
Wheel diameter: 3 ft 7½ in.
Height from rail to top of gas lamp: 12 ft 7¼ in.

Worth mentioning is the fact that the extreme width over guard's lookouts, or 'duckets', was 9 ft 2 in. These duckets were without any mouldings. Many carriages later had their duckets altered so that the extreme width was now only 8 ft 9 in., and these could be identified as they *did* have mouldings on them.

BOGIE THIRDS

Nos. 2, 11-15, 20, 27-30 etc. (SR Nos. 1960-2113)

Body length: 48 ft. Body width : 8 ft. Bogie centres : 32 ft.
Compartments: Eight (5 ft 9⅝ in. between partitions). Seats 80.
Tare weight: 20 tons 6 cwt.; 21 tons if electrically lit.
Diagram No. 161 (SR No. 64). Built 1894-1905.

These eight-compartment Thirds were the most numerous type of bogie carriage on the LB&SCR, no fewer than 152 being built from 1894 to 1905; two more joined their number in 1911, having been originally Seconds but built in 1897/9 to the same design.

The first of the series were built by Cravens Ltd of Darnall, Sheffield, in 1894 and numbered 532 to 539. The next series, one year later, was also contractor-built, this time by Brown, Marshalls & Co. of Birmingham, who turned out 34 of the Thirds, consecutively numbered 1201 to 1234. All the rest were built at Brighton. Lighting was by gas for all coaches built between 1894 and 1900, but electric lighting on J. Stone's system was fitted to new vehicles built from 1902 onwards. Only four of the gaslit coaches were converted to electricity before 1923, these being Nos. 1212, 1264, 1266 and 1267.

Bogie Seconds Nos. 67 and 30 were reclassified Thirds and renumbered 1604 and 1722 respectively, the former in the second half of 1911 and the latter in the half-year ending December 1912. No. 1604, which was close-coupled, was working in seven-coach 'block' set No. 8B with 50 ft Thirds Nos. 1603/05, which had started life as second/third Composites. At the time of its alteration to close-coupling, Second No. 67 had been converted to electric lighting without dynamo, the current being supplied by the dynamo on an adjacent coach.

Few of the eight-compartment Thirds were formed into set trains in LB&SC days. Five-set No. 9 included No. 612; its booked workings in 1921 included the 6.30 am Brighton to Horsted Keynes and 7.40 am return, 10.08 am Brighton to Victoria and 2.00 pm return, 5.09 pm Brighton to Haywards Heath and 6.04 pm return (in company with the slip portion off the 5.08 pm from London Bridge), and, with a Pullman car attached, the 7.30 pm Brighton to Victoria and 12.05 midnight return. Five-sets Nos. 5 and 31 each included one Third, two Composites and two bogie brake vans and were allocated to Brighton-Portsmouth services. Third No. 1221 was in six-set No. 23 (7.23 am Brighton to London Bridge and 4.10 pm return via East Grinstead). Set No. 108, which included Third No. 11, was noteworthy in being really three different sets, which ran as a complete train between Ashurst and Victoria. The down train left Victoria at 3.45 pm, the front four coaches for Brighton via Eridge, the middle three for Eastbourne via Eridge, and the rear three slipped at Ashurst for Tunbridge Wells. Third No. 11 was in the Brighton portion, which formed the 8.05 am up via Eridge the next morning.

All the Thirds duly received their allotted Southern numbers during overhauls between 1924 and 1927; Nos. 691/93, 703/05/32/44 were renumbered at Brighton during 1924, but all the rest were done at Lancing. A few more of the Thirds were formed into sets by the Southern, but most remained as 'loose' coaches for strengthening. Set 108 was renumbered as SR set 935 and as such remained on the 3.45 pm Victoria to Brighton via Uckfield until about 1932. Close-coupled set No. 8B became SR set 942 in November 1924 and steam heating was installed; when this set was withdrawn in 1928 for conversion into electric stock No. 2112 (formerly 1604) did not form part of the conversion and was refitted with long buffers, altered from Westinghouse to vacuum braking in October 1928 and re-entered service on the main line. It was finally withdrawn in 1933.

The following examples were converted to push-and-pull trailers by the SR:

2002	9.25	1967, 2048, 2110	12.25
2007/38/39/61	10.25	1963	1.26
1995, 2063	11.25		

Ten were formed with driving trailer Composite Brakes 6927-36 into Sets 751 to 760, No. 2063 being paired with elliptical-roofed driving trailer Third Brake No. 3830 in Set 980. Set 980 was disbanded about 1928, however, and No. 3830 worked as a single coach on Brighton-Kemp Town services; No. 2063 was spare and during 1931/2 it was berthed at Chertsey for strengthening trains as required, being withdrawn in 1932. The other ten Thirds also were withdrawn in 1931/2, nine being replaced in push-and-pull sets 751-759 by eight-compartment Thirds, formerly Composites and originally AC electric driving trailers. The Third in Set 760 was not replaced and the set was therefore disbanded, its driving trailer Composite Brake No. 6936 becoming 'loose'.

Two subsequent push-and-pull conversions had a much longer life. Nos. 1960 and 2087, altered in 1931/2, went to sets 651 and 650 which ran until the late 1950s. No. 2087 received a new underframe in November 1930, and was altered from gas lighting to electricity; it was the only one of the gaslit Thirds to be so altered by the Southern Railway.

Withdrawal of the Thirds, whether gaslit or electrically lit, was rapid in the early 1930s and after February 1934 only four remained, these being the two push-and-pull conversions and two latterly in six-set No. 873, Nos. 2032 and 2084. In March 1936 these two were sent across to the Isle of Wight, renumbered 2410 and 2411, and formed into Set 489. Sending carriages to the Isle of Wight was a virtual guarantee of long life, and so No. 2411 lasted until February 1956 and its fellow until March 1959, by which time it was 57 years old. Nos. 1960 and 2087, the two push-and-pull trailers, lasted equally well on the mainland, being withdrawn in October 1958 and September 1959 respectively. The bodywork, although not the underframe, of No. 2087 was 64 years old !

EIGHT-COMPARTMENT THIRDS (DIAGRAM No. 161)

No.	Built	Set	SR No.	Re-No.	Set	Wdn	No.	Built	Set	SR No.	Re-No.	Set	Wdn
2	6.03		1960	7.26	651	10.58	428	6.00		1983	7.24	895	4.32
11	6.03	108	1961	9.25	935	2.34	532	6.94		1984	9.24		2.33
12	6.04		1962	2.26		2.34	533	6.94		1985	2.26	763	10.30
13	6.04		1963	2.26	758	2.32	534	6.94		1986	3.25		1.33
14	6.04		1964	10.26		3.31	535	6.94		1987	11.25	904	9.31
15	6.00		1965	7.24		4.31	536	6.94		1988	8.26		9.33
20	6.03		1966	11 26		2.33	537	6.94		1989	3.26		11.30
27	6.04		1967	1.26	757	6.32	538	6 94		1990	7.26		4.31
28	6.03		1968	4.26		9.33	539	6.94		1991	7.27		1.32
29	6.04		1969	6.26		2.33	578	12.02		1992	7.27		9.33
30	6.03		1970	2.26		3.32	579	6.00		1993	1.25		4.32
33	6.04		1971	8.26		12.30	580	6.01		1994	2.26		4 32
35	6.00		1972	6 24	884	4.32	581	6.02		1995	12.25	756	5.32
37	6.03		1973	7.27		10.32	583	12.04		1996	1.26	924	2.32
45	6.04		1974	8.27		2.33	587	6.00		1997	9.27		10.32
47	6.04		1975	2.26		4.31	588	12 01		1998	10.27		4.32
53	6.02		1976	4 26		4.32	589	6.00		1999	6.27		2.33
55	6.02		1977	9.26		1.33	590	6.02		2000	1.25		2.33
57	6.05		1978	5 25		11.33	595	12.04		2001	10.24	762	11.33
61	12.03		1979	7.26	932	2.34	596	6.01		2002	11.25	753	6.32
72	6.05		1980	8.27		1.31	597	6.01		2003	10.25		1.33
309	6 05		1981	1.26	924	2.32	598	6.00		2004	9.24		4.31
350	6.05		1982	5.27		11.30	600	6.00		2005	3.26		2.34

No.	Built	Set	SR No.	Re-No.	Set	Wdn	No.	Built	Set	SR No.	Re-No.	Set	Wdn
601	6.00		2006	1.26		9.33	727	12.04		2060	11 24		9.33
603	6.01		2007	11.25	755	4.32	728	6.03		2061	11.25	751	10.31
604	6.01		2008	4.26		4.31	732	12.02		2062	2.24		9.33
606	12.01		2009	8.27		11 33	733	12.02		2063	2,26	980,L	4.32
607	12 01		2010	3.26		2.34	734	12.02		2064	8.24		3.31
608	12.00		2011	9.27		10.32	735	6.03		2065	8.26		6.31
609	12.00		2012	2.25		11.33	738	6 03		2066	2.25	921	11 33
610	12.98		2013	9.27		10.32	740	12 03		2067	2.27		10.31
612	12.98	9	2014	10.26		4.31	741	12 03		2068	12.24		2.34
613	12 98		2015	12.25		1.33	742	6.03		2069	3.25		9.33
614	12.98		2016	4.25		1.33	744	12.03		2070	6.24	921	4.32
615	12.98		2017	6.27		4.31	745	12 03		2071	7.26		4.31
622	6.99		2018	10.24		9.33	746	12.03		2072	4.25		2.33
628	12.04		2019	8.26	936	10.30	1201	6.95		2073	2.26	923	4.32
631	12.04		2020	7.25		2.34	1202	6.95		2074	10.26		1.32
633	12.03		2021	7.26	932	10.30	1203	6.95		2075	4.27		4.31
656	6.99		2022	6.25		9.33	1204	6.95		2076	4.25		4.31
658	6.99		2023	1.26		3.32	1205	6.95		2077	4.25		4.32
659	6.99		2024	8.24		11.33	1206	6.95		2078	6.27		1.33
660	6.99	31	2025	1.25		12.32	1207	6.95		2079	1.25		4.31
662	12.00		2026	7.27		10.31	1208	6.95		2080	6.25		4.32
663	12.04		2027	8.24		1.33	1209	6.95		2081	8.24		12.30
666	12.04		2028	10.26		10.32	1210	6.95		2082	8.26		1.33
667	12.99		2029	9.27		9.33	1211	6.95		2083	6.24		2.33
668	12.99		2030	4.25		6.31	1212	6.95		2084	4.26	873	-
669	12.99		2031	4 26		4.31	1213	6.95		2085	4.25		2.33
670	6.02		2032	9.24	873	-	1214	6.95		2086	7.25		8.30
672	12.99		2033	10.24		9.33	1215	6.95		2087	8.27	650	9.59
674	12.99		2034	6.27		10.32	1216	6.95		2088	3.26		2.34
675	6.05		2035	8.26	936	2.34	1217	6.95		2089	6.26		4.32
678	6.02		2036	2.27		10.32	1218	6.95		2090	7.25		4.31
680	12.99		2037	1.25		10.32	1219	6.95		2091	1.27		4.31
681	6.02		2038	11.25	754	12.31	1220	6.95		2092	8.27		2.33
684	6.02		2039	9.24	752	10.31	1221	6.95	23	2093	12.25		3.31
687	12.99		2040	4.25	904	6.31	1222	6.95		2094	2.25		2.33
688	12.99		2041	7 26		9.33	1223	6.95		2095	3.27		9.30
689	12.99		2042	9.26		11.30	1224	6.95		2096	9.27		4.31
690	12.99		2043	4.27		10.31	1225	6.95		2097	9.26		1.33
691	12.04		2044	8.24		10.32	1226	6.95		2098	3.26		1.33
693	12.00		2045	6.24	894	4.31	1227	6.95		2099	1.27		4.32
694	6.02		2046	1.25		2.32	1228	6.95		2100	8.24		6.31
695	12.02		2047	10.25	916	2.32	1229	6.95		2101	1.25		9.30
696	12.02		2048	1.26	760	4.31	1230	6.95	5	2102	11.24	921	11.33
697	12.02		2049	11.27		10.31	1231	6.95		2103	7.26		8.30
698	12.02		2050	10.27		4.32	1232	6.95		2104	1.26		12.32
701	12.00		2051	8.26		1.33	1233	6.95		2105	4.26		4.31
702	6.01		2052	10.26		10.32	1234	6.95		2106	3.27		3.31
703	12 02		2053	2.24	842	10.32	1263	6.98		2107	12.25		10.30
704	6 01		2054	8.26		2.34	1264	6.98		2108	1.27		4.32
705	6.01		2055	2.24		11.33	1265	6.98		2109	10.25		12.30
714	12.01		2056	2 25		2.33	1266	6.98		2110	1.26	759	11.31
720	12.01		2057	10.24		9.33	1267	6 98		2111	8.26		1.33
721	12.03		2058	9.26		10.31	1604	6.99	8B	2112	11.24	942	3.33
722	12.01		2059	7.26		5.31	1722	6.97		2113	2.27		4.32

Some coaches, after withdrawal, had their bodies removed from the underframes and sent to various locations where they were grounded as huts. The following were noted:

2012	Woking	2083	Gillingham (Kent)
2025, 2104	Newhaven Harbour 6.47	2103	New Cross Gate
2068	Three Bridges Loco Yard 9.46	2108	Eardley 2.48
1961	Littlehampton 12.46		

In 1931, 13 ten-coach sets were formed for special traffic on the Central Section. The identity of the coaches in these sets is unknown, but the formation of the sets *is* known. Each was composed of six eight-compartment Thirds, two Composites, a Third Brake and a six-wheeled brake van. Numbered 863 to 872, 878, 886 and 892, the sets were berthed at New Cross Gate or Eardley when not in use. All were withdrawn about 1933.

BOGIE THIRD

No. 1235 (SR No. 2114)

Body length 48 ft. Body width 8 ft. Bogie centres: 32 ft.
Compartments: Nine (5 ft 2¾ in. between partitions). Seats : 90.
Tare weight: 20 tons 10 cwt. Diagram No. 160 (SR No. 65). Built 1896.

It was something of an achievement to cram nine compartments into a carriage body only 48 ft long, but it was done at the expense of passengers' comfort, the compartments being appallingly narrow; interlocked knees must have been the only answer for seated passengers. This solitary specimen was built at Brighton in 1896 and was lit by gas. The Southern fitted electric lighting and stripped out the Westinghouse brakes in April 1930, but the coach was withdrawn the following year.

No.	Built	SR No.	Re-No.	Set	Wdn
1235	12.96	2114	3.27	891	9.31

BOGIE LAVATORY THIRDS

Nos. 1314-19 (SR Nos. 2173-2178)

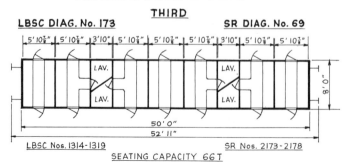

THIRD
LBSC DIAG. No. 173   SR DIAG. No. 69

LBSC Nos. 1314-1319   SR Nos. 2173-2178
SEATING CAPACITY 66 T

Body length: 50 ft. Body width: 8 ft. Bogie centres: 33 ft.
Compartments: Seven (5 ft 10⅞ in. between partitions). Seats: 66.
Tare weight: 20 tons 18 cwt. Diagram No. 173 (SR No. 69).
Four lavatories, with access from four compartments. Built 1900.

These six lavatory carriages, ordered to be built by the Gloucester Railway Carriage & Wagon Co. in 1900, were quite an innovation for the 'Brighton'; very few carriages were lavatory-fitted at that time, and certainly no third-class ones. They were of sufficient interest to be noted by *The Locomotive* in its May 1901 issue, although that magazine was in error in stating that there were two lavatories in each vehicle. Excepting No. 1314, they were electrically lit.

The Southern fitted vacuum brakes during 1925/6, and in 1930 stripped the Westinghouse brakes of all save No. 2178 (ex-1319). No. 2177 (ex-1318) was given a new underframe in 1931, and this coach outlasted the others of its type by six or so years. On withdrawal in 1940, No. 2177 was used for Mess and Tool Van No. 1543 S, Locomotive Running Department Eastleigh. It was finally withdrawn in May 1957.

BOGIE LAVATORY THIRDS (DIAGRAM No. 173)

No.	Built	SR No.	Re-No.	Set	Wdn
1314	12.00	2173	10.27		2.34
1315	12.00	2174	6.26	854	1.32
1316	12.00	2175	12.26	855	4.32
1317	12.00	2176	10.24	856	10.31
1318	12.00	2177	9.26	853	4.40
1319	12.00	2178	10.24	922	3.32

BOGIE LAVATORY THIRDS

Nos. 1322, 1323 (SR Nos. 2115, 2116)

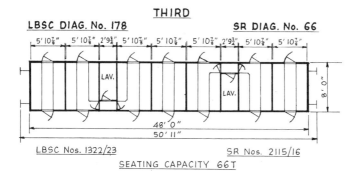

THIRD
LBSC DIAG. No. 178   SR DIAG. No. 66

5' 10⅞"   5' 10⅞"   2'9¾"   5' 10⅞"   5' 10⅞"   5' 10⅞"   2'9¼"   5' 10⅞"   5' 10⅞"

LAV.

LAV.

8' 0"

48' 0"
50' 11"

LBSC Nos. 1322/23   SR Nos. 2115/16
SEATING CAPACITY 66 T

Body length: 48 ft. Body width: 8 ft. Bogie centres: 32 ft.
Compartments: Seven (5 ft 10⅞ in. between partitions). Seats: 66.
Two lavatories, with access by short corridors from four compartments.
Tare weight: 20 tons 16 cwt. Diagram No. 178 (SR No. 66). Built 1905.

These two Lavatory Thirds were built at Brighton in 1905; externally they were similar to the half-dozen built five years previously, with frosted-glass windows between the second and third, fifth and sixth compartments. Internally the lavatories were arranged so that each was shared by two compartments (an arrangement never found on the neighbouring South Eastern & Chatham Railway), a short corridor connecting the two compartments and leading past the lavatory.

Both coaches had electric lighting. The Southern added vacuum brakes to the existing Westinghouse system in January 1926. No. 2115 (ex-1322) was formed into four-set 862, which in 1928 was booked to work the 8.50 am Victoria to Portsmouth and 4.30 pm return services. Withdrawal of both Lavatory Thirds came about in 1932.

No.	Built	SR No.	Re-No	Set	Wdn
1322	6.05	2115	3.26	862	10.32
1323	6.05	2116	1.24		4.32

BOGIE SECONDS

Nos. 30, 67 (SR Nos. 2113, 2112)

Body length: 48 ft. Body width: 8 ft. Bogie centres: 32 ft.
Compartments: Eight (5 ft 9⅝ in. between partitions). Seats: 80.
Tare weight: 20 tons 6 cwt. Diagram No. (as Thirds) 161 (SR No. 64).
Built 1897/9.

The only 48 ft bogie Seconds built by the LB&SCR were these two, Nos. 30 and 67, in 1897 and 1899 respectively. They were identical to the numerous eight-compartment Thirds and had gas lighting.

No. 67 is believed to have been altered to close-coupling in about 1909 and placed in suburban 'block' seven-set No. 8B in replacement of Composite No. 30. The gas lighting was replaced by electricity, though without its own dynamo, the current being supplied by the dynamo on an adjacent coach (probably 48 ft First No. 67). The confusion caused by having two coaches with the same number in a set was not destined to last long, for in the second half of 1911 Second No. 67 was altered to 3rd class and renumbered 1604; at the same time second/third Composites Nos. 233 and 150 were renumbered as Thirds Nos. 1603 and 1605.

The other eight-compartment Second, No. 30, was not altered to close-coupling or even given electric lighting; but in the second half of 1912 it was downgraded to 3rd class because of the abolition of Second Class on main-line services (except Newhaven boat trains) and renumbered 1722 in the 3rd class series.

For the further history of these coaches as Thirds see page 13.

BOGIE COMPOSITES

Nos. 14-16, 22, 23, 33-62, etc. (SR Nos. 5872-5991)

Body length: 48 ft. Body width: 8 ft. Bogie centres: 32 ft.
Compartments: Three 1st class (7 ft 4½ in. between partitions) and four 2nd class (6 ft 2¼ in. between partitions). Seats: 18 1st and 40 2nd class.
Tare weight: 21 tons 4 cwt. Diagram No. 88 (SR No. 327). Built 1894-1905.

Also Nos. 203, 209 (SR Nos. 5992/93): dimensions as above, but one of the 2nd class compartments upgraded to 1st class. Seats: 24 1st and 30 2nd class.
Diagram No. 89 (SR No. 328). Built 1902, 1898.

In 1894 the first of Robert Billinton's bogie Composites began to appear. They were 1st/2nd Composites, numbered 260 to 270, and were delivered from the Lancaster Railway Carriage & Wagon Co. Each had three 1st-class compartments in the centre of the vehicle with two 2nd-class compartments at each end. During the following year the Birmingham Railway Carriage & Wagon Co. constructed for the LB&SCR a further 51 Composites to the same design, these being numbered 421 to 441 and 33 to 62. Birmingham built four more during 1896/7, Nos. 472 to 475, but subsequent batches were built by Brighton Works, the last appearing in 1905.

Gas lighting was standard until 1902, after which new vehicles were fitted with electric lighting on Stone's system. Those recorded as being electrically lit were Nos. 14-16, 22/3, 79-83, 92/4/7/9, 101/03/04/24/29/48/57/58/61/83/89, 205/07/13, 375/82, 401/02/06/08, 501-10/15/19-21. In addition, Nos. 480 to 483, built in 1898, were electrically-lit, presumably having been converted from gas lighting at some stage before 1923.

Nos. 203 and 209 are believed to have been built new as Composites with three 1st-class and four 2nd-class compartments and later altered, one of the 2nd-class compartments becoming a rather mean 1st-class one. No. 203, built in 1902, had electric lighting, but No. 209 of 1898 was gaslit.

On 23rd December, 1899, two of the Composites were damaged beyond repair in a bad collision at Wivelsfield, when the 5.35 pm from Newhaven was hit by the 5.45 pm from Brighton, which was running late. The two bogie Composites that were demolished were both in the Newhaven train, towards the rear; they were Nos. 53 and 59, and were only four years old. Also destroyed were two six-wheeled Guard's Vans, one at the front of the Brighton train, the other at the rear of the Newhaven. The guard and two passengers were killed.

In 1913 No. 72 was altered to all-First, renumbered 272 in the 1st-class list and given a coat of arms for working with the Royal Train. Seating capacity was 42.

Few of the Composites were placed in set trains, most running as loose stock either for strengthening trains or as reserves for forming 'scratch' sets. Most of the sets were reformed in the 1920s, and only four LB&SC sets containing these Composites were retained as·such by the Southern Railway. Three-set No. 53, with Composite No. 79 (SR 5906), became SR set No. 792, and was dual-braked - Westinghouse and vacuum. Five-set No. 77, with Composite No. 129 (SR

5919), was booked to work the 9.25 am Portsmouth to Victoria and 4.53 pm return in 1917 and 1921; as SR set 889 it worked the 10.28 am Portsmouth to Victoria and 4.54 pm (not Saturdays) or 7.30 pm (Saturdays) return in 1928. The set was withdrawn towards the end of 1932. Four-set No. 105, with Composite No. 78 (SR 5905) worked between Brighton, Chichester, Midhurst, Horsham and Victoria in 1917 and 1921, returning to Brighton via Horsham. As SR No. 858, it worked between Portsmouth and London Bridge on a two-day diagram during 1931. Set No. 108 was the unique triple-portioned train used in the 3.45 pm Victoria to Brighton via Uckfield, the middle portion being for Eastbourne and the rear portion being slipped at Ashurst for Tunbridge Wells. Composites Nos. 54 and 423 were included in this train. The set became SR No. 935, still being used on the 3.45 pm until about 1932. The up workings were the 8.10 am from Brighton, 7.55 am from Eastbourne (combined at Eridge) and the 9.50 am from Tunbridge Wells (attached at Ashurst).

All the coaches were given vacuum braking by the SR from 1924 onwards; those converted from 1928 onwards had the Westinghouse brake equipment removed at the same time. Three gaslit coaches were altered to electric lighting in 1929: Nos. 5892, 5957 and 5973. Five others were discovered to have been equipped only with through pipes for steam heating but no heaters, which were installed during 1926: these being Nos. 5884/91, 5926/59/76. No. 5973 received a new underframe, which increased the weight of the vehicle to 23 tons, in January 1930. Nos. 5886 and 5915 had the first class seating altered from three-a-side to four-a-side, increasing the capacity from 18 to 24.

The Composites were seen on the Eastern Section of the SR, No. 5964 being in the train that was derailed at Bearsted on 20th August, 1927, and one turned up in the Westerham branch train during June 1930. However, withdrawal was rapid in the early 1930s and all but two were gone by February 1934. These two were retained for further use in the Isle of Wight. The first-class seating was altered to four-a-side - necessitating the issue of a new diagram No. 374 - and the vehicles were sent over in May 1936. Nos. 5942 and 5973 became 6362 and 6363 and were both formed in Set 489 until about 1948. However, as most other ex-LB&SC bogie carriages on the Island had 54 ft bodies, these two short Composites were rather non-standard and were both withdrawn about 1955 after closure of the Sandown-Newport line.

COMPOSITES (DIAGRAM No. 88)

No.	Built	Set	SR No.	Re-No.	Set	Wdn	No.	Built	Set	SR No.	Re-No.	Set	Wdn
14	6.04		5872	12.24		9.33	39	6.95		5883	3.27	895	3.34
15	6.03		5873	4.27		2.33	40	12.95		5884	2.26		10.30
16	6.04		5874	5.27		4.32	41	6.95		5885	9.24		3.31
22	12.02		5875	6.24		9.31	42	6.95		5886	9.25		4.32
23	6.04		5876	8.25		10.30	43	6.35		5887	10.26	915	10.31
33	6.95		5877	6.24	884	9.33	44	12.95		5888	10.26	915	4.31
34	6.95	22	5878	2.25		9.33	45	12.95		5889	4.26	894	2.33
35	6.95		5879	8.24		9.31	46	12.95		5890	11.26		4.31
36	6.95	26	5880	3.26		11.33	47	12.95		5891	12 26		6.31
37	6.95		5881	6.24	894	3.31	48	12.95		5892	3.26	846	1.32
38	6 95		5882	7.24	895	4.31	49	12.95		5893	12.25		11.33

No.	Built	Set	SR No.	Re-No.	Set	Wdn
50	12.95		5894	7.27		4.32
51	12.95		5895	7.26		1 31
52	12.95		5896	1.25		4.31
53	12.95		-	-		12.99
54	12.95	108	5897	9.25	935	12.32
55	12.95		5898	8.25		2.33
56	12.95		5899	4.27		6.32
57	12.95		5900	2.25		4.31
58	12.95		5901	2.26		2.32
59	12.95		-	-		12.99
60	12.95		5902	8.26		11.33
61	12.95		5903	11.24		3.32
62	12.95		5904	2.27		4.31
72	12.02		-	-		-
78	6.03	105	5905	6.24	858	11.33
79	12.04	53	5906	5.24	792	1.33
80	6.03		5907	6.26		4.32
81	6.03		5908	4.25	904	4.32
82	6.04		5909	2.25		2.31
83	6.03		5910	3.25		2.34
92	6.03		5911	6.26	924	12.31
94	6.03		5912	12.24		2.34
97	6.03		5913	10.25		2.33
99	12.02	31	5914	10.26		2 33
101	6.02	84	5915	10.26		10.30
103	6.03		5916	7.26		1.32
104	6.04		5917	8.24		11.33
124	12.04		5918	8.27		12.32
129	12.02	77	5919	6.25	889	10.32
148	6.04		5920	12.26		4.32
157	6.04		5921	11.26		4.31
158	6.04		5922	10.26		4.31
161	12.04		5923	6.26		2.33
183	12.04		5924	3.26		1.33
189	12.04		5925	4.25	911	12.31
205	12.04		5926	1.25		1.33
207	12.02		5927	9.25		3.32
208	12.98	31	5928	2.25	915	1.32
213	12.02		5929	1.26		3.31
260	6.94		5930	11.25		4.32
261	6.94		5931	11.25		9.33
262	6.94		5932	11.26	917	12.30
263	6.94		5933	6.27		4.32
264	6.94	90	5934	6.24	894	4.31
265	6.94	5	5935	11.26		12.31
266	6.94		5936	12.24		1.33
267	6.94	17	5937	10.26		12.30
268	6.94		5938	10.25		9.30
269	6.94		5939	10.24		12.30
270	6.94	45	5940	6.25		2.33
297	6.95		5941	2.27		4.31
298	6.95	7	5942	8.27	852	To IOW
375	12.02		5943	12.26		10.32
382	12.04		5944	6.27		10.32
401	12.02	79	5945	3.24	876	11.33
402	12.02		5946	6.24		4.31
406	12.04		5947	4.26		2.33
408	12.04	74	5948	3.26	850	10.32
421	6.95		5949	12.24		2.33
422	6.95		5950	1.26		4.31
423	6.95	108	5951	9.25	935	6.31
424	6.95		5952	6.25		1.33
425	6.95	26	5953	1.25		6.31
426	6.95	32	5954	2.24	915	3.32
427	6.95	84	5955	2.27		5.31
428	6.95		5956	1.25		4.32
429	6.95		5957	1.25	829	2.34
430	6.95		5958	10.26		8.30
431	6.95		5959	11.26		4.31
432	6.95		5960	8.26		4.31
433	6.95	70	5961	11.25		2.33
434	6.95		5962	4.25		9.31
435	6.95	5	5963	10.24		10.30
436	6.95	7	5964	8.27		4.32
437	6.95		5965	1.25	895	4.32
438	6.95		5966	5.27		4.31
439	6.95		5967	2.25		2.34
440	6.95		5968	7.25	904	3.32
441	6.95		5969	12.25		4.32
472	12.96		5970	8.27		4.31
473	12.96		5971	11.25		5.31
474	6.97		5972	1.25		4.31
475	6.97		5973	1.25	890	To IOW
480	6.98		5974	11.25		11.31
481	6.98		5975	8.25		6.31
482	6.98		5976	1.25	860	2.34
483	6 98		5977	9.26	817	7.31
501	12.03		5978	7.27		9.33
502	12.03	3	5979	7.27		11.33
503	12.03		5980	12.26		11.33
504	12.03		5981	11.25		4.32
505	12.03		5982	8.26		4.31
506	12.03		5983	2.25		2.34
507	12.03		5984	7.26		9.33
508	12.03		5985	8.26		2.32
509	12.03		5986	9.26		3.31
510	12.03		5987	7.27		2.34
515	12.04		5988	6.27		12.32
519	6.05		5989	7.26		2.34
520	6.05		5990	6.25		1.33
521	6.05	9	5991	10.26		2.32

COMPOSITES (DIAGRAM No. 89)

No.	Built	Set	SR No.	Re-No.	Set	Wdn	No.	Built	Set	SR No.	Re-No.	Set	Wdn
203	12.02		5992	8.26		4.31	209	12.98	82	5993	2.24	873	9.33

Note: Nos. 53 and 59 were withdrawn following accident damage at Wivelsfield on 23rd December, 1899. No. 72 was transferred to First class No. 272, half-year ending December 1913. SR No. 7549, July 1926. Set 917, later Set 848. Withdrawn December 1931.

SR Nos. 5942/73 transferred to Isle of Wight in May 1936 as Nos. 6362/63 (SR Diagram No. 374); both ran in Set 489. They were withdrawn from service in March 1959 and December 1955 respectively.

The body of No. 5892, after withdrawal, was grounded at Blackheath, noted there in July 1947.

BOGIE COMPOSITES

Nos. 13, 30, 67, 476, 477 (SR Nos. 5868-5871)

Body length: 48 ft. Body width: 8 ft. Bogie centres: 30 ft.
Compartments: Two 1st class (6ft 6½ in. between partitions) and six 2nd class (5 ft 8½ in. between partitions). Seats: 12 1st and 60 2nd class.
Tare weight: 21 tons 3 cwt. if gaslit, 22 tons approximately if electrically lit.
Diagram No. 87 (SR No. 325 or 326). Built 1897-99. Makeup 22211222.

No. 415 (SR No. 6048)

Dimensions as above, but fitted out as four 1st class and four 3rd class compartments seating 24 and 40 respectively. Tare weight 23 tons approx. Diagram No. 104 (SR No. 331). Built 1901. Makeup 33111133.

A small number of Composites were built by Brighton between 1897 and 1901 with compartments of somewhat meagre dimensions. Probably the vehicles were intended for use in suburban services, where such things were expected. No. 476, dated 1897, was gaslit; Nos. 477 and 13 were turned out in 1898; and Nos. 30 and 67 were dated 1899, these last four having electric lighting. No. 415 of 1901 had exactly the same body design as the others, but two of the narrow compartments were designated first class, with the remaining four 5 ft 8 in. compartments being classified 'third' instead of 'second'. It is likely that all six coaches were built with close-coupling for working in 'block' sets, but from about 1910 five of them were given ordinary buffers and couplings for main-line work.

No. 477 however retained close-coupling with central 'block' at each end and the 1st-class seating was modified to seat four-a-side instead of three-a-side. It was placed in one of the seven-coach 'bogie block' suburban sets, probably No. 6B, which later became SR No. 941. This coach alone, as SR No. 5871, was given Diagram No. 326.

No. 30 seems to have been withdrawn by 1910, its number being taken by a six-wheeled former second-class coach in that year. The remaining four coaches had their 2nd-class accommodation altered to 3rd class in 1911/12, and in 1923 were taken into Southern Railway stock and renumbered 5868-71. No. 415 was retained as a Composite with four 1sts and four 3rds, being renumbered 6048 in 1926 as part of eight-set No. 932.

Nos. 5868-70 and 6048 were dual-braked between 1925 and 1927, and the Westinghouse brakes were taken off Nos. 5868/69 and 6048 in 1930. No. 477 remained in its Westinghouse 'block' set until 1928, when the other six vehicles were withdrawn for conversion to electric stock. However, No. 477 remained as a 'steam' Composite, being altered to long-buffered, converted to vacuum braking (only) and receiving its SR number 5871 in December 1928. It later found its way to local five-coach set No. 894, which included three bogies and two six-wheeled guard's vans, finally being withdrawn in 1933.

The Southern altered the 1st-class seating in Nos. 5868/70 from three-a-side to four-a-side. No. 5870 was in six-set 917 (four bogies and two six-wheeled vans), which in 1928 worked the 8.32 am Uckfield to London Bridge and 4.40 pm return. The set was disbanded late in 1930.

No. 6048 remained in Set 932 until its withdrawal early in 1934. This set was kept at New Cross Gate during the week, its only booked workings during 1931/2 being the Sunday 8.52 am London Bridge to Brighton and 5.50 pm return.

COMPOSITES (DIAGRAM No. 87)

No.	Built	Set	SR No.	Re-No.	Set	Wdn
13	12.98		5868	10.24		3.32
30	99			-	-	.10 ?
67	6.99		5869	6.27		4.32
476	6.97		5870	11.26	917	12.30
477	6.98	6B	5871	12.28	941,894	11.33

COMPOSITE (DIAGRAM No. 104)

No.	Built	Set	SR No.	Re-No.	Set	Wdn
415	6.01		6048	7.26	932	2.34

BOGIE LAVATORY COMPOSITES

Nos. 66, 71, 86, 108/15/16/40/69/87, 210/11, 374, 407/84-97, 528-32 (SR Nos. 5994-6025).

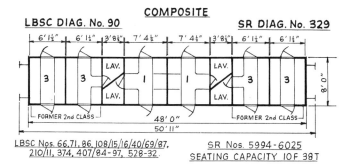

COMPOSITE

LBSC DIAG. No. 90   SR DIAG. No. 329

LBSC Nos. 66,71,86,108/15/16/40/69/87, 210/11, 374, 407/84-97, 528-32.

SR Nos. 5994-6025
SEATING CAPACITY 10F 38T

Body length: 48 ft. Body width: 8 ft. Bogie centres: 32 ft.
Compartments: Two 1st class (7 ft 4½ in. between partitions), four 2nd class (6 ft 1½ in.
between partitions) and four lavatories serving two 1st and two 2nd class
compartments. Seats: 10 1st and 38 2nd class.
Tare weight: 22 tons 2 cwt. if gaslit, 23 tons approximately, if electrically lit.
Diagram No. 90 (SR No. 329). Built 1898-1905.

Between 1898 and 1905, 32 Lavatory Composites were put into service by the
LB&SCR. They were quite well-appointed by the standards of the time, and in
each vehicle only the two end 2nd-class compartments were without lavatory
access. Fourteen of the coaches, Nos. 484 to 497, were built by the Gloucester
Railway Carriage & Wagon Company, but the others were produced by
Brighton Works. Only the earlier-built carriages - Nos. 66, 71, 108, 115, 116, 169
and 484 - had gas lighting, and all those built from late 1900 onwards were
electrically lit. No. 489 was dual-braked.

Second class was altered to third in 1912, but No. 187, which was allocated to
boat train stock, was retained as a 1st/2nd Composite until 1924.

Nine of the Lavatory Composites were recorded as having been formed in set
trains by 1917. Of these, No. 211 was in spare four-set No. 3 until c. 1920. Four-
set No. 14 included Composite No. 108 and worked in the 7.15 am Brighton to
London Bridge and 4.00 pm return; four-set 38 had Composite No. 497 and took
in the 6.45 am Hastings to London Bridge and 4.05 pm return. No. 488, in five-
set No. 62, worked in the 9.45 am Eastbourne to Victoria and 3.20 pm return;
whilst No. 491, formed in five-set No. 77, worked the 9.25 am Portsmouth to
Victoria and 4.53 pm return.

Most of these sets were altered or disbanded in the early 1920s, but No. 38
became part of SR No. 843, No. 62 became part of SR No. 888 and No. 77 was
wholly SR No. 889. In SR days most of the remaining Composites found their
way into sets.

During the mid-1920s vacuum brakes were added to the Westinghouse
equipment in all except Nos. 5999, 6017 and 6020. Later, Westinghouse brakes
were taken off Nos. 5994, 5999, 6000, 6002, 6003, 6006, 6008, 6011, 6012, 6014,
6017, 6020, 6022, 6024. Nos. 5999 and 6017/20 received vacuum brakes in 1929.
No. 5999 also had its gas lighting replaced by electricity at the same time. Two
vehicles that had been steam-piped only, Nos. 6003/04, were given full steam
heating equipment in 1926.

In the 1928 carriage working notice, 4-set 843, which included Composite No.
6020, was shown as working the 9.30 am Portsmouth to Victoria and 4.20 pm
return; the set was withdrawn in 1931 and No. 6020 was transferred to seven-
set No. 890, remaining there until February 1934. Four-set 844, which included
Composite No. 6008, also worked from Portsmouth: on the 8.25 am to London
Bridge and 1.50 pm return. Five-set 846, with Composite No. 6002, worked the
7.05 pm Eastbourne to London Bridge and 6.40 pm Victoria to Eastbourne in
1928. The 1.55 pm Littlehampton to Victoria and 6.40 pm return were booked
to be formed of five-set No. 860, which included Composite No. 6004. Five-set
888 included two of these vehicles, Nos. 6003/11; this set ran in the 9.20 am
Eastbourne to Victoria and 5.20 pm return services. Nos. 6023/25 were both in

Set 935 for the 3.45 pm Victoria to Brighton and Eastbourne via Eridge.
These lavatory Composites were all withdrawn in the early 1930s, the last
examples going in February 1934.

LAVATORY COMPOSITES (DIAGRAM No. 90)

No.	Built	Set	SR No.	Re-No.	Set	Wdn
66	12.00		5994	8.24		4.31
71	12.00	23	5995	1.25		2.33
86	6.01	75	5996	6.26	851	4.31
108	6.99	14	5997	5.24		1.33
115	12.98		5998	10.26	915	4.31
116	12 98	49	5999	12.25	923	4.31
140	6.01	105	6000	6.24	858	.33
169	6.99		6001	10.26		1.32
187	6.05		6002	8.24	846	1.32
210	6.01		6003	2.25	888	3.32
211	6.01	3	6004	5.24	860	2.34
374	6.05	40	6005	12.24	911	12.31
407	6.05		6006	3.25		1.33
484	12.00		6007	7.26		10.30
485	12.00		6008	5.27	844	10.31
486	12.00		6009	5.27		2.33
487	12.00		6010	6.27	885/31	2.34
488	12.00	62	6011	2.25	888	10.32
489	12.00		6012	10.26	857	4.31
490	12.00	59	6013	4.25	911	12.31
491	12.00	77	6014	6.25	889	10.32
492	6.01	17	6015	5.24	842	10.32
493	6.01		6016	4.26	764	10.30
494	6.01		6017	12.26	873	6.31
495	6.01		6018	12.26		6.31
496	6.01		6019	4.27	852	4.31
497	6.01	38	6020	7.25	843, 890	2.34
528	12.02		6021	8.24	916	4.32
529	12.02		6022	7.26	885	4.31
530	12.02	108	6023	9.25	935	3.31
531	6.02		6024	7.26		11.33
532	6.02	108	6025	9.25	935	2 34

BOGIE TRI-COMPOSITES

Nos. 106/18/39/47/71, 404/17, 533-47 (SR Nos. 6026-6047)

Body length: 48 ft. Body width: 8 ft. Bogie centres: 32 ft.
Compartments: Two 1st class (7 ft 10½ in. between partitions), two 2nd class (6 ft 8 in.
between partitions) and three 3rd class (5 ft 10½ in. between partitions). Seats: 12 1st,
20 2nd and 30 3rd class. Tare weight: 23 tons approx.
Diagram No. 99 (SR No. 330). Built 1901-03. Makeup 3211233.

Between 1901 and 1903 a range of tri-Composite carriages totalling 22 in
number was built at Brighton. The 1st-class compartments, which sat three-a-

side, were really sumptuous at 7 ft 10½ in. between partitions (the South Eastern's widest 'firsts' were 7 ft 6½ in.). Second-class compartments were quite generously-proportioned, and even the 3rd class was reasonable. Two of the carriages, Nos. 417 and 547, although having all the same compartment dimensions as the tri-Composites, seem to have been put into service from the start as 1st/3rd bi-Composites; these each seated 12 1st and 50 3rd class passengers. In 1912 the other twenty vehicles were altered to match, when second-class accommodation was abolished.

No. 118 was recorded as being formed in four-set No. 79, which worked between Horsham and Victoria in 1908, but by 1917 it was a 'loose' coach. Only three were in sets by then: Nos. 537/42 in five-set 25 and No. 546 in four-set No. 24. Both sets worked between Brighton and Hastings in 1917 and 1921, and in addition Set 24 worked in the 5.20 am from London Bridge to Brighton and 8.50 pm return.

These sets were disbanded in the early 1920s, and the SR renumbered all the Composites to 6026-47. Nos. 6026-32 and 6046/47 became dual-braked, and did not run in sets. Nos. 6033-45 retained their Westinghouse brakes until late 1929. These particular vehicles had been adapted by the LB&SCR to run as trailers, originally 'loose'. The SR placed them in push-and-pull sets Nos. 736-48, allocated in numerical order and paired with 'Balloon' driving trailer Third Brakes, which until the early 1920s had run singly. The visual mismatch of high-roof and arc-roof coaches was allowed to continue until 1931 when the Composites were withdrawn and replaced by spare high-roof Composites. Before then, Sets 736-48 had been converted to vacuum braking, in conjunction with the LB&SC system of air-control, on the following dates: November 1929 (Sets 736/39/40/41/43/47/48), December 1929 (Sets 742/44), January 1930 (Sets 737/38/46) and April 1930 (Set 745).

The allocations in August 1930 of push-and-pull sets formed with a 'Balloon' driving trailer and an arc-roof trailer Composite were:

Bognor	736
Brighton	738, 748
Horsham	Three (unidentified)
Littlehampton	Two (unidentified)
Relief	Four (unidentified)
Portsmouth	741

Of the dual-braked Composites, Nos. 6029/31/32 had their Westinghouse fittings removed in 1930. Nos. 6026-32/46/47 did not long outlast the Composites that had been converted to trailers, and the last example - No. 6029 - was withdrawn in February 1934.

TRI-COMPOSITES (DIAGRAM No. 99)

No.	Built	Set	SR No.	Re-No.	Set	Wdn
106	6.03		6026	10.27		11.33
118	6.03		6027	11.25		11.33
139	12.02		6028	10.24		4.32
147	12.02		6029	2.25		2.34

No.	Built	Set	SR No.	Re-No.	Set	Wdn
171	12.02		6030	5.27		9.33
404	6.03		6031	11.25		1.33
417	6.03		6032	8.26		4.32
533	6.02		6033	3.24	736	12.31
534	6.02		6034	5.25	737	2.32
535	6.02		6035	2.26	738	3.31
536	6.02		6036	2.25	739	10.31
537	6.02	25	6037	4.26	740	2.32
538	6.02		6038	1.26	741	4.32
539	6.02	59/21	6039	9.26	742	8.31
540	6.02		6040	8.27	743	12.31
541	6.02	75/21	6041	7.27	744	12.31
542	12.01	25	6042	9.25	745	12.31
543	12.01		6043	2.27	746	6.32
544	12.01		6044	6.27	747	12.31
545	12.01		6045	4.25	748	12.31
546	12.01	24	6046	6.27		4.32
547	12.01		6047	7.26		2.32

BOGIE TRI-COMPOSITE BRAKES

Nos. 516-518 (SR Nos. 6923-6925)

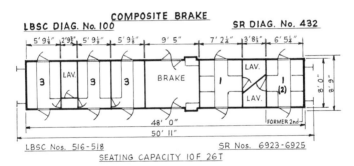

Body length: 48 ft. Body width: 8 ft (8 ft 9 in. over duckets).
Bogie centres: 32 ft. Compartments: One 1st class (7 ft 2¼ in. between partitions), one 2nd class (6 ft 5¼ in. between partitions) and three 3rd class (5 ft 9½ in. between partitions). Three lavatories - one to 1st class, one to 2nd class and one accessible from all 3rd class compartments. Seats: 5 1st, 5 2nd and 26 3rd class.
Tare weight: 19 tons 18 cwt. Diagram No. 100 (SR No. 432). Built 1905.

In 1905 Brighton built three Tri-Composite Brakes that had the very unusual feature of a centrally-placed guard's compartment with passenger compartments both sides of it. Of the LB&SC's neighbours, only the London & South Western had any examples of this type of carriage. The 'Brighton' Composite Brakes had the make-up 2, Lavs, 1, Guard, 3, 3, Lav, 3. A short side corridor, without partitions, connected the three third-class compartments, thus enabling all their occupants to have access to a rather small lavatory compartment. The guard's compartment, 9 ft 5 in. long, included side duckets adjacent to the 1st class compartment, and double doors on each bodyside. The guard's doors, adjacent to the ducket on each side, opened inwards but the other two doors opened outwards.

The carriages appeared in umber brown with white upper panels, the mouldings of which were picked out in brown, but at the first repainting they appeared in all-over brown. In 1912 the second-class compartment in each vehicle was upgraded to first class, and the seating capacity was now 10 1st, 26 3rd class.

As all three Composite Brakes were both Westinghouse- and vacuum-braked, it seems likely that they were intended for through workings between the LB&SCR and L&SWR: probably the Brighton to Plymouth service. The carriages were 'loose stock' until Southern days. No. 6923 (formerly 516) was then formed in three-set No. 857, with Composite No. 6012 and Third Brake No. 3804, remaining therein until 1931, when it reverted to loose stock. No. 6924 (formerly 517) was for a short time in two-set No. 735 with Composite No. 6258, but was 'loose' again by 1931. No. 6925 (formerly 518) was in three-set No. 778 until its withdrawal early in 1933; its 1928 workings included the 8.33 am Seaford to London Bridge and 5.20 pm Victoria to Seaford. During 1931 No. 6923 was based at Hawkhurst station for working the 7.23 am to Paddock Wood, returning thence at 7.20 pm. No. 6924 was allocated to the Dunton Green - Westerham branch, on which it worked most of the trains, being berthed overnight at the terminus. Both coaches had had their braking system altered from Westinghouse to vacuum in 1930, but were withdrawn only two years later.

TRI-COMPOSITE BRAKES (DIAGRAM No. 100)

No.	Built	SR No.	Re-No.	Set	Wdn
516	6.05	6923	7.25	857, L /31	4.32
517	6.05	6924	10.26	735, L /31	2.32
518	6.05	6925	11.24	778	2.33

BOGIE FIRSTS

Nos. 79-97, 141-148 (SR Nos. 7578-7604)

Body length: 48 ft. Body width: 8 ft. Bogie centres: 32 ft.
Compartments: Six (7 ft 9⅞ in. between partitions). Seats: 36.
Tare weight: 21 tons approximately if gaslit, 22 tons approximately if electrically lit.
Diagram No. 49 (SR No. 514). Built 1894-1904.

As part of its carriage renewal programme in the 1890s, the LB&SCR ordered from the Lancaster Railway Carriage & Wagon Co. 19 bogie Firsts to the standard body length of 48 ft. Numbered 79 to 97, they were delivered between 1894 and 1896. All were illuminated by gas, and the compartments sat three-a-side in great luxury. A further eight of these Firsts were built at Brighton in 1903/04 to the same dimensions, but were lit by electricity; the battery boxes and dynamo increased the weight of each carriage by just under a ton. Of the earlier series, Nos. 86 and 91 were converted to electric lighting by the LB&SC. By 1917 Nos. 90 and 95 had been formed in nine-set 17, working between London and Brighton; No. 96 was in four-set 14; No. 83 was in five-set 23; No. 144 was in three-set 55, working between Victoria and Brighton and Victoria and Tunbridge Wells; No. 94 was in four-set 71, working between Hastings and Victoria; No. 145 was in five-set 77 (Portsmouth-Victoria); and No. 85 was in five-set 109, working between London and Brighton. Four years later, two more Firsts found themselves formed into set trains: No. 143 in seven-set No. 49 and No. 79 in three-set 51. Set 14 was disbanded, Set 23 worked Brighton-London Bridge services, Set 49 worked between Bognor and London Bridge, and Set 51 between Eastbourne and Victoria.

The Southern Railway renumbered all the Firsts consecutively to 7578-7604 between 1924 and 1927 at Lancing, at the same time adding vacuum brake equipment to all except No. 7593. Westinghouse air brake gear was removed in 1929/30 from Nos. 7578/83/84/87/90-94/96/7601, and vacuum braking fitted to No. 7593 in April 1929. Other modifications included increasing the seating capacity of No. 7588 to 48 (i.e. four-a-side instead of three-a-side) and replacing the underframe of No. 7596 in 1930 by a new one. Electric lighting replaced gas in Nos. 7578/83/84/87/96 during 1929/30.

Two of the Firsts were formed into three-sets 781/2, which in the 1920s worked two-day diagrams that took in the 8.27 am Forest Row to Victoria and 5.50 pm Victoria to Tunbridge Wells, and the 8.58 am Tunbridge Wells to London Bridge and 5.05 pm from London Bridge, slipped for Three Bridges and Forest Row. No. 7601 was in five-set 889, working between Portsmouth and Victoria, and No. 7578 was part of five-set 891, which was booked for the 2.55 pm London Bridge to Oxted and 3.59 pm return, and the 5.11 pm London Bridge to Brighton and 9.00 pm return in the 1928 carriage workings. A First was part of six-set 911 (Bognor-Victoria) and there were two in seven-set 922 (Bognor-London Bridge). About 1929 Set 924 was increased to eight coaches, including First No. 7586, and this worked between Victoria and Coulsdon North on weekdays, and on the Oxted line on Sundays, in 1931.

Set 842 seems to have had three Firsts allocated to it in succession: No. 7594 until about 1928, No. 7590 until about 1931, and finally No. 7601, transferred from Set 889.

With the exception of No. 7596 - which had a new frame - all the Firsts were withdrawn between late 1930 and mid 1934. The body of No. 7581 was sold out of service in October 1930, probably as living quarters. No. 7598 also was purchased with the intention of converting it to a dwelling; the body was removed from the frame at Chichester and taken to West Chiltington in 1931. There it remained until 1989.

The Bluebell Railway, which had spent years hunting for an LB&SC carriage to run on its line, tracked down this body and arranged for its removal to Horsted Keynes station in September 1989. On arrival there No. 7598 was placed on a temporary underframe (far too long for it) and it then occupied one of the platform roads at Horsted Keynes where visitors could inspect the results of its gradual restoration. Although there were holes in the bodywork in places, much of the timber was sound and once cleaned and varnished looked as good as new. All the compartment partitions and seats had been stripped long ago, so the interior was still an empty shell; but it was fascinating to poke about inside and examine what remained. It is, as far as is known, the only ordinary ex-LBSC Billinton bogie carriage body in existence.

BOGIE FIRSTS (DIAGRAM No. 49)

No.	Built	Set	SR No.	Re-No.	Set	Wdn	No.	Built	Set	SR No.	Re-No.	Set	Wdn
79	6.94	51	7578	3.27	891	10.31	93	12.95		7592	8.24		1.33
80	6.94		7579	12.26		9.33	94	6 96	71	7593	5.25	848	12.30
81	6.94		7580	7.27		4.32	95	6.96	17	7594	5.24	842	3.31
82	6.94		7581	3.26		9.30	96	12.96	14	7595	3.27		11.30
83	6.94	23	7582	8.24		1.34	97	12.96		7596	12.25		10.39
84	6.94		7583	12.26	782	1.32	141	6.03		7597	8.24		3.31
85	6.94	109	7584	4.25	911	2.32	142	6.03		7598	9.25		10.31
86	6.94		7585	11.26		1.34	143	6.03	49	7599	10.24	922	3.31
87	6.94		7586	2.26	924	2.32	144	6.03	55	7600	10.24	922	3.31
88	6.94		7587	6.24	781	9.31	145	6.03	77	7601	6.25	889, 842	10.32
89	6.94		7588	1.27		4.31							
90	6.94	17	7589	7.27		7.34	146	6.03		7602	10.26		3.32
91	6.94		7590	11.25	842	4.34	147	6.04		7603	9.24		4.31
92	12.95		7591	1.25		5.31	148	12.04		7604	7.26		4.31

BOGIE LAVATORY FIRSTS

Nos. 129-140 (SR Nos. 7605-7616)

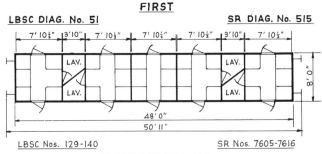

Body length: 48 ft. Body width: 8 ft. Bogie centres: 32 ft.
Compartments: Five (7 ft 10½ in. between partitions).
Four lavatories, with access from four compartments. Seats: 26.
Tare weight: 22 tons 4 cwt. Diagram No. 51 (SR No. 515). Built 1900/1.

Twelve Lavatory Firsts were constructed by Brighton during 1900/01 and put into service on the main line. Each had five compartments of exceptional width, of which only the centre one had no lavatory access. All the carriages were electrically-lit from the outset.

Only four had been placed in three-coach set trains by 1917: No. 134 in Set 85, No. 140 in Set 86, No. 139 in Set 88, and No. 132 in Set 94. Of these, Nos. 85 and 94 worked between Eastbourne and Victoria, No. 86 between Hastings and London Bridge, while No. 88 was spare. To these, seven-set No. 49 was added by 1921 and included Lavatory First No. 130.

On being acquired by the SR, all twelve were renumbered at Lancing between 1924 and 1926, all but two finding their way into sets. In 1925/6 vacuum brake equipment was fitted to all but No. 7613, which received it in April 1929; Westinghouse air brake equipment was then removed from Nos. 7605/08/10/12/13/15/16 during 1929/30.

In 1928 the following sets included a Lavatory First in their formation:

5-set 846:	7.05 am Eastbourne to London Bridge, 6.40 pm Victoria to Eastbourne.
4-set 853:	9.15 am Victoria to Hastings and 3.45 pm return.
4-set 854:	Spare.
4-set 855:	'Rover' set.
4-set 856:	7.30 am Eastbourne to London Bridge and 12.14 pm return.
5-set 862:	8.50 am Victoria to Portsmouth and 4.30 pm return.
7-set 890:	10.05 am Brighton to London Bridge and 11.48 am return; 4.08 pm Brighton to London Bridge and 6.18 pm return.
7-set 922:	8.10 am Bognor to London Bridge and 1.20 pm (Saturdays) or 5.50 pm (not Saturdays) return.
8-set 923:	7.10 am Brighton to London Bridge and 4.00 pm return.

No. 7610 in Set 853 was withdrawn in April 1931 and replaced by No. 7607, formerly 'loose', this coach remaining in the set until January 1934. By September 1931 only four sets remained in use with a Lavatory First in the formation:

4-set 853:	7.27 am London Bridge to Ramsgate via Redhill and Dover Marine; 4.55 pm Ramsgate to Charing Cross via Dover Marine.
4-set 862:	8.03 am London Bridge to Brighton via East Grinstead; 11.30 am Brighton to London Bridge via Redhill.
8-set 890:	Brighton-London Bridge-Eastbourne-Ashford-Eastbourne-Brighton.
6-set 923:	Spare at Eardley.

BOGIE LAVATORY FIRSTS (DIAGRAM No. 51)

No.	Built	Set	SR No.	Re-No.	Set	Wdn	No.	Built	Set	SR No.	Re-No.	Set	Wdn
129	12.00		7605	3.26	862	10.32	135	6.01		7611	7.25		8.31
130	12.00	49	7606	10.24	922	3.31	136	6.01		7612	6.26	846	10.32
131	12.00		7607	2.26	853	1.34	137	6.01		7613	12.25	923	1.34
132	12.00	94	7608	10.24	856	11.31	138	6.01		7614	8.25	890	3.32
133	6.01		7609	3.26		4.31	139	6.01	88	7615	4.26	855	6.34
134	6.01	85	7610	9.26	853	4.31	140	6.01	86	7616	6.26	854	10.31

BOGIE LAVATORY FIRSTS

Nos. 149, 150 (SR Nos. 7617, 7618)

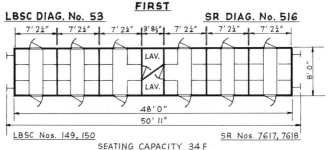

FIRST

LBSC DIAG. No. 53   SR DIAG. No. 516

LBSC Nos. 149, 150   SR Nos. 7617, 7618

SEATING CAPACITY 34 F

Body length: 48 ft. Body width: 8 ft. Bogie centres: 32 ft.
Compartments: Six (7 ft 2¼ in. between partitions).
Two lavatories, with access from two compartments. Seats: 34.
Tare weight: 22 tons approximately. Diagram No. 53 (SR No. 516). Built 1905.

Only two of this type of Lavatory First were built, both at Brighton in 1905. By reducing the width of the compartments and reducing the number of lavatories, an extra passenger compartment was fitted in to the 48 ft body as compared with the Lavatory Firsts of 1900. The two lavatories were placed in the centre of the coach, one to each of the 1st-class compartments next to them. Both carriages were lit by electricity.

Three-set 16 comprised First No. 149 and two Slip Third Brakes rebuilt from six-wheelers; it worked between London and Hastings in 1917. Three-set 81 comprised First No. 150 and two other Slip Third Brakes rebuilt from former six-wheeled vehicles and also worked between London and Eastbourne or Hastings. Although still unchanged four years later, both sets had been disbanded by 1923. The Southern numbers were applied at Lancing; No. 7617 went to five-set No. 888, but its companion remained as a 'loose' coach until withdrawal in 1933.

No. 7617 was dual-braked in March 1926 and No. 7618 in December 1925. Set 888 worked in 1928 with two Pullman cars the 9.20 am Eastbourne to Victoria and 5.20 pm return. No. 7617, damaged in a collision at Eastbourne on 21st May, 1930, was withdrawn and replaced by five-compartment Lavatory First No. 7612, from Set 846.

BOGIE LAVATORY FIRSTS (DIAGRAM No. 53)

No.	Built	Set	SR No.	Re-No.	Set	Wdn
149	6.05	16	7617	2.25	888	6.30
150	6.05	81	7618	7.27		1.33

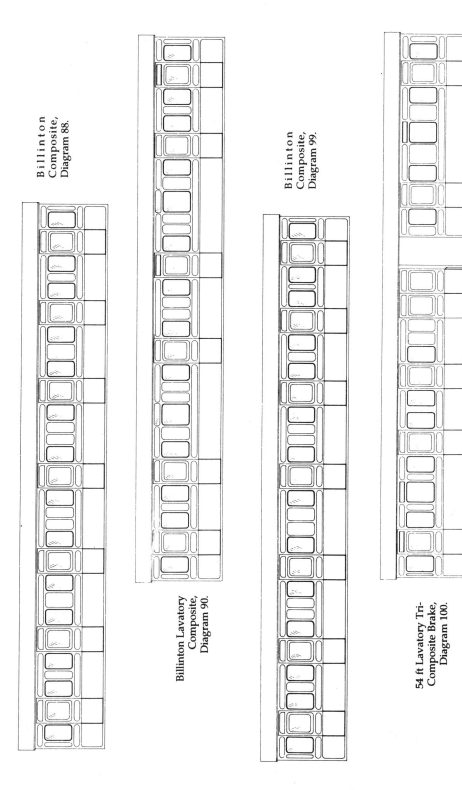

Billinton
Composite,
Diagram 88.

Billinton
Composite,
Diagram 99.

Billinton Lavatory
Composite,
Diagram 90.

54 ft Lavatory Tri-
Composite Brake,
Diagram 100.

BOGIE FIRST

No. 272 (SR No. 7549)

Body length: 48 ft. Body width: 8 ft. Bogie centres: 32 ft. Compartments: Seven (three being 7 ft 4½ in. between partitions and four being 6 ft 2¼ in.). Seats: 42. Tare weight: 21 tons approximately.
Diagram No. 66 (SR No. 511). Built 1902.

This coach, originally built in 1902 as a Composite with three 1st-class and four 2nd-class compartments (No. 72 in the Composite list), was re-upholstered as an all-First, No. 272, in the second half of 1913 for working in the Royal Train, for which it was given a coat of arms. Renumbered SR 7549 in July 1926 and converted to dual braking, it was transferred to six-set 917, which in 1928 was booked to work the 8.32 am Uckfield to London Bridge and 4.40 pm return trains. In 1931 it went to four-set 848 in replacement of withdrawn First No. 7593, and worked the 6.53 am West Worthing to London Bridge and 3.35 pm Victoria to West Worthing; but in December 1931 it, too, was withdrawn.

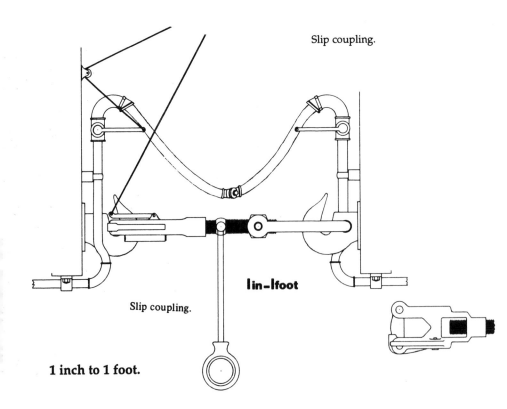

Slip coupling.

Slip coupling.

lin-lfoot

1 inch to 1 foot.

Chapter Three

Bogie Block Sets

Billinton's seven-coach close-coupled suburban 'Block' sets were constructed between 1898 and 1901. The first four sets were turned out in 1898/9 by Brighton, but the great majority were built by the Birmingham Railway Carriage & Wagon Co. during 1900/1, Brighton turning out four additional sets during those years.

Formation of most of the sets was: seven-compartment Third Brake, nine-compartment 2nd/3rd Composite, eight-compartment 1st/2nd Composite, seven-compartment 1st, another 1st/2nd Composite, another 2nd/3rd Composite and a Third Brake. Some sets, however, seem to have had two Firsts and only one 1st/2nd Composite.

Two Third Brakes and two Firsts were built at Brighton during 1897 to the 'Block' design, then two complete sets during 1898 and two more in 1899. The railway press of the day noted that 'one of the new suburban bogie trains has appeared during the Easter traffic'.

On 25th January, 1899, the LB&SCR announced its decision to order 15 trains of bogie suburban stock on capital account, plus five on revenue account. (*Railway Magazine* Vol. 4 p. 203.) On 28th July, 1899, a contract was signed with the Birmingham Railway Carriage & Wagon Co. for 20 close-coupled suburban block sets, each of seven vehicles and each costing £9,644. By the end of 1900, ten sets had been delivered; by April 1901 there were 16 running in traffic; and the remaining four had arrived before the end of the year.

All the carriages had steel underframes and ran on Fox's pressed-steel bogies of 8 ft wheelbase. Except at the outer ends, couplings were by means of a central block and buffer, there being no side-buffers. Electric lighting was provided by J. Stone & Co.'s axle-driven dynamo and battery on about four vehicles in each set, and by through connections on the remaining three vehicles. Overall length of each set was 353 ft 5 in. and the carriage bodies were either 48 ft or 50 ft long, 8 ft wide (9 ft 2 in. over guard's duckets) and 11 ft 9¼ in. high from rail to the top of the roof. Each set accommodated no fewer than 520 seated passengers - 120 1st, 160 2nd and 240 3rd class. An unusual feature was the presence of coloured glass toplights over the bodyside windows: blue to indicate a 1st class compartment, red for 2nd class, and yellow for 3rd class. After the last set was put into service the coloured glass was replaced by white frosted glass in the ventilating lights above the windows (*Railway Magazine* Vol. 8 p. 477) and the class designation was moved from its normal position on the doors to the etched glasses in the toplights.

First-class compartments originally had a single armrest in the centre of each seat as they were intended to accommodate four passengers a side, but later the armrest was removed. Second-class compartments were not very spacious, and sat five-a-side. Third-class compartments were horribly cramped, and moreover each alternate compartment partition went up only as far as the seat-back. However, by the current standards of suburban travel, the Bogie Blocks

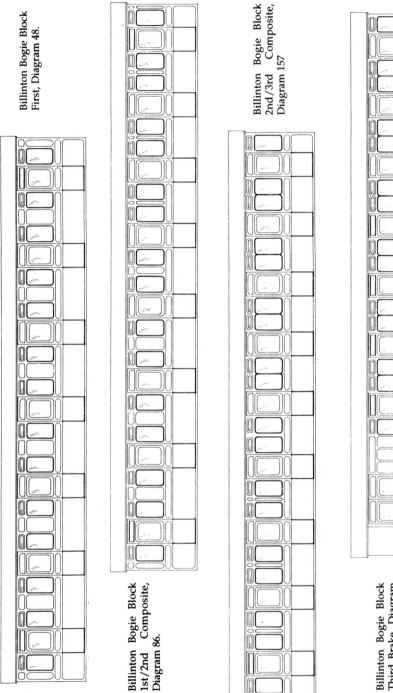

Billinton Bogie Block
First, Diagram 48.

Billinton Bogie Block
1st/2nd Composite,
Diagram 86.

Billinton Bogie Block
2nd/3rd Composite,
Diagram 157

Billinton Bogie Block
Third Brake, Diagram
158.

were good. The *Railway Magazine* noted in 1901 that in all the compartments artistic platinotype photographs were replacing monochrome views of scenery on the LB&SCR.

While the Birmingham-built sets were being delivered Brighton Works built two more in 1900 and two in 1901, and by summer 1901 there were 28 close-coupled seven-coach block trains in service.

Details of the carriages forming these sets now follow.

BOGIE FIRSTS

Nos. 3, 22, 30, 33, 56, 58, 59, 61, 63, 67, 68, 98-100 (built at Brighton), 201-220 (built by BRC&W). SR Nos. 7543-7577.

Body length: 48 ft. Body width: 8 ft. Bogie centres: 32 ft.
Compartments: Seven (6 ft 8¾ in. between partitions). Seats: 56.
Tare weight: 20 tons 4 cwt. (21 tons with dynamo).
Diagram No. 48 (SR Nos. 510, 512 or 513).

BOGIE COMPOSITES (1st/2nd)

Nos. 27, 59, 68, 142, 277, 299, 498 (built at Brighton), 548-587 (built by BRC&W). SR Nos. 6049-6095.

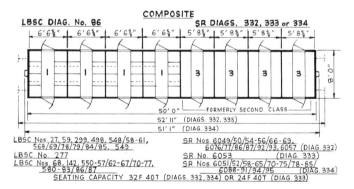

Body length: 50 ft. Body width: 8 ft. Bogie centres: 33 ft.
Compartments: Four 1st class (6 ft 6⅝ in. between partitions) and four 2nd class (5 ft 8⅝ in. between partitions). Seats: 32 1st, 40 2nd.
Tare weight: 21 tons (22 tons with dynamo). Diagram No. 86 (SR Nos. 332, 333 or 334).

BOGIE COMPOSITES (2nd/3rd)

Nos. 19, 25, 85, 88, 95, 141, 150, 175, 193, 204, 206, 233, 478, 479, 499, 500 (built at Brighton), 588-627 (built by BRC&W). Renumbered randomly as all-Thirds, 1911. SR Nos. 2117-2172 - not in same order.

Body length: 50 ft. Body width: 8 ft. Bogie centres: 33 ft.
Compartments: Four 2nd class (5 ft 8⅝ in. between partitions) and five 3rd class (5 ft 2⅝ in. between partitions). Seats: 40 2nd, 50 3rd.
Tare weight: 21 tons (22 tons with dynamo).
Diagram No. (as all-Third) 157. (SR Nos. 67 or 68).

BOGIE THIRD BRAKES

Nos. 584, 585, 594, 708, 710, 718, 1236/40/61/62/68/70-73, 1320/21 (built at Brighton), 1274-1313 (built by BRC&W). SR Nos. 3760-3802.

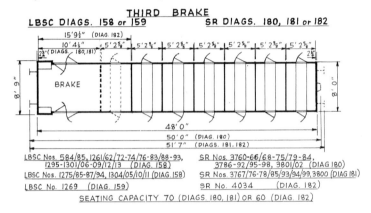

THIRD BRAKE

LBSC DIAGS. 158 or 159   SR DIAGS. 180, 181 or 182

LBSC Nos. 584/85, 1261/62/72-74/76-83/88-93, 1295-1301/06-09/12/13 (DIAG. 158)
SR Nos. 3760-66/68-75/79-84, 3786-92/95-98, 3801/02 (DIAG 180)
LBSC Nos. 1275/85-87/94, 1304/05/10/11 (DIAG. 158)
SR Nos. 3767/76-78/85/93/94/99, 3800 (DIAG 181)
LBSC No. 1269 (DIAG. 159)
SR No. 4034 (DIAG. 182)

SEATING CAPACITY 70 (DIAGS. 180, 181) OR 60 (DIAG. 182)

Body length: 48 ft. Body width: 8 ft (9 ft 2 in. over duckets - later 8 ft 9 in.). Bogie centres: 32 ft.
Compartments: Seven (5 ft 2⅝ in. between partitions). Seats: 70.
Tare weight: 19 tons 18 cwt. (20 tons with dynamo).
Diagram No. 158 (SR No. 180 or 181).

BOGIE THIRD BRAKE

No. 1269 (built at Brighton), SR No. 4034.

As above, but with only six compartments, seating 60 passengers.
Diagram No. 159 (SR No. 182).

The twenty Birmingham-built sets are presumed to have been formed in numerical sequence from the start, though whether they had set numbers initially is unknown. Later, they bore the numbers 60B to 79B.

3rd Bke	1274	1276		1312
2nd/3rd	588	590		626
1st/2nd	548	550	and so on	586
First	201	202	until	220
1st/2nd	549	551		587
2nd/3rd	589	591		627
3rd Bke	1275	1277		1313

Four of the Brighton-built sets are believed to have included Composites of a different design, Nos. 13, 30, 67 and 477; these were 48 ft vehicles each with two 1st-class and six 2nd-class compartments. Formations of these sets, based on building dates of the individual coaches, were probably as shown:

Built	6/98	12/98	6/99	12/99
3rd Bke	1261	1268	1270	1272
2nd/3rd	479	19	85	233
1st/2nd	477	13	67	30
First	22	56	61	67
First	33	58	63	68
2nd/3rd	478	25	88	150
3rd Bke	1262	1269	1271	1273

Other Brighton-built sets had the standard formation:

Built	6/00	12/00	6/01	12/01
3rd Bke	1320	594	710	584
2nd/3rd	95	141	499	206
1st/2nd	277	59	415	142
First	100	3	30	59
1st/2nd	299	27	498	68
2nd/3rd	175	204	500	193
3rd Bke	1321	708	718	585

Composite No. 415 of 1901, although having the same body design as Nos. 13, 30, 67 and 477, had four 1st- and four 2nd-class compartments, two of the 'firsts' being very narrow indeed. Composite No. 30 was withdrawn c. 1909 and replaced by an all-Second, No. 67 of 1899.

All the 'Block' sets ran in the suburban area, and often outside it, making regular outings to Dorking and possibly down the main line too at busy times. They could be seen on Lingfield race specials. Where high capacity was needed, there they would be found.

Third Brakes Nos. 1302 and 1303 were removed from their set following accident damage at Peckham Rye in 1904 and stored. From 1910 several sets were disbanded, their Third Brakes being required for rebuilding into electric Driving Trailer Composites for the South London line. In each of these reconstructions, six of the seven 3rd-class compartments were retained, and in the space formerly occupied by the seventh compartment and the guard/luggage compartment two new 1st-class compartments, each being 6 ft wide between partitions, and a driver's compartment, were built. The carriages then ran with the original 1909-built South London line A.C. motor coaches. The numbers of the coaches converted, and their new 'electric series' numbers, are shown below; it will be noted that the two Peckham Rye accident victims were included in the scheme.

Converted 6.1910		Converted 6.1911		Converted 12.1912	
Old No.	New No.	Old No.	New No.	Old No.	New No.
594	3225	1268	4057	708	4065
1236	3226	1320	4058	1321	4066
1240	3227	710	4059	1302	4067
1270	3228	718	4060	1303	4068
1271	3229				
1284	3230				

This resulted in the disbanding of several sets and the reformation of some others, Nos. 1302/03 from Set 74 being replaced by Nos. 1274 ex-Set 60 and 1295 ex-Set 70. (Set numbers for block trains were in use by 1906.)

In 1911 second class was abolished in the suburban area and the 2nd/3rd Composites were altered to all-3rds and renumbered into the Third Class series. The renumbering was not carried out to any noticeable system; such was the haste in which it was done that it seems clear new numbers were merely allocated on the spot as carriages or sets entered Works. The following table would seem to indicate as much:

Old No.	New No.	Old No.	New No.	Old No.	New No.	Old No.	New No.
597	1524	616	1561	620	1597	609	1690
596	1525	617	1562	621	1598	608	1691
479	1529	614	1563	233	1603	206	1708
478	1530	615	1564	150	1605	193	1709
500	1531	627	1565	594	1620	141	1719
499	1532	626	1566	595	1621	85	1727
624	1533	605	1568	612	1626	204	1731
601	1534	604	1569	613	1627	88	1734
618	1535	610	1572	622	1631	599	1738
589	1537	611	1573	623	1632	25	1752
592	1553	602	1584	591	1652	625	1768
593	1554	603	1585	590	1653	19	1773
606	1555	619	1590	598	1687	600	1778
607	1556	588	1592	175	1688	95	1781

All-Second No. 67 was renumbered Third No. 1604.

Even before the renumbering, some of the block trains had been split up, and the process continued into 1912, when in March of that year *Railway & Travel Monthly* reported that the bogie block trains were being fitted with full-size buffers to make them suitable for use on the main line. However, not all the sets were so-fitted, and three Brighton-built and 14 Birmingham-built sets (Nos. 6B, 8B, 12B, 61-4B, 67-9B, 71-4B, 76B, 77B and 79B) remained in use as close-coupled sets, most of them in their original formations. All the remaining coaches were given long buffers and formed into different sets.

Long-buffered Thirds (22): 1531-35/37/90/92, 1687/88/90/91, 1719/27/31/34/38 /52/68/73/78/81.
Long-buffered 3rd Brakes (10): 1269/75/85-87/94, 1304/05/10/11.
Long-buffered Composites (16): 27, 59, 277/99, 498, 548/58-61/68/69/78/79/84/85.
Long-buffered Firsts (13): 3, 30, 56, 58, 61, 63, 98, 201/06/07/11/16/19.

The following 'main-line' sets contained former 'Block' carriages in 1917 (principal workings shown):

5-set 15	(Composite 299 and Third 1592): London Bridge, Mitcham Junction, London Bridge, Horsham, Brighton, Worthing, Brighton, Horsham, London Bridge.
4-set 18	(3rd Brake 1275, First 201, Compos 549, 548): 9.24 am Epsom to London Bridge and 3.15 pm (Saturdays) or 5.15 pm (not Saturdays) return.
4-set 28	(3rd Brake 1294, Composites 568, 569): 8.13 am Epsom to Victoria, Victoria-Cheam-Victoria, 12.27 pm Victoria to Epsom.
3-set 30	(First 58): Tunbridge Wells and London Bridge.
4-set 35	(Composite 59, First 3): Brighton, London Bridge, Tunbridge Wells, Brighton.
5-set 37	(First 211): Oxted line. By 1921 this set was disbanded and No. 211 went to 5-set No. 78, which worked between Brighton and Victoria.
4-set 38	(First No. 56): 6.45 am Hastings to London Bridge and 4.05 pm return.
3-set 110	(3rd Brakes 1269/85, Composite 558): Clapham-Junction Kensington.

By 1921, in addition, Firsts Nos. 30 and 216 had been formed into ten-set No. 40, which ran between Brighton and London on the main line.

What happened to the other long-buffered carriages is not known, although some of them were formed in eight-coach bogie suburban sets 75L and 81L, also five-coach set 82L, the formations of which are not recorded, although apparently these did become SR sets Nos. 936, 932 and 924.

In some of the long-buffered former 'Block' carriages, the first-class compartments were altered to seat three passengers each side: Composite No. 277 and Firsts Nos. 3, 30, 56, 58, 61 and 98. Other modifications included the replacement of the toplights on all carriages by normal panelling and the fitting of steam heating apparatus to Sets 6B, 61B, 63B, 67B, 69B, 72B, 73B, 77B and 79B by 1923 (No. 12B was through-piped and then given heaters after 1923). In each set, the electric lighting equipment was arranged so that four carriages had dynamos and three did not, but in Sets 6B, 68B, 71B, 72B, 73B and 76B *all* the coaches were fitted with dynamos. In the other sets the arrangement was always that one of the Third Brakes had a dynamo and the other did not, one of the Thirds had one and the other did not, and *either* one Composite *or* the First was without the dynamo.

The 17 remaining seven-coach 'Block' trains continued working in the suburban area, each set finishing its day's work at a different station from the one whence it had started. The berthing points included Coulsdon, Epsom Town, New Cross, Sutton and Wallington. One set in 1921 did have a regular out-and-home working, however: No. 73B, based at Horsham, was found on the 8.20 am to London Bridge, from which it then ran empty to Eardley for cleaning, continuing later empty to Victoria for the 6.00 pm to Horsham. Three of the long-buffered sets made up from former 'block' carriages were berthed at Coulsdon for regular booked services in 1921. Eight-set No. 81L worked the 8.58 am to London Bridge, returning on the 1.32 pm (Saturdays) or 5.42 pm (not Saturdays) to Coulsdon. Five-set No. 82L formed the 9.40 am to Victoria and 5.27 pm return. Ten-set No. 75L ran up as the 7.55 am to Victoria, returning on

Saturdays at 12.41 pm. Except on Saturdays it was divided at Victoria into two five-coach portions, one of which returned to Coulsdon at 4.53 pm and the other at 5.52 pm; the portions were reunited at Coulsdon to form the up train next morning.

After 1923 the remaining unheated 'Block' sets - Nos. 8B, 12B, 62B, 64B, 68B, 71B, 74B and 76B - were fitted with steam heaters. The Southern renumbered the 17 sets 941 to 957 in the same order as the LB&SC set numbers, and between 1924 and 1926 12 of the sets were repainted in Southern livery with their new carriage numbers applied; the remaining five sets never appeared in SR colours as in 1927 the decision was made to withdraw all 17 of them for conversion into D.C. electric trains. None was ever given vacuum brakes, for the same reason, and all ended their days equipped only with Westinghouse air brakes. Withdrawal began with Set 951 in September 1927 and the last three sets - Nos. 943, 946 and 956 - went in November 1928.

The usual method was to withdraw three sets at a time, as this provided 21 coaches which could then be adapted into seven three-car electric trains. This process went on until 42 units had been completed, each of which was formed Motor Third Brake, Trailer Composite, Motor Third Brake *or* Motor Composite Brake, Trailer Composite, Motor Third Brake. Eight-compartment Motor Third Brakes were fabricated from the old Thirds or Third Brakes, whilst seven-compartment Motor Composite Brakes and ten-compartment Trailer Composites used the bodies of the old 1st/2nd Composites. Nine-compartment Trailer Composites used up all the old Firsts.

All were mounted on new 62 ft underframes and, where necessary, new compartments were added to bring the bodies up to the required length. Very clever thinking was involved to decide how to make the best use of all the original vehicles, at the same time ensuring that the standard provision for all three-car electric units - seven firsts and 18 thirds - was maintained. It meant that two distinct batches of units had to be constructed concurrently: Nos. 1631-57, each with two eight-compartment Motor Third Brakes and a Trailer Composite with seven 1st class and two 3rd class compartments; and Nos. 1702-16, with one Motor Third Brake, one Motor Composite Brake (three 1sts and four 3rds) and a Trailer Composite with four 1sts and six 3rds, the first-class ends of both carriages being adjacent to each other.

For example, Units 1631 and 1702 were formed at the same time from six coaches of block set No. 951; one Third Brake, one Third and the First going to Unit 1631 and the other Third Brake and the two Composites making up Unit 1702; the left-over Third was put aside to be formed into a later unit. Exactly the same happened with Set 953, which was carved up to make electric units 1632 and 1703.

The actual reconstruction of the bodies, which was carried out by Ashford Works, involved the following: Motor Third Brakes used the seven-compartment Third Brakes, with an extra compartment built on and new steel-panelled driving ends and guard's compartments. The nine-compartment Thirds each lost a compartment and were converted to Motor Third Brakes in the same way. Trailer Composites made from ex-Firsts used all seven of the original compartments plus a newly-built 3rd-class compartment at each end.

Motor Composite Brakes were made from Composites, losing one of the original four 1st-class compartments and retaining all four of the original 3rd class. Trailer Composites made from Composites used all four of the 1st-class compartments and all four Thirds, plus two new 3rd-class compartments built on.

Thus the 42 electric units reused 126 'Block' vehicles, of which the breakdown was 34 Third Brakes converted to Motor Third Brakes (Diagram No. 672), 35 Thirds converted to Motor Third Brakes (Diagram Nos. 673 and 674), 15 Composites to Motor Brake Composites (Diagram No. 692), 27 Firsts to Trailer Composites (Diagram No. 762) and 15 Composites to Trailer Composites (Diagram No. 763).

Of the Thirds, 34 were taken from close-coupled sets and one, No. 2163 (Motor Third Brake 8666), was long-buffered; all 34 of the close-coupled Third Brakes were reused, the long-buffered examples being kept in steam sets for a couple more years; all 30 close-coupled Composites were 'electrified', the remaining 17 long-buffered ones being retained as steam stock; and 19 close-coupled plus eight long-buffered Firsts were converted, leaving seven which remained as steam stock until withdrawal in 1931.

Units 1631 to 1657 comprised Motor Third Brakes Nos. 8617-70 in pairs and in numerical order, and Trailer Composites Nos. 9675-9701 in order. Units 1702-16 comprised Motor Third Brakes Nos. 8671-85, Trailer Composites Nos. 9702-16 and Motor Composite Brakes Nos. 8837-51, all in numerical order. Some of the units were put into service on 25th March, 1928, but full electric services on the Central Section suburban lines began on 17th June. Most of the units went into service during 1929.

On 9th July, 1928, the 7.22 pm London Bridge to Epsom Downs had just left London Bridge when it was hit side-on by a light engine. Unit 1702 was derailed. Later it was found that the centre trailer, No. 9702, was not worth repairing, so a 'new' trailer was fabricated by using two ex-LB&SC six-wheeled bodies, SR Nos. 1901 and 1922. This took the number of the withdrawn vehicle, 9702.

These conversions of Bogie Block sets into electric units left several long-buffered former 'Block' carriages in service for a time, but almost all eventually found their way into electric trains. The first to be altered were twelve nine-compartment Thirds, LB&SC Nos. 1531-35/37/90, 1688, 1727/68/78/81, which between February and April 1926 were adapted to run as two-car trailer sets Nos. 1111-13/15-17, vehicle Nos. 9121-32. All these were reformed in 1934, one ex-LBSC vehicle remaining in each set and the other being transferred to another set, its place taken by a 62ft trailer using lengthened ex-LSW bodywork.

In 1930 two more Thirds were rebuilt into Motor Third Brakes: these were numbered 8747/48 and were formed into Units 1770/71. The other cars making up these units were adapted from former A.C. electric stock. Finally, in January 1932, five more three-car motor units were made up using up most of the remaining Thirds, Third Brakes and Firsts. These were Units 1797-1801. Units 1797/98 comprised Motor Third Brakes Nos. 8586-89 converted from Thirds; and Units 1799-1801 comprised Motor Third Brakes Nos. 8590-95 converted from Third Brakes. Centre trailers of all five units were adapted from Firsts, with two new 3rd-class compartments, and were numbered 9666-70. Any remaining steam-hauled former 'Block' carriages were withdrawn during 1930-32.

The units made from former Bogie Block carriages had the narrowest third-class compartments on the Southern Electric; these, combined with the rough riding of motor coaches generally, made them just about the most uncomfortable electric trains to ride in, particularly in the peak periods. In the 1940s the decision was made to increase the length of the three-car units to four cars, at the same time abolishing the separate trailer sets. Unit 1709 was the first of this type of motor unit to be augmented, in June 1943, and it was renumbered 4250. The additional trailer, No. 9722 (ex-A.C.) was taken from Unit 1722; however, most of the later augmentations of units comprising vehicles of LB&SC origin employed a newly-built steel trailer. Several units were withdrawn without ever being augmented: these were Nos. 1632/33/35/40/41/46/54-7, 1702/05/08/10-12/70/99, 1800. The augmented units were renumbered into a new 4XXX series, but they did not last long in their new identities, most being scrapped in 1948 and 1949.

Several units suffered accident damage in the 1940s.

Unit 1799:   8590 damaged by enemy action at Elmers End 28.5.41. Unit reformed.
Unit 1633:   8622 accident damage Waddon 4.11.42. Unit disbanded.
Unit 1770:   Accident damage at South Croydon, 24.10.47. 8747 and remainder of unit withdrawn.
Unit 4250:   Accident damage, Herne Hill, 6.11.47. Whole unit withdrawn.
Unit 4607:   8595 accident damage at Crayford, 11.2.48. 8595 cut up, and 8594 to spare, later withdrawn.
Unit 1800:   Involved in a mishap at South Bermondsey, 10.5.48. Unit withdrawn.

The accident at South Croydon was very serious. In dense fog, Unit 1770, working the 8.04 am Tattenham Corner to London Bridge, hit the 7.33 am Haywards Heath to London Bridge train, which had been brought to a stand. All the cars of Unit 1770 were damaged beyond repair, and the centre vehicle had to be cut up on site. Thirty-two passengers were killed and 183 injured in the disaster.

The Herne Hill accident, a few days later, involved augmented unit No. 4250 which, while working the 6.58 pm Holborn Viaduct to West Croydon via Tulse Hill, was hit a glancing blow by the 4.15 pm Ramsgate to Victoria steam train. Motor Third Brake No. 8678 had the sides of all eight compartments torn out, and trailer No. 9722 had its body detached from the underframe. Both vehicles were cut up on site.

The last units in service comprising bodywork made from 'Bogie Block' sets were Nos. 4613 (old 1652), 4576 (old 1704), 4578 (old 1713) and 4581 (old 1715). They were withdrawn in September and October 1949, after a life, in one form or another, of nearly fifty years. Thanks to the Southern's 'make do and mend' policy, that life had been extended further than was really desirable.

THIRDS (DIAGRAM No. 157)

LBSC No.	Built	Set	SR No.	Re-No.	Set No.	DC No.	Re-No.	Unit	Wdn
1524	12.00	64B	2117	5.25	947	8654	10.28	1649, 4257	49
1525	12.00	64B	2118	5.25	947	8653	10.28	1649, 4257	49
1529	6.98	6B	-	-	941	8650	10.28	1647, 4610	2.49
1530	6.98	6B	-	-	941	8652	10.28	1648, 4606	1.49
1531	6.01		-	-		9121	2.26	1111	7.42
1532	6.01		-	-		9122	2 26	1113, 1097	.42
1533	12.01	78B, L	-	-		9123	2.26	1111, 1070	.47
1534	12.00	66B, L	-	-		9124	3.26	1112	.47
1535	6.01	75B, L	-	-		9125	3.26	1113	.42
1537	6 00	60B, L	-	-		9126	3 26	1112, 1111	3.48
1553	6.00	62B	2127	6.26	945	8632	7.28	1638, 4523	1.49
1554	6.00	62B	2128	6.26	945	8630	7.28	1637, 4522	1.49
1555	12.00	69B	-	-	950	8646	9.28	1645, 4604	6.49
1556	12.00	69B	-	-	950	8648	9.28	1646	11.48
1561	6.01	74B	2131	11.24	954	8655	10.28	1650, 4575	2.49
1562	6.01	74B	2132	11.24	954	8656	10.28	1650, 4575	2.49
1563	6.01	73B	-	-	953	8620	10.27	1632	11.48
1564	6.01	73B	-	-	953	8640	8.28	1642, 4525	1.49
1565	12 01	79B	2135	3.24	957	8641	9.28	1643, 4601	6.49
1566	12.01	79B	2136	3.24	957	8642	9.28	1643, 4601	6.49
1568	12.00	68B	2137	7.25	949	8628	7.28	1636, 4605	2.49
1569	12.00	68B	2138	7.25	949	8626	7.28	1635	11.48
1572	6.01	71B	-	-	951	8618	9.27	1631, 4585	1.49
1573	6.01	71B	-	-	951	8638	8.28	1641	10.48
1584	12.00	67B	2141	6.26	948	8636	8.28	1640	11.48
1585	12 00	67B	2142	6.26	948	8634	8.28	1639, 4524	6.49
1590	6.01	75B, L	-	-		9127	4.26	1117	.45
1592	6.00	60B, 15	2144	8.25	890	8589	1.32	1798, 4584	6.49
1597	12.01	76B	2145	12.24	955	8667	5.28	1656	11.48
1598	12.01	76B	2146	12.24	955	8668	5.28	1656	11.48
1603	12 99	8B	2147	11.24	942	8644	9.28	1644, 4562	1.49
1605	12.99	8B	2148	11.24	942	8643	9.28	1644, 4562	1.49
1620	6.00	63B	2149	12.23	946	8664	12.28	1654	11.48
1621	6.00	63B	2150	12.23	946	8665	12.28	1655	11.48
1626	6.01	72B	-	-	952	8670	4.28	1657	1.49
1627	6.01	72B	-	-	952	8669	4.28	1657	1.49
1631	12.01	77B	2153	4.24	956	8658	11.28	1651, 4608	2.49
1632	12.01	77B	2154	4.24	956	8663	12.28	1654	11.48
1652	6.00	61B	2155	2.24	944	8622	7.28	1633	12.42
1653	6.00	61B	2156	2.24	944	8624	7 28	1634, 4603	2.49
1687	12.00	65B, L	2157	7.25		8587	1.32	1797, 4583	2.49
1688	6.00		-	-		9128	4.26	1116	4.42
1690	6.01	70B, L	2159	8.24		-	-		6.32
1691	6.01	70B, L	2160	11.26		8748	6.30	1771	.48
1708	12.01	12B	2161	2.25	943	8662	11.28	1653, 4614	1.49
1709	12.01	12B	2162	2.25	943	8660	11 28	1652, 4613	9.49
1719	12.00		2163	4.26		8666	12.28	1655	11.48
1727	6.99		2164	8.24		9129	2.26	1115	.42
1731	12.00		2165	8.26		8747	6.30	1770	10.47

LBSC No.	Built	Set	SR No.	Re-No.	Set No.	DC No.	Re-No.	Unit	Wdn
1734	6.99		2166	4.24	979	8588	1.32	1798, 4584	6.49
1738	12.00	65B, L	2167	9.26	817	-	-		12.30
1752	12.98		2168	8.26		8586	1.32	1797, 4583	2.49
1768	12.01	78B, L	-	-		9130	4.26	1117, 1195	.45
1773	12.98		2170	7.27		-	-		12.30
1778	12.00	66B, L	2171	12.24		9131	4.26	1116, 1197	.42
1781	6.00		2172	7.24		9132	3.26	1115, 1196	.47

SR Diagram No. 67 (close-coupled) and 68 (long-buffered).
L = Loose vehlcle.

THIRD BRAKES (DIAGRAM No. 158)

LBSC No.	Built	Set	SR No.	Re-No.	Set No.	DC No.	Re-No.	Unit	Wdn
584	12.01	12B	3760	2.25	943	8659	11.28	1652, 4613	9.49
585	12.01	12B	3761	2.25	943	8661	11 28	1653, 4614	1.49
594	12.00								
708	12.00								
710	6.01								
718	6.01								
1236	.96								
1240	6.97								
1261	6.98	6B	-	-	941	8645	9.28	1645, 4604	6.49
1262	6.98	6B	-	-	941	8647	9.28	1646	11.48
1268	12.98								
1270	6.99								
1271	6.99								
1272	12.99	8B	3764	11.24	942	8637	8.28	1641	10.48
1273	12.99	8B	3765	11.24	942	8639	8.28	1642, 4525	1.49
1274	6.00	60B, 74B	3766	11.24	954	8649	10.28	1647, 4610	2.49
1275	6.00	60B, 18	3767	8.25	923	8591	1.32	1799	.48
1276	6.00	61B	3768	2.24	944	8621	7.28	1633	11.48
1277	6.00	61B	3769	2.24	944	8623	7.28	1634, 4603	2.49
1278	6.00	62B	3770	6.26	945	8629	7.28	1637, 4522	1.49
1279	6.00	62B	3771	6.26	945	8631	7.28	1638, 4523	1.49
1280	6.00	63B	3772	12.23	946	8685	12.28	1716, 4582	6.49
1281	6.00	63B	3773	12.23	946	8684	12.28	1715, 4581	9.49
1282	12.00	64B	3774	5.25	947	8681	10.28	1712	8.48
1283	12.00	64B	3775	5.25	947	8682	10.28	1713, 4578	10.49
1284	12.00	65B, L							
1285	12.00	65B, 110	3776	9.26	817	-	-		12.30
1286	12.00	66B, 81L	3777	7.26	932	8590	1.32	1799	5.41
1287	12.00	66B, 81L	3778	7.26	932	8594	1.32	1801, 4607	2.48
1288	12.00	67B	3779	6.26	948	8677	8.28	1708	.49
1289	12.00	67B	3780	6.26	948	8678	8.28	1709, 4250	11.47
1290	12.00	68B	3781	7.25	949	8625	7.28	1635	11.48
1291	12.00	68B	3782	7.25	949	8627	7.28	1636, 4605	2.49
1292	12.00	69B	-	-	950	8679	9.28	1710	7.48
1293	12.00	69B	-	-	950	8680	9.28	1711	11.48
1294	6.01	70B, 28	3785	8.24	916	-	-		10.31

LBSC No.	Built	Set	SR No.	Re-No.	Set No.	DC No.	Re-No.	Unit	Wdn
1295	6.01	70B, 74B	3786	11.24	954	8651	10.28	1648, 4606	1.49
1296	6.01	71B	-	-	951	8617	9.27	1631, 4585	1.49
1297	6 01	71B	-	-	951	8671	10.27	1702	9.48
1298	6.01	72B	-	-	952	8674	10.27	1705	11.48
1299	6.01	72B	-	-	952	8675	7.28	1706, 4577	1.49
1300	6.01	73B	-	-	953	8619	10.27	1632	11.48
1301	6.01	73B	-	-	953	8672	10.27	1703, 4256	.49
1302	6 01	74B, L							
1303	6.01	74B, L							
1304	6.01	75B, 82L	3793	1.26	924	8593	1.32	1800	5.48
1305	6.01	75B, 82L	3794	1.26	924	8595	1.32	1801, 4607	2.48
1306	12.01	76B	3795	12.24	955	8673	10.27	1704, 4576	9.49
1307	12 01	76B	3796	12.24	955	8676	7.28	1707, 4602	6.48
1308	12.01	77B	3797	4.24	956	8683	11.28	1714, 4563	2.49
1309	12.01	77B	3798	4.24	956	8657	11.28	1651, 4608	2.49
1310	12.01	78B, 75L	3799	8.26	936	-	_		10.30
1311	12.01	78B, 75L	3800	8.26	936	8592	1.32	1800	5.48
1312	12.01	79B	3801	3.24	957	8635	8.28	1640	11.48
1313	12.01	79B	3802	3.24	957	8633	8.28	1639, 4524	6.49
1320	6.00								
1321	6.00								

SR Diagram No. 180 (close-coupled) and 181 (long-buffered).

THIRD BRAKE (DIAGRAM No. 159)

LBSC No.	Built	Set	SR No.	Re-No.	Set No.	DC No.	Re-No.	Unit	Wdn
1269	12.98	?, 110	4034	9.26	817	-	-		12.30

COMPOSITES (DIAGRAM No. 86)

LBSC No.	Built	Set	SR No.	Re-No.	Set No.	DC No.	Re-No.	Unit	Wdn
27	12.00		6049	1.26	890	-	-		4.32
59	12.00	35	6050	7.26		-	-		5.31
68	12.01	12B	6051	2.25	943	8851	12.28	1716, 4582	6.49
142	12.01	12B	6052	2.25	943	9716	12.28	1716, 4582	6.49
277	6.00		6053	10.24		-	-		1.33
299	6.00	?, 15	6054	1.26	924	-	-		A
498	6.01	?, 81L	6055	7.26	932	-	-		2.34
548	6.00	60B, 18	6056	8.25	749	-	-		3.32
549	6.00	60B, 18	6057	8.27	750	-	-		4.32
550	6.00	61B	6058	2.24	944	9707	7.28	1707, 4602	6.48
551	6.00	61B	6059	2.24	944	8842	7.28	1707, 4602	6.48
552	6.00	62B	6060	6.26	945	8844	8.28	1709, 4250	11.47
553	6.00	62B	6061	6.26	945	9709	8.28	1709, 4250	11.47
554	6.00	63B	6062	12.23	946	8850	12.28	1715, 4581	9.49
555	6.00	63B	6063	12.23	946	9715	12.28	1715, 4581	9.49
556	12.00	64B	6064	5.25	947	9713	10.28	1713, 4578	10.49
557	12.00	64B	6065	5.25	947	8848	10.28	1713, 4578	10.49
558	12.00	65B, 110	6066	9.26	817	-	-		12.30

LBSC No.	Built	Set	SR No.	Re-No.	Set No.	DC No.	Re-No.	Unit	Wdn
559	12.00	65B, 75L	6067	8.26	936	-	-		10.30
560	12.00	66B, 81L	6068	7.26	932	-	-		2.34
561	12.00	66B, 81L	6069	7.26	932	-	-		2.34
562	12.00	67B	6070	6.26	948	8843	8.28	1708	.49
563	12.00	67B	6071	6.26	948	9708	8.28	1708	.49
564	12.00	68B	6072	7.25	949	8841	7.28	1706, 4577	1.49
565	12.00	68B	6073	7.25	949	9706	7.28	1706, 4577	1.49
566	12.00	69B	-	-	950	8846	9.28	1711	11.48
567	12.00	69B	-	-	950	9711	9.28	1711	11.48
568	6.01	70B, 28	6076	8.24	916	-	-		10.32
569	6.01	70B, 28	6077	8.24	916	-	-		10.32
570	6.01	71B	-	-	951	9702	10.27	1702	7.28
571	6 01	71B	-	-	951	8837	10.27	1702	9.48
572	6.01	72B	-	-	952	8840	10.27	1705	11.48
573	6.01	72B	-	-	952	9705	10.27	1705	11.48
574	6.01	73B	-	-	953	9703	10.27	1703, 4256	.49
575	6.01	73B	-	-	953	8838	10.27	1703, 4256	.49
576	6.01	74B	6084	11.24	954	8847	10.28	1712	8.48
577	6.01	74B	6085	11.24	954	9712	10.28	1712	8.48
578	6.01	75B, 82L	6086	1.26	924	-	-		A
579	6.01	75B, 82L	6087	1.26	924	-	-		A
580	12.01	76B	6088	12.24	955	8839	10.27	1704, 4576	9.49
581	12.01	76B	6089	12 24	955	9704	10.27	1704, 4576	9.49
582	12.01	77B	6090	4.24	956	9714	11.28	1714, 4563	2.49
583	12.01	77B	6091	4.24	956	8849	11.28	1714, 4563	2.49
584	12.01	78B, L	6092	6.27		-	-		10.31
585	12.01	78B, L	6093	7.27		-	- .		6.31
586	12.01	79B	6094	3.24	957	8845	9.28	1710	7.48
587	12.01	79B	6095	3.24	957	9710	9.28	1710	7.48

SR Diagram No. 332 (long-buffered); 333 (No. 6053 only) and 334 (close-coupled).

A   6054 renumbered Third 2121, 10.28. Withdrawn 2.32.
6086 renumbered Third 2122, 10.28. Withdrawn 7.31.
6087 renumbered Third 2123, 9.28. Withdrawn 2.34.

FIRSTS (DIAGRAM No. 48)

LBSC No.	Built	Set	SR No.	Re-No.	Set No.	DC No.	Re-No.	Unit	Wdn
3	12.00	35	7543	9.26	817	-	-		12 30
22	6.98	6B	-	-	941	9691	10.28	1647, 4610	2.49
30	6.01	?, 40	7544	6.26		9669	1.32	1800	5.48
33	6.98	6B	-	-	941	9690	9.28	1646	11.48
56	12.98	38	7545	8.25	843	9668	1.32	1799	.47
58	12.98	30	7546	4.27	786	9667	1.32	1798, 4584	6.49
59	12.01	12B	7552	2.25	943	9696	11.28	1652, 4613	9.49
61	6.99		7547	1.26		9666	1.32	1797, 4583	2.49
63	6.99		7553	5.27		9680	7.28	1636, 4605	2.49
67	12.99	8B	7554	11.24	942	9685	8.28	1641	10.48
68	12.99	8B	7555	11.24	942	9686	8.28	1642, 4525	1.49

Stroudley bogie First No. 77 of 1889 (Diagram No. 43). Note the spoked wheels and the lightweight construction of the bogies, which lacked headstocks.

Stroudley Inspection Saloon No. 72 of 1889, as rebuilt in 1900 with partly-enclosed ends and Pullman bogies. As SR No. 7969 the vehicle was withdrawn in 1930.   *Lens of Sutton*

Billinton eight-compartment Third No. 728, built in 1903 (Diagram No. 161); here shown in Marsh livery. Became SR No. 2061, a push-and-pull trailer, in 1925.

Locomotive Publishing Co.

Gloucester RC & W Co.-built Billinton Lavatory Third No. 1319, new in 1900 (Diagram No. 173). This coach, which was equipped with gas lighting, became SR No. 2178.

Gloucester RC&W Co.

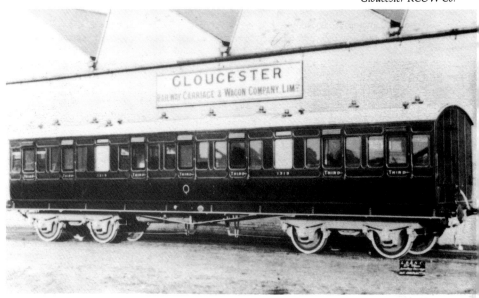

Lavatory Composite No. 484, built by the Gloucester RC&W Co. in September 1900, and gas lighted (Diagram No. 90). This later became SR No. 6007. *Gloucester RC&W Co.*

In this scene of Lancing Works, among examples of elliptical-roofed carriage stock, is Billinton Lavatory Composite No. 497 (built by Gloucester RC & W Co. in 1901) which later became SR No. 6020. *Lens of Sutton*

Billinton Lavatory Composite Brake with central guard's compartment, No. 518, built in 1905 (Diagram No. 100). It is in Marsh livery and carries a destination board reading 'Brighton'. The coach became SR No. 6925 after Grouping.

The only existing Billinton coach body today: six-compartment 48 ft First No. 142 (SR No. 7598) is here shown mounted on a temporary underframe and being shunted at Horsted Keynes, Bluebell Railway, by 'Rooter' No. 55 *Stepney* on 10th September, 1989. *Author*

Billinton 'Bogie Block' set at Forest Hill on London Bridge to Crystal Palace service, being
worked by a class 'E2' 0-6-0 tank engine in 1926.   *Rev. A.W.V. Mace*

SR DC electric unit 1705: Motor Brake Composite No. 8840 was converted from Billinton 'Block'
Composite No. 572 and Trailer Composite No. 9705 (part shown on right) from 'Block'
Composite No. 573, both in October 1927.   *Lens of Sutton*

Twelve-wheeled King's Saloon No. 562 (Diagram No. 37) built in 1897. It became SR No. 7970 in 1925.

The LB&SC Royal Train (five saloons, with the 12-wheeled Royal Saloon in the centre) passes Hackbridge, headed by class 'B4' No. 42 *His Majesty*.

ROYAL TRAIN 1906

An up LB&SC Royal Train leaves Portsmouth Dockyard (South Railway Jetty) in charge of Marsh's class '13' No. 24.

D. Cullum Collection

Panter nine-compartment Third No. 634, built in 1905 (Diagram No. 185); it was adapted for Ambulance Train No. 25 in 1915. *Locomotive Publishing Co.*

Panter Lavatory Third Brake No. 810 of 1906 (Diagram No. 190); here shown in a troop train at Lewes with the Lewes Volunteers assembled on the platform. No. 810 was adapted for Ambulance Train No. 25 in 1915. Also visible are a six-wheeled Third and a Billinton 48 ft bogie First (Diagram No. 49), in Marsh livery.

Panter Lavatory Second No. 233, built in 1905. Altered to Third No. 1679 in 1912, it was rebuilt to seven-compartment Lavatory First Brake No. 9 a year later (Diagram No. 42). As SR No. 7768 it was withdrawn in 1940. *Locomotive Publishing Co.*

Panter Lavatory Tri-Composite No. 629 of 1905 (Diagram No. 103). This carriage became SR No. 6200.

Panter First Brake No. 27 of 1905 (Diagram No. 54) painted, as were all the elliptical-roofed carriages, in umber and white. No. 27 became SR No. 7772.

Panter Third Brake as SR No. 3816 in push-and-pull set 734, with the former lavatory compartment at the inner end blanked off. The carriage was built in 1906 as LB&SC No. 605.

Panter Third Brake No. 4054 in about 1938, formed in SR set No. 882. The carriage was built in 1906 as LB&SC Second Brake No. 37.   E. Jackson

Panter Composite, SR No. 6189, as running in push-and-pull set 750 with 'Balloon' Third Brake No. 3845 at Horsham, 16th July, 1938. The Composite was built in 1905 as No. 522 and withdrawn in 1943.   H.C. Casserley

A push-and-pull set including one of the Composites in the 6189-91 series enters Dorking North on a service from Horsham about 1938 in charge of class 'D1/M' locomotive No. 2229.

Lens of Sutton

A Panter Composite in the SR 6193-98 series (SR Diagram No. 344) built in 1905.   *E. Jackson*

Panter Composite No. 6284, built as LB&SC No. 526 in 1907 with 10 ft-wheelbase bogies for the Newhaven Boat Train. It was fitted as a push-and-pull trailer in 1931 and formed with Third Brake No. 3836 in Set 741 ; withdrawn in 1941.   *E. Jackson*

Panter 56 ft Composite SR No. 6286, built as LB&SC No. 73 in 1906 and push-and-pull fitted in 1931 for Set 736; it was withdrawn in 1940.   *E. Jackson*

One of the Panter First Brakes built in 1905 and numbered in the SR series 7772-74; here shown at New Cross Gate formed in a five-coach set, 22nd June, 1935.   *L.E. Brailsford Collection*

Former 'City Limited' Lavatory First, built in 1907, with body dimensions of 54 ft x 9 ft. The SR number series was 7638-40. Set No. 933 is here shown with replacement First Brake at the end, possibly ex-South Eastern & Chatham.   *E. Jackson*

Former 'City Limited' Saloon First Brake No. 7770 in SR race set No. 933 at Lingfield in 1938. Corridor First No. 7641 is next to it. *E.R. Lacey*

SR Race Set No. 933 (former 'City Limited' stock, passing Belmont on Derby Day, 1935. Behind class 'I3' locomotive No. 2086 is Corridor Saloon First Brake No. 7770 (LB&SC No. 31) and next to that is the unique six-compartment Corridor First No. 7641 (LB&SC No. 151).

D. Cullum Collection

LB&SC Ambulance Train No. 14 at Lovers Walk, Brighton, in 1915 ; Coach No. 14H, converted from Panter four-compartment Lavatory Third Brake, is the end vehicle.

Ambulance Train No. 14, which also included some London & North Western carriages, worked in France ; here it is shown divided, having arrived at Le Tréport to unload the wounded into motor ambulances for transfer to the hospital ship. Coach 14D is nearest the camera.

Arnault, Le Tréport

LBSC No.	Built	Set	SR No.	Re-No. No.	Set	DC No.	Re-No.	Unit	Wdn
98	6.97		7548	6.26	921	9670	1.32	1801, 4607	2.48
99	6.97		7556	7.26		9699	12.28	1655	11.48
100	6.00	21	7557	6.26	921	-	-		3.31
201	6.00	60B, 18	7558	9.24	845	9698	12.28	1654	11.48
202	6.00	61B	7559	8.24	944	9677	7.28	1633	11.48
203	6.00	62B	7560	6.26	945	9681	7.28	1637, 4522	1.49
204	6.00	63B	7561	12.23	946	9697	11.28	1653, 4614	1.49
205	12.00	64B	7562	5.25	947	9693	10.28	1649, 4257	.49
206	12.00	65B, L	7563	7.25		9682	7.28	1638, 4523	1.49
207	12.00	66B, L	7564	6.27		9679	7.28	1635	11.48
208	12.00	67B	7565	6.26	948	9683	8.28	1639, 4524	6.49
209	12.00	68B	7566	7.25	949	9678	7.28	1634, 4603	2.49
210	12.00	69B	-	-	950	9689	9.28	1645, 4604	6.49
211	6.01	70B, 37, 78	7568	4.27		9687	9.28	1643, 4601	6.49
212	6.01	71B	-	-	951	9675	9.27	1631, 4585	1.49
213	6.01	72B	-	-	952	9701	4.28	1657	1.49
214	6.01	73B	-	-	953	9676	10.27	1632	11.48
215	6.01	74B	7572	11.24	954	9692	10.28	1648, 4606	1.49
216	6.01	75B, L, 40	7573	4.26		9694	10.28	1650, 4575	2.49
217	12.01	76B	7574	12.24	955	9700	5.28	1656	11.48
218	12.01	77B	7575	4.24	956	9695	11.28	1651, 4608	2.49
219	12 01	78B, L	7576	8.26		9688	9.28	1644, 4562	1.49
220	12.01	79B	7577	3.24	957	9684	8.28	1640	11.48

SR Diagram No. 510 (long-buffered - seats three-a-side); No. 512 (long-buffered - seats four-a-side) and No 513 (close-coupled).

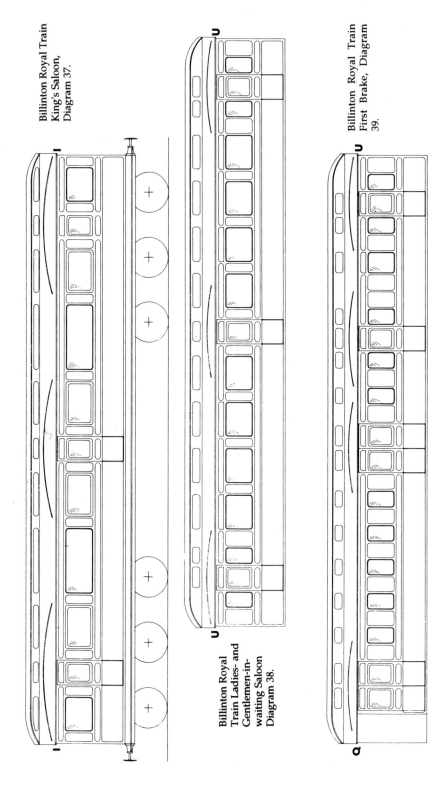

Billinton Royal Train
King's Saloon,
Diagram 37.

Billinton Royal
Train Ladies- and
Gentlemen-in-
waiting Saloon
Diagram 38.

Billinton Royal Train
First Brake, Diagram
39.

Chapter Four

The Royal Train

In 1897 a new Royal Train was built to replace the old six-wheel saloon built by Stroudley in 1871. This train, intended primarily for the use of Edward, Prince of Wales, consisted of five clerestory-roofed carriages, the bodies of which were all 52 ft in length. Edward's saloon, which ran on six-wheeled bogies and had a body width of 8 ft 9 in., was the centre vehicle of the set. The other carriages were 8 ft wide and eight-wheeled: two saloons, one for the gentlemen-in-waiting and the other for Princess Alexandra's ladies-in-waiting, and two lavatory brake firsts with a few seats for railway and other officials.

Prince Edward's saloon, No. 562, consisted of three compartments, one each for him, Princess Alexandra, and the servants. There were three lavatory compartments. The Royal Saloon was not gangwayed to the adjacent vehicles as Edward desired privacy on his journeys. Windows had etched borders, and there was a false arch in the clerestory, the decoration of which was in white lincrusta picked out in gold. The walls under the sidelights were fawn lincrusta also picked out in gold. In Edward's compartment the mouldings were mahogany, but in Alexandra's they were maple. The panels between the sidelights were of satinwood with a floral marquetry design inlaid with a variety of other woods. Both saloons were sumptuously furnished, with dark green Morocco leather upholstery for the Prince and Utrecht stamped velvet for the Princess; and carpets were crimson and grey-green Axminster, respectively. Pale green silk was used for the curtains and for the shades to the electric lights. Each of the Royal compartments had an electric heater. The servants' compartment had Morocco leather seating, a folding table, a bell indicator and hat and coat hooks. Four of the large windows in each bodyside were droplights, with a drop of 8 in.

The saloon for the ladies-in-waiting, No. 563, had four compartments with two lavatories. The clerestory and dados had lincrusta in white and fawn, but not picked out in gold. Sycamore panelling and mahogany mouldings decorated the walls, and upholstery was of blue silk plush with a blue Axminster carpet. The saloon for the gentlemen-in-waiting, No. 564, was identical in layout and decoration except that the colour scheme was green. Two of the large windows in each bodyside were droplights, with a drop of only 6 in.

The lavatory Brake Firsts (Nos. 565 and 566) had seating of the normal 1st-class type for ten passengers in two compartments. A short side passage connected them and gave access to the lavatory, which was between the two compartments. One carriage had upholstery in dark blue figured plush with carpet and fittings to match, and the other was in red. Only No. 565 was equipped with a dynamo to give electric lighting supply to all five vehicles. The guard's compartment at each end incorporated side lookouts, the extreme width of which was 9 ft 2 in., and there were four large windows in the ends, overlooking the track.

51

Externally, all five vehicles were finished in varnished mahogany with gilt lining; none were subsequently painted in umber brown.

The train was used frequently by Edward as Prince of Wales, and from 1901 as King Edward VII, on his journeys to Epsom Downs for Derby Day, and journeys to Singleton, for West Dean House, and to Eastbourne, are also recorded.

On 2nd February, 1901, the Royal Train was used to convey the body of Queen Victoria from Gosport (London & South Western Railway) to Victoria Station. In addition to the five LB&SC carriages there were two bogie Firsts and a Great Western funeral carriage to convey the coffin. Among the Royal personages were Edward VII and Kaiser Wilhelm II. Leaving Royal Clarence Yard, Gosport, at 8.45 am the train arrived at Fareham nine minutes later; here engines were changed and the train's direction of travel was reversed. Because the various carriages had not been placed where the mourners had expected them to be there was considerable delay while they sorted themselves out, and in consequence the funeral train left Fareham about ten minutes late. However, Driver Walter Cooper was instructed to make up time, and this he did; arrival at Victoria was two minutes *early*! The King had no cause for complaint about unpunctuality, and the German Emperor was so pleased about the fast running he sent his equerry to congratulate the driver and fireman.

The train was not used as a Royal Train by the Southern Railway, who preferred the South Eastern & Chatham train. In May 1924 all five vehicles emerged from Lancing Works in Southern green, Nos. 562-4 being renumbered 7970-72 and the Brake Firsts, No. 565/6, becoming 7766/7. They were now made available for use by ordinary first class passengers, the set train (numbered 925) being placed on the 8.33 am Eastbourne to London Bridge business service, returning at 5.05 pm. Two or three elliptical-roofed coaches were also formed into the set, as otherwise the seating capacity of the train would have been unacceptably low; all the original furniture was retained for a couple of years. Later it was retrimmed in a less comfortable style, and in spring 1926 vacuum brake equipment was added to the original Westinghouse air-brake gear. By September 1928 Set 925 had been taken off its Eastbourne workings, having been replaced by newly-built corridor stock, and the formation was then: Brake First 7766, elliptical-roofed Third 2179, Saloon Firsts 7972 and 7970, elliptical-roofed lavatory Third 2338, and Brake First 7767.

Set 925 seems to have been reduced to four vehicles by 1930 and was kept at Eastbourne for working bank holiday reliefs and special trains. In May the Brake Firsts became vacuum-braked only. Nos. 7970/72 lost their Westinghouse gear in September 1930 and No. 7971 did so two months later; these three saloons were then used for the conveyance of private parties. In 1931 the set was disbanded.

The two Brake Firsts were withdrawn in 1932, and No. 7971 went a year later. Nos. 7970 and 7972 are recorded as having been sold out of service, probably as dwellings: the King's Saloon in March 1933 and the other in March 1934.

ROYAL SALOON

No. 562, built 12.1897. SR No. 7970.

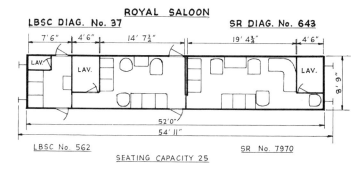

Body length: 52 ft. Body width: 8 ft 9 in. Height, rail to top of clerestory: 13 ft 1 in. Bogie centres: 34 ft. Bogie wheelbase: 5 ft 9 in. plus 5 ft 9 in. Compartments: Three. Lavatories: Three, one per compartment. Seats: 25. Tare weight: 27 tons 9 cwt. Diagram No. 37 (SR No. 643). Sold March 1933.

ROYAL SALOON

Nos. 563, 564, built 12.1897. SR Nos. 7971, 7972.

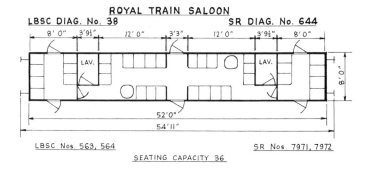

Body length: 52 ft. Body width: 8 ft. Height, rail to top of clerestory: 13 ft 1½ in. Bogie centres: 35 ft. Bogie wheelbase: 8 ft. Compartments: Four. Two lavatories, accessible from all compartments. Seats: 28, later 36. Tare weight: 22 tons 2 cwt. Diagram No. 38 (SR No. 644).
No. 7971 withdrawn c. 12.1933, No. 7972 sold March 1934.

ROYAL TRAIN FIRST BRAKE

Nos. 565, 566, built 12.1897. SR Nos. 7766, 7767.

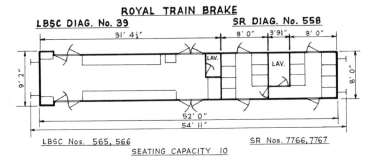

ROYAL TRAIN BRAKE

LBSC DIAG. No. 39   **SR DIAG. No. 558**

LBSC Nos. 565, 566   SR Nos. 7766, 7767

SEATING CAPACITY 10

Body length: 52 ft. Body width: 8 ft (9 ft 2 in. over duckets). Height, rail to top of clerestory: 13 ft 1½ in. Bogie centres: 35 ft. Bogie wheelbase: 8 ft. Compartments: Two (8 ft between partitions). One lavatory with access from both compartments. Also one lavatory for use of the guard. Seating capacity: Ten. Tare weight: 20 tons 4 cwt. Diagram No. 39 (SR No. 558). Nos. 7766/67 both withdrawn 2.1932.

I

Q

U

Chapter Five

Elliptical-Roofed Carriages
Built During Marsh's Superintendency

Billinton's replacement as locomotive, carriage and wagon superintendent was Douglas Earle Marsh, who was formally appointed on 23rd November, 1904. From May 1889 he had been assistant Works manager at Swindon, moving in December 1895 to Doncaster where he was chief assistant mechanical engineer for the Great Northern Railway.

Under Marsh was instituted a policy of forming the carriages into set trains, which in normal circumstances would not be altered or divided. Each train was given a set number, painted on the solebar of every carriage within the set, and in addition the number usually appeared on the brake-ends of the set, painted in very large figures. New carriages built from 1905 onwards were mostly formed into set trains from the outset, each one specifically intended to work a particular service or group of services. Between 1906 and 1910 many of Billinton's six-wheeled carriages were rebuilt into bogie coaches, the great majority being formed into standard three-coach sets, each formed of a Third Brake, a Composite and another Third Brake. However, there were still plenty of carriages not attached to sets; they were known as 'spares' and would be used to strengthen normal trains or make up temporary non-set trains. The commonest formation for Branch Trains without a set number was a bogie Composite, a bogie Third and a six-wheeled Brake Van.

Several sets were built to a new design with high elliptical roof. Between July 1906 and June 1907 one of these sets, No. 12, was regularly employed on a through train that ran between Brighton and Paddington via the West London and Hammersmith & City lines; the up train left Brighton at 11.30 am and returned from the Great Western's domain at 3.40 pm. Unfortunately this potentially useful service was withdrawn after a year; even the employment of the best and newest carriage stock did not seem to attract the passengers. Elliptical-roofed stock was also used on the 'Crowborough Express', complete with roofboards, in 1907-8.

Marsh resigned on 19th July, 1911.

Between 1905 and 1907 a new series of carriages for main-line train services was built to the designs of Albert Harry Panter, who from 1904 was manager of the carriage and wagon construction branch of the Locomotive and Carriage Department. The most outstanding feature of these carriages was a high elliptical roof, the top of which was 12 ft 11½ in. above rail level, in stark contrast to the hitherto standard arc roof. There were many different types of what came to be known as 'Balloon' carriages, all being produced in fairly small quantities. Body length and width, however, were standardised at 54 ft and 8 ft 6 in. respectively; these dimensions prohibited the carriages from passing through Crystal Palace and Leigham Court Tunnels.

When new the elliptical stock was painted in a new umber and white livery; the umber was on all the bodywork below the waist and on all mouldings, and the white, lined in pale yellow, was on all the panels above the waist. When varnished it would have looked creamy. Carriage ends were plain umber. Unfortunately this attractive livery was short-lived, and from 1910 all repaints were in plain umber with yellow lining. Lettering was gold, shaded blue.

BOGIE THIRDS

Nos. 6, 7, 16, 48, 87, 627/34/35, 737/39/47/50/59/71 (SR Nos. 2179-85)

Body length: 54 ft. Body width: 8 ft 6 in. Bogie centres: 37 ft.
Compartments: Nine (5 ft 10½ in. between partitions). Seats: 90.
Tare weight: 24 tons 1 cwt. Diagram No. 185 (SR No. 70). Built 1905/6.

These 14 non-lavatory Thirds were built in 1905 and 1906. Originally, only the two end compartments were designated for smokers. Right from the start most of these Thirds were formed into set trains with contemporary elliptical stock. However, in 1915 seven were withdrawn from passenger service and converted into ambulance coaches for Train No. 25, together with other elliptical coaches, and none was returned to passenger service after World War I, although the underframes were reused for new arc-roofed coach bodies in 1922.

In the October 1917 carriage workings, No. 739 was in nine-set No. 4 working the 3.40 pm Victoria to Brighton and 5.55 pm return. No. 635 was in eight-set 47 (8.10 am Brighton to Victoria and 10.05 am return; 2.50 pm Brighton to Victoria and 6.35 pm return). No. 627 was found in four-set 50, a spare train which was withdrawn by 1921, its stock being dispersed. No. 771 was formed in five-set 61, which worked the 8.15 am Brighton to London Bridge and 2.08 pm (Saturdays) or 6.08 pm (not Saturdays) return.

By 1921 Set 4 had been broken, Third No. 739 being transferred to 11-set 87 (10.00 am Victoria to Newhaven Harbour and 5.45 pm return). No. 747, formerly 'loose', went to six-set 13, which was booked for the 4.25 pm Victoria to Brighton and 9.50 pm return, and loose coach No. 16 was formed into the London Bridge portion of Set 27: the 8.33 am from Eastbourne and 5.05 pm return.

The seven remaining Thirds all passed to the Southern Railway in 1923, and new numbers 2179-2185 were painted on at Lancing during overhauls between 1924 and 1927. All seven vehicles were fitted with vacuum brake equipment in addition to their existing air-brake gear in 1925/6. No 2179 (LB&SC No. 16) ran in Set 925 with the former Royal Train stock between Eastbourne and London Bridge between 1924 and about 1928. Nos. 2184/5 were both in 10-set 934 until the early 1930s. In 1928 this set worked up from Brighton to London Bridge at 8.15 am, but once in London it was divided into two five-coach portions which returned to Brighton at 2.40 pm and 7.20 pm, being reunited in time to work the up train next morning. No. 2184 was later transferred to five-set 840, whilst No. 2185 went to seven-set 879 in replacement of No. 2180, which was required as a trailer for push-and-pull set 738 in 1931. No. 2183 was formed in the 1920s into seven-set 881, in which it remained until its withdrawal in 1936; it worked three return trips between Brighton and Victoria daily. No. 2181 was in five-set No.

882, which stayed intact until 1940. With three Pullman cars included, this set worked in 1928 the 3.35 pm Brighton to Victoria and 5.35 pm return; 7.35 pm Brighton to Victoria and 10.05 pm return services.

Five-set No. 893 included Third No. 2182, and this (with three Pullmans) worked the 8.05 am Brighton to Victoria and 6.35 pm return. In 1931 the workings included the 8.05 am up, but on Saturdays the set returned from Victoria at 1.10 pm. Except on Saturdays Set 893 returned at 6.05 pm, and there were additional journeys at 7.35 pm to Victoria and 10.05 pm return.

About 1930 No. 2179 was adapted as a Trailer Third for push-and-pull set No. 979, working with Driving Trailer Third Brake No. 3289, an elliptical-roofed open coach. This was a non-standard formation, as most push-and-pull sets included some 1st-class accommodation. Set No. 979 was reserved for working between Brighton and The Dyke, later becoming a relief set with no regular workings. In about 1936 it was renumbered 733, and by 1939 it was working the Midhurst branch.

The underframe of No. 2183 on withdrawal in 1936 was transferred to the body of Composite No. 6241 (Set 718), but was badly damaged by enemy action at Bramley in 1942. No. 2180 was converted to a Yard Wagon No. 1644S at Lancing Works in June 1941, and remained there until November the same year.

The body of No. 2179 after withdrawal in July 1942 was grounded at Orpington for some years, and the body of No. 1644S (formerly 2180) was grounded at Lancing Works for many years. Gomshall station received the body of No. 2181; it was still there in June 1948.

THIRDS (DIAGRAM NO. 185)

No.	Built	Set No.	SR No.	Re-No.	Set No.	Wdn
6	6.06	AMB 25	-	-		12.15
7	6.06	AMB 25	-	-		12.15
16	6.06	27, /21	2179	5.24	925, 979, 733	7.42
48	6.06		2180	11.24	879, 738 /31	6.41
87	6.06	AMB 25	-	-		12.15
627	12.05	50	2181	5.27	882	12.40
634	12.05	AMB 25	-	-		12.15
635	12.05	47	2182	9.25	893, 880 /39	4.40
737	12.05	AMB 25	-	-		12.15
739	12.06	4, 87 /21	2183	2.27	881	10.36
747	12.06	13, /21	2184	9.26	934, 840	12.40
750	12.06	AMB 25	-	-		12.15
759	12.06	AMB 25	-	-		12.15
771	12.06	61	2185	9.26	934, 879 /31	1.39

BOGIE LAVATORY THIRDS

Nos. 1324, 1325 (SR No. 2338)

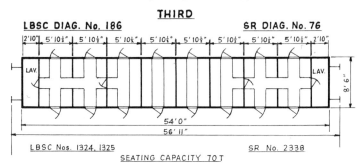

Body length: 54 ft. Body width: 8 ft 6 in. Bogie centres: 37 ft. Compartments: Eight (5 ft 10½ in. between partitions). One lavatory at each end, each with access from three compartments by means of central aisle. Seats: 70. Tare weight: 23 tons. Diagram No. 186 (SR No. 76). Built 1905.

Both these Lavatory Thirds were built during the second half of 1905 and showed the results of quite advanced thinking, for they were almost 'non-gangwayed open Thirds' with central walkway. To this day this layout is regarded as the only proper way to allow passengers to distribute themselves, whether in main-line or suburban carriages. In the Panter coaches, only the two central compartments were of the then-normal 'isolated' type, without access to the lavatories; the other six were available to passengers who desired 'facilities'.

Unfortunately No. 1325 was destined to have a very short life as it was wrecked in a bad accident at Stoats Nest (Coulsdon) on 29th January, 1910. The 3.40 pm Brighton to Victoria was composed mostly of elliptical-roofed stock built in 1905: Third Brake No. 804, Lavatory Third No. 1325, Lavatory Composite No. 113, Composite No. 525, Lavatory Composite No. 77 and Third Brake No. 803, together with three Pullman cars and a six-wheeled brake van. As the train approached Stoats Nest the rear six vehicles became detached, No. 1325 and others leaving the rails and swinging broadside across the track; No. 1325 crashed into the platform ramp, killing two bystanders and also five of the 71 passengers who were travelling in the carriage. The body of No. 1325 was destroyed although its underframe remained intact. It was found that a wheel on the leading bogie had shifted along the axle until it was an inch out of gauge, and upon fouling a crossover it had caused the couplings to part. Although 60 tons of pressure was supposedly needed to get a wheel on to its axle, only 11 tons were needed to remove the wheel from the axle of No. 1325; so the LB&SCR immediately gave orders that stricter methods of testing the fixing of wheels to axles must in future be used.

No. 1324, the surviving Lavatory Third, was not recorded as being in a set train in the last few years of the LB&SC, and in May 1924 it was renumbered as Southern 2338 and, along with Third No. 2179, placed in Set 925, which was formed otherwise of four or five former Royal Train vehicles. Vacuum brakes were fitted in April 1926 and Westinghouse brakes were removed in May 1930. A year later Set 925 was disbanded, and No. 2338 was transferred to Set 840 in about 1933 or 1934. This remained in use until late 1940, when No. 2338 and the other coaches in the set were withdrawn. It is recorded that No. 2338 had fouled a structure while working on the London to Bognor route on 20th August, 1937; why this should be is unclear, as elliptical roofed stock regularly worked over this route until electrification in July 1938.

LAVATORY THIRDS (DIAGRAM No. 186)

No.	Built	Set No.	SR No.	Re-No.	Set No.	Wdn
1324	12.05		2338	5.24	925, 840	12.40
1325	12.05		-	-		12.10

After withdrawal, the body of No. 2338 was taken off its underframe and sent to Woking, where it was grounded as temporary accommodation during World War II.

BOGIE THIRD BRAKES

Nos. 802, 803, 804 and 809

Body length: 54 ft. Body width: 8 ft 6 in. Bogie centres: 37 ft. Compartments: Five (5 ft 10½ in. between partitions). Seats: 50. Tare weight: 21 tons 10 cwt. Diagram No. 187. Built 1905.

All four of these Third Brakes were built during the second half of 1905. Of the five compartments, the two nearest the luggage compartment were reserved for smokers. The guard's and luggage compartment was entered by means of two sets of double doors each side. The guard was able to view the passing scene through two small windows in the body end.

Nos. 803 and 804 were in the train that was involved in the Stoats Nest derailment described in the previous section, but they were little damaged; No. 803 at the rear was derailed, but the front Third Brake, No. 804, was in the part of the train unaffected by the accident.

All four Third Brakes were appropriated for use in Ambulance Train No. 14 in April 1915, but were never returned to passenger service when finished with. Consequently they were not given Southern numbers. It is believed that their underframes were used for a series of arc-roofed coaches built in 1922.

BOGIE LAVATORY THIRD BRAKES

Nos. 602/17/18/24/26/51/53/57, 709/13/19/26, 810/11/29/30/35/45 (SR Nos. 3805-14/18/19)

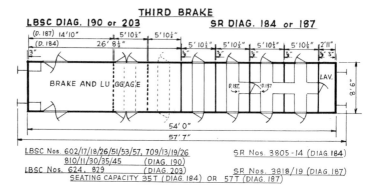

Body length: 54 ft. Body width: 8 ft 6 in. Bogie centres: 37 ft.
Compartments: Four (5 ft 10½ in. between partitions). One lavatory at opposite end to brake section, with access from three compartments by means of central aisle. Seats: 35. Tare weight: 22 tons 5 cwt.
Diagram No. 190 (SR No. 184). Built 1906.

Eighteen four-compartment Lavatory Third Brakes were built during 1906. The make-up included a long luggage compartment, with two sets of double doors on each bodyside, accommodation for the guard (who was able to view the track through two small windows in the body end), one 'isolated' compartment, three compartments with pairs of seats each side of a central walkway, and a small lavatory compartment at the far end.

At an unrecorded date, two of the vehicles, Nos. 624 and 829, were rebuilt with two additional compartments, with consequent reduction in length of the luggage compartment from 26 ft 8½ in. to 14 ft 10 in. and increase in seating capacity from 35 to 57 each. At the same time, the third compartment from the inner end was isolated from lavatory access and an extra seat put in; the second compartment was also given an extra seat where part of the walkway had been. The layout thus was four 'isolated' compartments seating 40 passengers, and two with lavatory access seating 17. The new Diagram No. for these two coaches was 203 (SR No. 187).

In April 1915 No. 626 was withdrawn from service and rebuilt into an Ambulance Train coach. No. 651 was so-rebuilt in May, and in December 1915 Nos. 653, 719, 810 and 811 went to Ambulance Train No. 25. None of these vehicles was returned to passenger service.

All the remaining twelve Lavatory Third Brakes were running in set trains in 1917. No. 726 was in Set No. 1 on the 9.20 am Brighton to London Bridge and 6.00 pm return, though by 1921 the carriage had been transferred to Newhaven

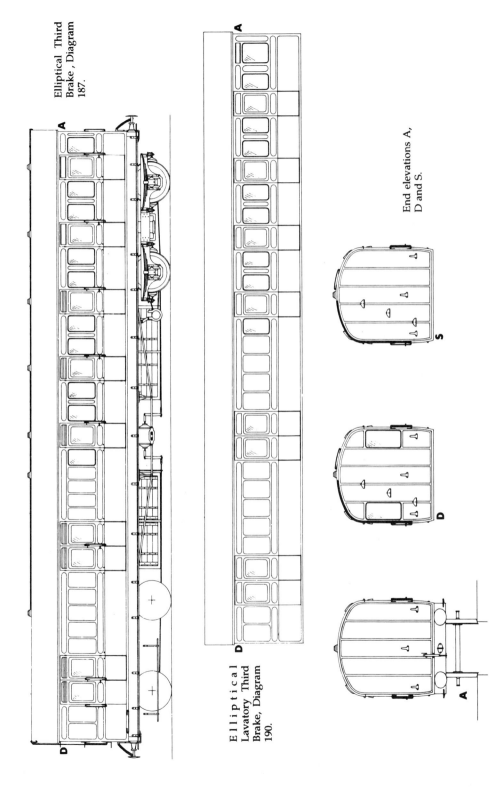

Elliptical Third
Brake , Diagram
187.

Elliptical
Lavatory Third
Brake, Diagram
190.

End elevations A,
D and S.

Boat Set No. 87. No. 713 was in Set No. 4, disbanded by 1921. Nos. 617/8 were both in six-set No. 13 (4.30 pm Brighton to Victoria and 9.50 pm return) and Nos. 657 and 835 (the latter noted as slip-fitted) were in Set 27, which was actually two separate sets working between Eastbourne and London Bridge and Eastbourne and Victoria. Nos. 709 and 830, formed in eight-set 47, worked between Brighton and Victoria; No. 845 in four-set 60 worked between West Worthing and London Bridge, being detached from Set No. 1 on the down journey; and No. 602 was in five-set 61 (Brighton and London Bridge).

Both rebuilt six-compartment Third Brakes were formed in seven-set 46, whose regular weekday workings took in the 7.46 am Bognor to London Bridge and 5.08 pm return (8.15 am Angmering to London Bridge and 5.08 pm return in 1921).

Between 1924 and 1927 the ten four-compartment Third Brakes were renumbered 3805 to 3814, the six-compartment pair becoming 3818/9 in September 1924, certain coaches from Set 46 remaining in what became SR Set No. 926 (which was spare by 1928). About 1931, No. 3818 was transferred to Set 840, which formed part of the 8.05 am Brighton to Victoria and 1.10 pm (Saturdays) or 6.35 pm (not Saturday) return; and later No. 3819 was adapted to work as a push-and-pull driving trailer in Set 735, allocated to Bognor in the mid-1930s. The lavatory was removed and seating capacity increased to 58.

In 1928 four-set 841 included Third Brake No. 3813, working between London, Horsham and Bognor; in the mid-1930s this coach was 'loose', berthed at Eardley, but later was noted by R. E. Tustin in four-set 840 along with No. 3805 (ex Set 934). Five-sets 879 and 880 included Third Brakes Nos. 3808 and 3809; the former worked the 3.15 pm Victoria to Eastbourne and 5.20 pm return, the latter the 8.18 am Brighton to Victoria and 12.05 pm return, the 2.35 pm Brighton to Victoria and 4.35 pm return, plus extra trips on Saturdays at 6.05 pm up and 8.05 pm down. Nos. 3806/7 were both in five-set 881, on the 7.35 am Brighton to Victoria and 9.05 am return, 11.05 am Brighton to Victoria and 12.35 pm (Saturdays) or 3.35 pm (not Saturdays) return, plus extra trips except on Saturdays at 6.05 pm up and 8.05 pm down. No. 3810 was in five-set 882 (Brighton and Victoria), whilst Nos. 3811/14 were both found in five-set 883, which in 1928 regularly worked the 9.35 am Brighton to Victoria, 11.15 am Victoria to Eastbourne and 2.20 pm return, finishing with the 6.05 pm (not Saturdays) or 11.05 pm (Saturdays) Victoria to Brighton. Finally, No. 3812 was in four-set 893 (Brighton-Victoria). All these sets in traffic included two or three Pullman cars. Generally speaking, elliptical-roofed stock was still in use for many of the 'best' trains on the Brighton line until electrification in 1933.

Except for No. 3809, all the vehicles became dual-braked in 1925/6; air brake equipment was removed from Nos. 3811/14 in November 1930, and No. 3809 was converted to vacuum braking in May 1929.

The sets were still very busy in 1931, as the following shows:

879 - 8.15 am Brighton to London Bridge, 7.20 pm (not Saturdays) return. Saturdays only: 2.40 pm London Bridge to Brighton, 6.35 pm Brighton to London Bridge and 9.20 pm return.

*880 - Not Saturdays: 12.05 pm Victoria to Brighton and 2.35 pm return, 4.35 pm Victoria to Brighton and 6.05 pm return.

*881 - Not Saturdays: 7.35 am Brighton to Victoria and 9.05 am return, 11.05 am Brighton to Victoria and 3.35 pm return.

882 or 883 - 8.10 am Lewes to London Bridge. Next day work:

882 or 883 - 5.18 am London Bridge to Brighton via Horsham, 10.05 am Brighton to Bognor. Bognor-Barnham local workings. 2.18 pm Bognor to Victoria, 5.08 pm Victoria to Lewes via East Grinstead.

* Plus two Pullman cars.

None of the Third Brakes was withdrawn immediately after electrification of the Brighton line, as other work was found for them. They still worked to Eastbourne until 1935, after which some were withdrawn; those remaining could be found on the Oxted line and on London-Bognor services. After 1938 only Nos. 3805/10/12/13/19 remained in service; Nos. 3805/13 were in five-set 840, 3810 in five-set 882 and 3812 in three-set 893, whilst No. 3819 was the push-and-pull fitted specimen in Set 735, which lasted until October 1941. The other sets, which after 1937 presumably worked on the Oxted line as that was practically the only steam service remaining which they could work, were withdrawn at the end of 1940.

Four are known to have become grounded bodies in the 1940s:

Nos. 3805/12/13/19 at Dorking North, Plymouth, Redhill Loco and Wembley Hill trading estate respectively.

LAVATORY THIRD BRAKES (DIAGRAM No. 190 or 203*)

No.	Built	Set No.	SR No.	Re-No.	Set No.	Wdn
602	6.06	61	3805	9.26	934, 840	12.40
617	6.06	13	3806	5.26	881	10.36
618	6.06	13	3807	5.26	881	10.36
626	6.06	AMB 14	-	-		4.15
651	6.06	AMB 14	-	-		5.15
653	6.06	AMB 25	-	-		12.15
657	6.06	27	3808	1.27	879	8.35
709	12.06	47	3809	11.24	880	1.39
713	12.06	4	3810	5.27	882	12.40
719	12.06	50, AMB 25	-	-		12.15
726	12.06	1, 87/21	3811	4.24	883	12.37
810	12.06	AMB 25	-	-		12.15
811	12.06	AMB 25	-	-		12.15
830	12.06	47	3812	9.25	893	12.40
835	12.06	27	3813	3.27	841, L, 840/36	12.40
845	12.06	60	3814	4.24	883	12.37
624*	6.06	46	3818	9.24	926, 840/31	12.35
829*	12.06	46	3819	9.24	926, 735/34	10.41

BOGIE LAVATORY THIRD BRAKES

Nos. 605 and 654 (SR Nos. 3816 and 3817)

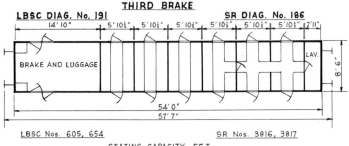

Body length: 54 ft. Body width: 8 ft 6 in. Bogie centres: 37 ft.
Compartments: Six (5 ft 10½ in. between partitions). One lavatory at opposite end to brake section, with access from three compartments by means of central aisle.
Seats: 55. Tare weight : 22 tons 10 cwt.
Diagram No. 191 (SR No. 186). Built 1906.

Only two of this type of six-compartment Lavatory Third Brake were built, both in the first half of 1906. They differed from the two vehicles later rebuilt as six-compartment Third Brakes (Diagram 203) in that three compartments had lavatory access, whilst in Diagram 203 only two did, so that the seating capacity was 57 as opposed to 55. Externally the two types looked identical, with one set of double doors each side of the luggage compartment, which was 14 ft 10 in. long internally. They featured the normal two small windows in the brake-end.

No. 605 was formed in the four-coach Eastbourne-Victoria portion of Set 27, and was noted as having slip apparatus. The set worked up on the 11.40 am to Victoria, returning (coupled to three-set 81 from Victoria to Polegate) at 5.20 pm to Eastbourne. No. 654 was in seven-set No. 4 until 1921, when it presumably became 'loose' for a time. This set worked with two Pullman cars between Victoria and Brighton.

After the Grouping, No. 605 was renumbered 3816 at Lancing in March 1927 and was formed in four-set 841 until 1932, when it was adapted as a driving trailer Third Brake for push-and-pull set No. 734; the lavatory was removed but it seems the frosted-glass windows were left in place, thus inducing passengers to believe the lavatory was still there - until they boarded the train! Seating capacity was increased to 56. The 1935 allocations show that Set 734 was one of six elliptical-roofed push-and-pull sets based at Bognor for local working. By summer 1939 it was allocated to Horsham.

No. 654 gained its Southern number, 3817, in November 1924 at Lancing and went to Set 880, whose workings were described in the previous section. Vacuum brakes were substituted for air in May 1929. Set 880, reduced to three coaches (3817, 6197, 3809) in about 1934, was withdrawn in January 1939, but

Set 734 lasted until May 1941. No. 3816 was then transferred to Yard Wagon No. 1636S at Lancing Works, where it remained until November 1945. The body was then grounded there.

BOGIE LAVATORY THIRD BRAKES (DIAGRAM No. 191)

No.	Built	Set No.	SR No.	Re-No.	Set No.	Wdn
605	6.06	27	3816	3.27	841, 734 /32	5.41
654	6.06	4	3817	11.24	880	1.39

BOGIE LAVATORY SECONDS

Nos. 233 and 234 (SR Nos. 4045 and 7768)

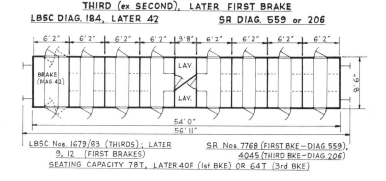

THIRD (ex SECOND), LATER FIRST BRAKE
LBSC DIAG. 184, LATER 42   SR DIAG. 559 or 206

LBSC Nos. 1679/83 (THIRDS); LATER   SR Nos. 7768 (FIRST BKE – DIAG. 559),
9, 12 (FIRST BRAKES)   4045 (THIRD BKE – DIAG. 206)
SEATING CAPACITY 78T, LATER 40F (1st BKE) OR 64T (3rd BKE)

Body length: 54 ft. Body width: 8 ft 6 in. Bogie centres: 37 ft.
Compartments: Eight (6 ft 2 in. between partitions). Two lavatories in centre, each with access from adjacent compartment. Seats: 78.
Tare weight: 24 tons 6 cwt. Diagram No. 110, later 184. Built 1905.

Only two of this design of Lavatory Second were built; lavatories were well designed but none too generously provided. The 'Brighton' did not treat its second-class passengers as well as the neighbouring South Eastern & Chatham did, for while that railway provided central armrests in its compartments, which therefore seated four-a-side, the LB&SC did not and second-class compartments seated five-a-side just as the 3rd-class did; the only difference was that the compartment width was a little more ample. Only two smoking compartments were provided in each of these two vehicles, being one of the two adjacent to a lavatory, and one at one end of the carriage.

Upon the abolition of second class in 1912 these two vehicles were downgraded to third class and renumbered 1679 and 1683, the diagram number being altered to 184; however, they did not remain in this form for very long. During the first half of 1913 both were rebuilt to First Brakes for a 1st-class-only set known as Members' Race Train No. 99. The alteration entailed stripping one end compartment and replacing it with a rather cramped guard's and luggage compartment which had the usual set of double doors each side and two windows in the end overlooking the track. Seating capacity in each of the Lavatory First Brakes was now 40 (three-a-side) and the new diagram number was 42. The coaches were renumbered 9 and 12 in the first-class list. Seven-set No. 99, which also included five lavatory Firsts, all of which had started life as Seconds, was kept for working race specials to Epsom Downs, Lingfield and other places on the LB&SC which had racecourses.

Set 99 was partly disbanded by the SR, three of the coaches - including No. 12 - remaining in what became Set 927. No. 9 went to Set 929.

In April 1925 No. 12 was altered to dual braking and reclassified Third Brake, SR No. 4045; with the seating back to five-a-side the number of passengers carried amounted to 64. Air brakes were removed in February 1929. Until 1931, 11-set No. 927, which included Third Brake No. 4045, was kept as a relief boat train for Newhaven workings.

It was then reduced to six coaches, still including No . 4045 , and was kept at Eardley sidings when not needed for Newhaven duties. As a five-coach set from the mid-1930s it lasted until June 1937, when No. 4045 was among those coaches withdrawn. Its SR Diagram Number was 206.

By contrast No. 9 was retained by the SR as a First Brake, altered to dual braking in October 1925 and renumbered 7768 in March 1927 (SR Diagram No. 559). It was formed in nine-set No. 929, which was also a relief Newhaven boat train until about 1931. Reduced to four coaches, Set 929 was then berthed at Eardley for special traffic. However, by 1934 it had been increased to nine coaches, all of which were Firsts (some taken from various other disbanded sets), and kept for race traffic. No longer to be found in its home territory, it was now Western Section stock, one of two elliptical-roofed sets permitted to run on the ex-L&SW lines. The 1934/5 berthing station of Set 929 was Brentford, and in 1936 it was Barnes. The entire set, including First Brake No. 7768, was withdrawn in June 1940. The body of the First Brake was taken off its wheels and grounded at Haywards Heath.

No.	Built	Third	Re-No.	1st Bke	Re-No.	Set	SR No.	Re-No.	Set	Wdn
233	12.05	1679	6.12	9	6.13	99	7768	3.27	929	6.40
234	12.05	1683	6.12	12	6.13	99	4045	4.25	927	6.37

BOGIE LAVATORY SECONDS

Nos. 15, 54, 83, 235 and 236 (SR Nos. 7622, 2339/40, 4495, 2342)

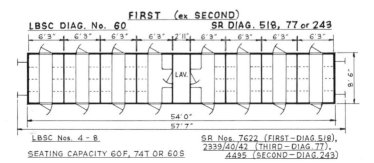

FIRST (ex SECOND)
LBSC DIAG. No. 60   SR DIAG. 518, 77 or 243

6'3" 6'3" 6'3" 6'3" 2'11" 6'3" 6'3" 6'3" 6'3"

LAV.

8' 6"

54' 0"
57' 7"

LBSC Nos. 4 - 8
SEATING CAPACITY 60F, 74T OR 60S

SR Nos. 7622 (FIRST-DIAG.518),
2339/40/42 (THIRD-DIAG.77),
4495 (SECOND-DIAG.243)

Body length: 54 ft. Body width: 8 ft 6 in. Bogie centres: 37 ft.
Compartments: Eight (6 ft 3 in. between partitions). One lavatory in centre, accessible from adjacent two compartments. Seats: 60.
Tare weight: 23 tons 18 cwt. Diagram No. 120, later 60. Built 1906/7.

Of these five Lavatory Seconds, three were built at Brighton in 1906, whilst two more came out during the following year. Similar in appearance to Nos. 233/4, the chief difference was that there was only one lavatory, centrally-placed, which had to be shared between the two compartments next to it; this lavatory actually had two doors, so that any occupant had to be careful to lock both, otherwise there would be the risk of having his or her privacy invaded. What happened if two passengers entered from both compartments simultaneously does not bear contemplation. The SE&C also possessed one carriage with this less than felicitous arrangement, but the Southern sealed off one of the doors; it does not seem to have bothered to do the same with these LB&SC carriages, however.

In 1912 all five coaches were reclassified Firsts and renumbered 4, 5, 6, 7 and 8 in the first-class list; seating remained at four-a-side (60 *in toto*) and the diagram number was altered to 60. Together with the former Lavatory Seconds that were altered to First Brakes, they were all formed into Members' Race Train No. 99, a seven-coach set composed entirely of first-class vehicles. One hopes the punters failed to notice how narrow their compartments were, after having paid the exorbitant first-class fares charged by the Brighton Company.

Race set No. 99 maintained its formation until 1923, when it was partly disbanded. Nos. 7 and 8 remained in what became SR Set No. 927, which, together with one of the former Seconds converted to a First Brake and eight additional elliptical-roofed vehicles, was a relief Newhaven Boat set between 1924 and 1931.

When dealing with these five lavatory Firsts, the Southern in its renumbering scheme managed to give them three separate classifications, First, Second and Third, which meant that three diagrams had to be drawn for what was really only one design of coach.

No. 4 remained as a First (SR Diagram No. 518) with 60 seats and was renumbered 7622 in September 1924. It was placed in nine-set 926, a spare set formed of various elliptical-roofed carriages, and given vacuum brake equipment in addition to the existing air brakes in March 1926. No. 7622 was still in Set 926 in 1931, by which time the set had been reformed and reduced to eight coaches for working (with two Pullman cars) the 10.05 am Brighton to Victoria and 12.05 pm return on Saturdays, and the 3.35 pm Brighton to Victoria and 5.35 pm return on all weekdays. No. 7622 was transferred to nine-set 934 in about 1934; this was a first-class-only race set kept at Brentford on the Western Section for race traffic. Set 934 was berthed at Barnes for the same purpose during 1936, and lasted until November 1940.

No. 7 was altered back to Second Class, seating 60, and renumbered 4495 in April 1925 (Diagram No. 243). It remained in Set 927, even when eventually downgraded to Third Class in June 1934 and renumbered (yet again) to 2333; by now Set 927 was only five coaches. As a Third, No. 2333 was now Diagram No.

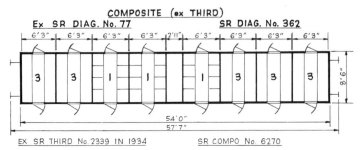

EX SR THIRD No. 2339 IN 1934   SR COMPO No. 6270

SEATING CAPACITY 24F 50T

77. Withdrawal came in June 1937.

Nos. 5, 6 and 8 were altered to Thirds, seating 74 passengers (Diagram No. 77). The first two were renumbered 2339/40 in July 1924, and went to Set 933. No. 8 became 2342 in April 1925, remaining in Set 927.

Ten-set No. 933 was noted in the 1928 carriage working notice as the Members' Race Train, but by 1931 it had been reduced to eight vehicles with the departure of Thirds 2339/40 to Set 926, which as mentioned above also contained First No 7622, one of the former Lavatory Seconds. When Set 926 was itself disbanded, about 1934, No. 2339 was renumbered 6270 as a Composite, but No. 2340 was given three more years of life in four-set No. 883 when it replaced Composite No. 6199. This set was condemned complete in December 1937.

Finally, No. 2342, in Set 927, had its air-brake equipment stripped in February 1929, and survived the various reformations of the set until, like No. 2333 (ex-4495), it was condemned in June 1937.

The reclassification of No. 2339 to Composite No. 6270 was done to create an additional push-and-pull set, No . 735, in April 1934. Three compartments were upgraded to first-class, seating four-a-side, and the lavatory was stripped, an empty space being left where it had been. The new diagram number was 362. No. 6270, formed with Third Brake No. 3819, lasted until October 1941.

No.	Built	1st No.	Re-No.	Set	SR No.	Re-No.	Set No.	Wdn
15	6.07	4	1912	99	7622	9.24	926, 934	11.40
54	6.07	5	1912	99	2339	7.24	933, 926	10.41
83	12.06	6	1912	99	2340	7.24	933, 926, 883	c. 12.37
235	6.06	7	1912	99	4495*	4.25	927	6.37
236	6.06	8	1912	99	2342	4.25	927	6.37

*   4495 renumbered Third 2333, 6.34.

BOGIE SECOND BRAKES

Nos. 355 and 356.

Body length: 54 ft. Body width: 8 ft 6 in.
Compartments: Four (6 ft 3 in. between partitions). Seats: 40.
Tare weight: 22 tons. Diagram No. 115, later 188. Built 1905.

Only two of these four-compartment non-lavatory Second Brakes were built, both during the second half of 1905. They did not stay as Seconds for very long, for in 1913 they were reclassified third class and renumbered 1780 and 1736. In this form they had an even shorter life: in April 1915 No. 1780 was withdrawn for use in Ambulance Train No. 14, and in December of the same year No. 1736 went to Ambulance Train No. 25. Neither was returned to ordinary passenger use after World War I; the bodies were broken up and the underframes may have been re-used for new coaches built in 1922.

BOGIE LAVATORY SECOND BRAKES

Nos. 37 and 89 (SR Nos. 4054 and 3815)

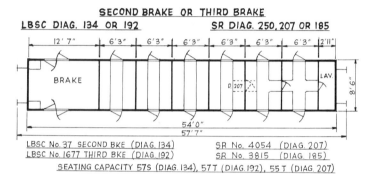

SECOND BRAKE OR THIRD BRAKE
LBSC DIAG. 134 OR 192   SR DIAG. 250,207 OR 185

LBSC No. 37 SECOND BKE (DIAG. 134)   SR No. 4054 (DIAG. 207)
LBSC No. 1677 THIRD BKE (DIAG. 192)   SR No. 3815 (DIAG. 185)
SEATING CAPACITY 57S (DIAG. 134), 57T (DIAG.192), 55T (DIAG. 207)

Body length: 54 ft. Body width: 8 ft 6 in. Bogie centres: 37 ft.
Compartments: Six (6 ft 3 in. between partitions). One lavatory at opposite end to brake, with access from two compartments by means of central aisle. Seats: 57. Tare weight: 22 tons 15 cwt. Diagram No. 134 or 192 (3rd class); SR Diagram No. 250 (2nd class) or 185 (3rd class). Built 1906.

In 1906 two Lavatory Second Brakes were built at Brighton; each had six compartments, of which two had lavatory access. There was a guard's and luggage compartment, 12 ft 7 in. long, with a set of double doors each side. As was standard practice on the 'Brighton', the guard's door opened inwards. Two windows overlooked the track at the brake end of the coaches.

No. 37 was formed in Newhaven Boat Train Set No. 87, and consequently was retained as a second-class vehicle until 1925, second-class being required for through bookings to and from the Continent. No. 89, in contrast, was reclassified Third in 1912 and renumbered 1677 (Diagram No. 192). It does not seem to have been formed in any set train.

During World War I, the Newhaven Boat train did not run as the port was closed to civilian traffic. Set 87, in a reduced form and with its second-class coaches temporarily running as Thirds, was allotted to the 11.40 am Victoria to Brighton and 3.40 pm return, and the 5.35 pm Victoria to Brighton and 7.30 pm return. After the War Set 87 returned to its full strength of ten vehicles plus

Pullman car and daily (including Sundays) worked the 10. 00 am Victoria to Newhaven and 5. 35 pm return services.

No. 37 was allotted an SR number in the second-class series, and given the SR diagram number 250, but was actually transferred to Third Brake at the time of its overhaul in October 1925. Vacuum brakes were fitted and the carriage was given its new diagram number 207. Actual renumbering to SR 4054 was not carried out until May 1927, by which time the carriage had been formed in five-set No. 882. It stayed in this set until withdrawal in December 1940.

Third Brake No. 1677 was dual-braked and renumbered SR 3815 in September 1925; it was placed in five-set 893 (which worked in traffic with three Pullman cars in the 1920s). In 1927 a central gangway was cut between the second and third compartments (viewed from the lavatory end), reducing the seating capacity from 57 to 55 but giving a further nine passengers lavatory access. The SR diagram number was in consequence altered from 185 to 207. No. 3815 remained in Set 893 until its withdrawal in December 1940, although by then it was only three coaches, presumably working on the Oxted line.

No.	Built	Re-No.		Set No.	SR No.	Re-No.	Set No.	Wdn
37	1906			87	4054	5.27	882	12.40
89	1906	1677	6.12		3815	9.25	893	12.40

Both coaches maintained a sort of 'after-life' as grounded bodies for a few years after withdrawal: No. 4054 was at Weybridge and No. 3815 at Crawley.

BOGIE SECOND BRAKE

No. 91 (SR No. 4494, later 3801)

Body length: 54 ft. Body width: 8 ft 6 in. Bogie centres: 37 ft.
Compartments: Four (6 ft 3 in. between partitions). Seats: 40.
Tare weight: 22 tons 10 cwt. Diagram No. 134, later 170.
SR Diagram No. 251 (2nd class). Built 1907.

No. 91 was built in 1907 as a Boat Train Second Brake, formed *ab initio* in Set 87. Compartments seated five-a-side, and there were no lavatories. The brake and luggage compartment measured 28 ft 2½ in. internally, and there were two sets of double doors each side. The guard had the use of two small windows in the end of the body overlooking the track.

During World War I the Newhaven Boat Train ceased to run, but five of the carriages of Set 87, including both Brake Seconds and with the addition of two Pullman cars, ran two daily return services between Victoria and Brighton. The Brake Seconds ran temporarily as third class, but they were back to providing second-class accommodation after the War, when Set 87, as a ten-set plus Pullman car, could once again be seen majestically sweeping through Purley on its way to Newhaven, headed by a Marsh 'Atlantic' locomotive.

Some of the coaches of Set 87 were kept together for what became SR Set No. 927, which in the 1920s was one of two relief boat train sets. No. 91 became SR Second Brake No. 4494. By 1931 this set had been reduced from 11 vehicles to six, but must have been retained for occasional runs to and from Newhaven as it still included Second Brake No. 4494 and Second No. 4495; when not in use it was kept at Eardley. Most of the coaches had their air-brake equipment stripped and replaced by vacuum brakes in February 1929.

No. 4494 was reclassified and renumbered Third Brake 3801 (the second coach to bear that number) in June 1934. It remained in Set 927, now only five vehicles, until its withdrawal from service in June 1937.

No.	Built	Set	SR No.	Re-No.	Set No.	3rd Bke	Set No.	Wdn.
91	1907	87	4494	4.25	927	3801	927	6.37

BOGIE COMPOSITES

Nos. 522-525 (SR Nos. 6189-6192)

Body length: 54 ft. Body width: 8 ft 6 in. Bogie centres: 37 ft.
Compartments Four 1st class (7 ft 2 in. between partitions) and four 2nd class (6 ft 1 in. between partitions). Seats: 32 1st, 40 2nd (No. 522 only) or 24 1st, 40 2nd (Nos. 523-5). Tare weight: 25 tons 2 cwt.
Diagram No. 101 (SR No. 342 or 343). Built 1905. Make-up 22111122.

Four Composites, Nos. 522 to 525, were built at Brighton in 1905; no lavatories were included. No. 522 seated the first-class passengers at four-a-side, and remained so, but the other three were built with three-a-side first-class seating, which was the normal arrangement for mainline stock. The first-class compartments were placed in the centre of each coach, with two second-class compartments, each seating ten passengers, at the ends. One 1st and two 2nd class compartments were labelled 'Smoking'.

No. 525 suffered minor damage in the Stoats Nest derailment on 29th January, 1910, but was repaired and returned to traffic. The second-class accommodation was altered to third-class in 1912, but as the coaches remained in the Composite number series they did not need renumbering.

All four were working in set trains by 1917. No. 523 was part of four-set No. 60, which worked the 12.16 pm West Worthing to London Bridge and 6.00 pm return, being detached on the down journey from the 6.00 pm London Bridge to Brighton, which had worked up from Brighton at 9.20 am ; this employed six-set No. 1, which included Composite No. 524. No. 522, with the four-a-side seating, was in six-set No. 13 (Brighton-Victoria). All four sets were disbanded before or at Grouping.

The Southern renumbered the four Composites to 6189-92. No. 6192 was placed in five-set No. 880 in 1924, remaining there until withdrawal in 1934; vacuum brakes were fitted in May 1929. No. 6190, dual-braked in November 1925, was in nine-set No. 929 until autumn 1931, when it was withdrawn for conversion into a push-and-pull trailer; Set 929 was one of the relief boat trains. Both Nos. 6189 and 6191 were placed in ten-set No. 934, which in the 1920s worked between Brighton and London Bridge; both were withdrawn in late 1931, again for conversion into push-and pull trailers. Incidentally, No. 6190 had run as a first/second Composite since April 1927, with the first-class seating altered to four-a-side.

The three Composites adapted to run as push-and-pull trailers, apart from being given the necessary through connections, had one of the first-class compartments altered to third and a new Diagram was issued (No. 366). No. 6189 bore plates proclaiming the weight of the carriage to be 27 tons. Seating capacity of Nos. 6189/90 was now 24 1st, 50 3rd, and of No. 6191 was 18 1st, 50 3rd. The three trailers were paired with 'Balloon' driving open Third trailers in replacement of arc-roof trailer Composites, and were a much better visual match than the original Composites had been. Nos. 6189-91, from late 1931, ran in Sets 750, 740 and 747 respectively; the mid-1930s allocations were Nos. 740 and 750 at Horsham and No. 747 was a relief set.

Set 740 was withdrawn in 1940, Set 747 in 1942 and Set 750 in 1943. The body of No. 6189 was grounded at Lancing Works and that of No. 6191 at Eastleigh Works. No. 6189, together with its open Third Brake, had been the last Panter elliptical-roofed carriage to remain in passenger service.

BOGIE COMPOSITES (DIAGRAM No. 101)

No.	Built	Set No.	SR No.	Re-No.	Set No.	Wdn
522	12.05	13	6189	9.26	934, 750 /31	1.43
523	12.05	60	6190	6.26	929, 740 /31	12.40
524	12.05	1	6191	9.26	934, 747 /31	11.42
525	12 05	4	6192	11.24	880	3.34

BOGIE LAVATORY COMPOSITES

Nos. 3, 77, 87, 113, 127 and 419 (SR Nos. 6193-6198)

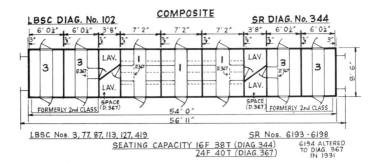

Body length: 54 ft. Body width: 8 ft 6 in. Bogie centres: 37 ft.
Compartments: Three 1st class (7 ft 2 in. between partitions) and four 2nd class (6 ft 0¼ in. between partitions). Four lavatories, each serving one compartment - two 1sts, two 2nds. Seats: 16 1st, 38 2nd class. Tare weight: 23 tons 15 cwt.
Diagram No. 102 (SR No. 344). Built 1905.

Brighton Works turned out these six Lavatory Composites during the half-year ending December 1905. The three first-class compartments were placed in the centre of each carriage, the middle compartment having no lavatory access, and there were two second-class compartments at each end, those at the extreme end also being without lavatory facilities. Seating was designed to be three-a-side in the first-class and five-a-side in the seconds. The latter were reclassified as Thirds in 1912.

Nos. 3 and 127 were both in Set No. 1, No. 87 was in Set 13, and No. 113 was found in Set 27 - or rather the six-coach London Bridge portion of Set 27, which left Eastbourne at 8.30 am and returned from London Bridge at 5.05 pm. The remaining two Composites were loose stock, and by 1921 the other four were also 'loose', the sets having been reformed or disbanded.

The Southern put the six Composites in six different sets from about 1924 onwards. Nos. 6194 and 6196 (formerly 77 and 113) had their third-class seating altered to second class, as the vehicles were formed in relief Newhaven boat trains: No. 6194 in Set 929 from April 1927 and No. 6196 in Set 927 from April 1925. Nos. 6193-95 were dual-braked in 1925 and No. 6198 in 1926; Nos. 6196/97 were altered from air to vacuum brakes in 1929, and in 1930 the air brake equipment was stripped from No. 6193.

In 1931 No. 6196 was transferred from Set 927 to four-set No. 841 in replacement of Composite No. 6286, which went to push-and-pull set 736. Second class was reclassified Third. The September 1931 workings of Set 841 included the 7.30 am Eastbourne to London Bridge and, except on Saturdays, the 6.05 pm Victoria to Brighton and 7.35 pm return, finishing with the 10.05 pm Victoria to Eastbourne. On Saturdays the set returned to Eastbourne on the 10.35 pm from London Bridge. Set 841 was disbanded early in 1932 and No. 6196 was later transferred to four-set No. 881, which ran in traffic until withdrawal in October 1936.

Only one of this type of Lavatory Composite was converted to a push-and-pull trailer: No. 6194, in 1931. Like the previous series of Composites, it was paired with an elliptical-roofed open driving trailer Third Brake, in this case No. 3841 in Set 746. The second-class seats were reclassified third-class and the lavatories were stripped, with additional seating installed across what had been the doorways so that the total capacity was now 18 1st and 40 3rd class seats. A new diagram had to be issued for the altered carriage (No. 367); this shows that the 1st-class seating was altered to four-a-side. Where the lavatories had been there were now just two empty spaces, each 3 ft 8 in. between partitions; one hopes that nothing was entombed therein. Set 746 was allotted to Eastbourne during 1934/5.

No. 6194 was withdrawn in July 1941 and the Third Brake was transferred to Set 750, lasting another 18 months. The body of No. 6194 was grounded as accommodation at Deptford Wharf. That of No. 6195 was grounded at Faversham, while the body of No. 6198 went to Guildford for a number of years.

BOGIE LAVATORY COMPOSITES (DIAGRAM No. 102)

No.	Built	Set No.	SR No.	Re-No.	Set No.	Wdn
3	12.05	1	6193	4.24	883	8.35
77	12.05		6194	5.26	929, 746 /31	7.41
87	12.05	13	6195	5.27	882	12.40
113	12.05	27	6196	3.24	927, 841, 881	10.36
127	12.05	1	6197	11.24	880	1.39
419	12.05		6198	9.24	926, 882 /34	12.40

The underframe of No. 6197 became Yard Wagon No. 1582S at Lancing Works in October 1940, but was condemned two months later.

BOGIE LAVATORY TRI-COMPOSITES

Nos. 628 and 629 (SR Nos. 6199 and 6200)

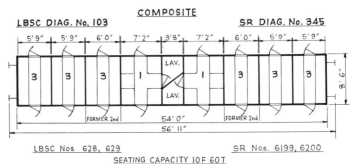

COMPOSITE

LBSC DIAG. No. 103   SR DIAG. No. 345

LBSC Nos. 628, 629   SR Nos. 6199, 6200

SEATING CAPACITY 10 F 60 T

Body length: 54 ft. Body width: 8 ft 6 in. Bogie centres: 37 ft.
Compartments: Two 1st class (7 ft 2 in. between partitions), two 2nd class (6 ft between partitions) and four 3rd class (5 ft 9 in. between partitions). Two lavatories with access from the two 1st class compartments only. Seats : 10 1st, 16 2nd, 40 3rd class.
Tare weight: 23 tons approximately. Diagram No. 103 (SR No. 345). Built 1905.

Only one design of Tri-Composite with high elliptical roof was evolved, and there were only two examples constructed, both during the half-year ending December 1905. They had a symmetrical layout: the two lavatories were in the centre, flanked by the 1st-class compartments; these were flanked by two 2nd-class compartments, which had four-a-side seating; and these in turn were flanked by four 3rd-class compartments, two at each end of the carriage. Only one of each class of compartment was labelled 'Smoking'.

In 1912 the second-class compartments were regraded as third class with five-a-side seating, the total capacity in each coach now being 10 1sts and 60 3rds.

No. 629 was formed in four-set No. 60, but this set did not last beyond 1922. No. 628 was 'loose' but from 1924, now renumbered 6199, it was in five-set No. 883. It was altered to dual-braking in October 1925. No. 629, renumbered 6200 in 1927, was part of two-set No. 734 which included slip-fitted First Brake No. 7775 and formed part of the 10.05 am Brighton to London Bridge (working with seven-set 890) and the Brighton portion of the 5.08 pm London Bridge to Angmering from 1928 until 1932.

In June 1934 No. 6200 was transferred to the reformed five-set No. 927, and when this was withdrawn in June 1937 the Composite was transferred again, this time to five-set No. 840, lasting until December 1940.

No. 6199, which from November 1930 had vacuum brakes only, was transferred from Set 883 to five-set No. 893 in about 1934 and, with Third Brakes Nos. 3812/15, lasted until December 1940.

It would seem that the LB&SC records of carriage weights cannot be entirely relied upon, as R.C. Riley noted weight plates affixed to these two Composites as 27 tons for No. 6199 and 25 tons for No. 6200.

The bodies of Nos. 6199 and 6200 were grounded at Hither Green Yard and Wimbledon Park Depot respectively, until the late 1940s.

No.	Built	Set No.	SR No.	Re-No.	Set No.	Wdn
628	12.05		6199	4.24	883, 893	12.40
629	12.05	60	6200	4.27	734, 927, 840	12.40

BOGIE LAVATORY COMPOSITES

Nos. 7, 120, 122 and 135

Body length: 55 ft. Body width: 8 ft 6 in.
Compartments: Four 2nd class (6 ft 3 in. between partitions) and four 3rd class (5 ft 10½ in. between partitions). Two lavatories, each with access from two compartments of each class. Seats: 37 2nd and 37 3rd class. Tare weight: 24 tons 4 cwt.
Diagram No. 119, later 189. Built 1906/7.

The only second/third Composites with elliptical roofs were these four 55 ft examples, of which No. 7 was built in 1906 and the other three in 1907. The second-class compartments were grouped at one end of the coach and the thirds at the other; at each extreme end was a lavatory which served the adjacent compartment and, by means of a through walkway, its neighbour.

In 1912 the second-class compartments were downgraded to third class, and in consequence the carriages became all-Thirds and had to be renumbered in the Third Class list. Nos. 7, 120, 122 and 135 became Nos. 1682, 1697, 1766 and 1732 in that order, and the new diagram number was 189.

Their life in this form was equally short, for in December 1915 all four were withdrawn and rebuilt as Ambulance Coaches for Train No. 25. When the requirement for these was over the bodies were scrapped and the underframes may have been reused for new carriage bodies built in 1922.

BOGIE LAVATORY COMPOSITES

Nos. 69, 198, 199, 212, 409, 411, 416 (SR Nos. 6271-6277)

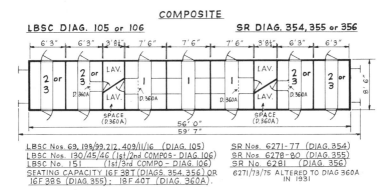

Body length: 56 ft. Body width: 8 ft 6 in. Bogie centres: 39 ft. Compartments: Three 1st class (7 ft 6 in. between partitions) and four 2nd class (6 ft 3 in. between partitions). Four lavatories, each serving one compartment - two 1sts, two 2nds. Seats: 16 1st and 38 2nd class. Tare weight: 24 tons. Diagram No. 105 (SR No. 354). Built 1906/7.

Nos. 130, 145, 146 and 151 (SR Nos. 6278-6281)

As above, but with 10 ft-wheelbase bogies at 39 ft centres. Tare weight: 27 tons 5 cwt. Diagram No. 106 (SR No. 355 and 356). Built 1907.

Eleven Lavatory Composites were built by Brighton in 1906/07; the last four, being intended for Boat Train No. 87, had bogies of ten feet wheelbase, presumably on the grounds that these would ride better than the standard 8 ft-wheelbase bogies. The layout of each carriage was three first-class compartments in the centre with two second-class compartments at each end; pairs of lavatories were placed between the 1sts and the 2nds, the central first-class and outermost second-class compartments being 'isolated'.

From 1912, all the carriages to Diagram 105 were altered to first/third Composites, the seating remaining unchanged; but Nos. 130, 145 and 146 continued as first/second Composites as they were Boat Train stock. No. 151 however was removed from Boat Train No. 87 and uniquely this 10 ft-wheelbase bogie carriage did have its second class altered to third. During World War I, No. 130 was temporarily removed from Set 87, which was used on Victoria-Brighton services; Nos. 145 and 146 remained in the set with their second-class accommodation being made available to third-class passengers. After the War, Set 87 was restored to Victoria-Newhaven services with No. 130 again forming part of the consist, but No. 151 was not returned to the set, instead forming part of Set No. 4, later disbanded.

The 1917 allocations of Diagram 105 to set trains included No. 199 in Eastbourne set No. 27, No. 416 in six-set No. 46 (7.46 am Bognor to London Bridge and 5.08 pm return) and No. 409 in West Worthing set No. 60. By 1921, No. 212 in addition was in ten-set No. 47 (which included three Pullman cars when in traffic). This worked the 8.05 am Brighton to Victoria and 10.05 am return from February 1921, also the 12.25 pm Brighton to Victoria and 6.35 pm return.

Also in 1921, five-set No. 60 worked the London Bridge portion of the 9.38 am West Worthing-Victoria, returning from London Bridge at 1.20 pm (Saturdays) or 5.56 pm (not Saturdays). The 1.20 pm was a Brighton train and the 5.56 pm one to Eastbourne, with the West Worthing portions formed in the rear.

Eight-set No. 46, which included a Pullman car, was now based at Angmering and worked up to London Bridge at 8.15 am on weekdays, returning on the 5.08 pm (which had a two-coach portion for Brighton in rear, slipped at Haywards Heath). The Pullman was not part of the 'permanent' set formation.

Between 1925 and 1927 the Composites were renumbered 6271-6281; the Southern sorted them into three diagrams, of which No. 354 was the group with 8 ft-wheelbase bogies, No. 355 were 1st/2nd Composites with 10 ft-wheelbase bogies, and No. 356 was the solitary 1st/3rd Composite with large bogies. Nos. 6271-73/75-77/81 became dual braked in 1925/6, and Nos. 6274/78-80 were

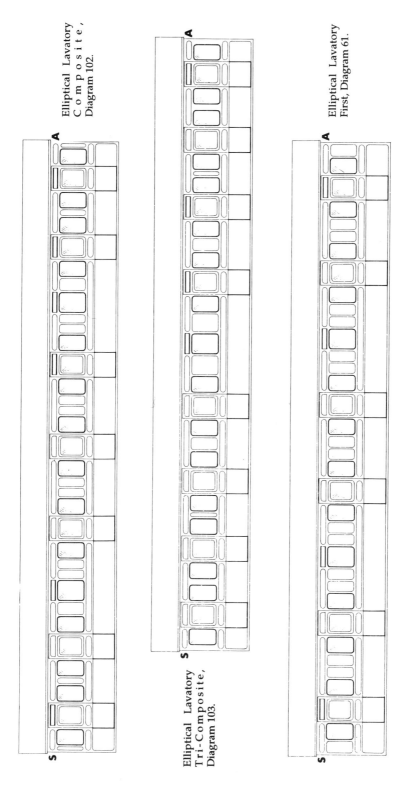

Elliptical Lavatory
C o m p o s i t e ,
Diagram 102.

Elliptical Lavatory
First, Diagram 61.

Elliptical Lavatory
Tri-Composite,
Diagram 103.

converted from air to vacuum brakes in February 1929. No. 6281 lost the Westinghouse equipment in November 1930. No. 6273 was altered to 1st/2nd accommodation in April 1925 and placed in relief boat set No. 927; No. 6275 was similarly altered in April 1927 for the other relief boat set, No. 929. Nos. 6278-80 were also formed in Set No. 927. All these Composites were removed in 1931 and converted to push-and-pull trailers. The other carriages were formed in sets with other elliptical-roofed vehicles (see list at end); workings of these sets have been described in previous sections.

In autumn 1931 six Lavatory Composites were withdrawn from main-line sets and adapted as trailers to run with open driving trailer thirds in replacement of arc-roof Composites. The lavatories were removed, merely leaving two empty spaces 3 ft 8½ in. between partitions, and extra seating was built across what had been the doorways, which were panelled over. Seating capacity was now 18 1st and 40 3rd; the coaches converted were Nos. 6271/73/75/78-80 and they were placed in push-and-pull sets 734/48/49/43/44/45 respectively. Diagram No. 360A was issued to cover the conversions. This diagram showed the 1st-class seating to be four-a-side, but the seating capacities shown against the sets listed in the Carriage Working Notices suggest that the 1st-class compartments did in fact remain as three-a-side.

In 1934/5 the allocations of the six elliptical-roofed push-and-pull sets containing these Composites were: 734, 744, 745, Bognor (Set 745 was reserved for Bognor-Barnham shuttle services); 743, Brighton; and 748, 749, Horsham. All these sets were used on local workings. Those at Horsham ran on the Guildford and Steyning lines and, until electrification in 1938, to Dorking and Three Bridges. Three sets were withdrawn in 1938, rendered surplus by electrification, and the remaining three went in 1939, 1941 and 1942.

BOGIE LAVATORY COMPOSITES (DIAGRAM Nos. 105 and 106)

No.	Built	Set No.	SR No.	Re-No.	Set No.	Wdn
69	12.06		6271	5.26	881, 734 /31	5.41
198	6.07		6272	9.26	934, 879 /31	1.39
199	6.07	27	6273	4.25	927, 748 /31	2.39
212	6.07	47 /21	6274	9.26	934, 893, 880 /39	4.40
409	6.07	60	6275	3.27	929, 749 /31	1.42
411	12.07		6276	1.27	879	8.35
416	12.07	46	6277	9.24	926, 840 /31	2.37
130	12.07	87	6278	4.25	927, 743 /31	11.38
145	12.07	87	6279	4.25	927, 744 /31	8.38
146	12.07	87	6280	4.25	927, 745 /31	8.38
151	12.07	87, 4	6281	4.24	883	12.37

Five of the coaches became service vehicles after withdrawal:

6271   to Yard Wagon 1635S at Lancing Works, May 1941.
6274   underframe to Yard Wagon 1583S at Lancing Works, October 1940. Withdrawn December 1940.
6277   underframe to Yard Wagon 1118S at Lancing Works, June 1937.
6273   underframe to Yard Wagon 1371S at Redbridge, May 1939
6275   to Yard Wagon 1716S at Lancing Works, January 1942. The body was grounded at Lancing after 1945.

BOGIE COMPOSITES

Nos. 73, 96, 110 (SR Nos. 6286, 6282, 6283)

Body length: 56 ft. Body width: 8 ft 6 in. Bogie centres: 39 ft.
Compartments: Four 1st class (7 ft 6 in. between partitions) and four 2nd class (6 ft 3 in. between partitions). Seats : 24 1st, 40 2nd.
Tare weight: 23 tons 15 cwt. Diagram No. 107 (SR No. 357). Built 1906/7.
No. 73 altered to Diagram No. 116 in 1911 (SR Diagram 359).

Nos. 526 and 527 (SR Nos. 6284 and 6285)

As Diagram 107, but with 10 ft-wheelbase bogies at 39 ft centres. Tare weight: 27 tons 7 cwt. Diagram No. 115 (SR No. 358). Built 1907.

The final design of elliptical-roofed Composite, of which five examples were constructed at Brighton in 1906/7, was in effect a lengthened version of Nos. 522-5, built in 1905; the compartments were arranged in the same way (first class in the centre, second class at the ends) but were more generously proportioned, the body being two feet longer. Nos. 526/7 were boat train stock, running in Set Train No. 87, and were fitted with bogies of 10 ft wheelbase, but were otherwise identical in appearance. There were no lavatories.

In 1911 there was a complaint about a shortage of first-class accommodation on the 5.20 pm Victoria to Eastbourne. On William Forbes' instructions the inner two second-class compartments on No. 73 were upgraded to first class, seating three-a-side, during the half-year ending December 1911. Consequently the seating capacity was now 36 1st, 20 2nd class, and new Diagram No. 116 was issued to cover this solitary specimen.

The October 1917 Carriage Workings indicate that No. 73 was still working in the 11.40 am Eastbourne to Victoria and 5.20 pm return as part of Set No. 27 ; in 1921 it was leaving Eastbourne two minutes later but still returned on the 5.20 pm, which also included Set 81 working through to Hastings, and a two-coach portion for Seaford. No. 110 was in six-set No. 46, No. 526 was temporarily in Set 47 but was later restored to Set 87, No. 96 was in five-set No. 61 (8.15 am Brighton to London Bridge and 2.08 pm (Saturdays) or 6.08 pm (not Saturdays) return) and No. 527 remained in Set No. 87.

All five Composites duly received their new numbers and SR green livery after 1923; Nos. 526/7 as SR Nos. 6284/5 were retained as first/second Composites and formed in relief boat train No. 929 until 1931. No. 73, the carriage with a higher proportion of first-class seating, became No. 6286 and was formed in four-set No. 841 until 1931. Vacuum brakes were added to the existing system on all five in 1925/6.

In autumn 1931 Nos. 6282-86 were all taken out of the mainline sets and adapted for use in two-coach push-and-pull sets in replacement of arc-roofed vehicles. In each case there were three first-class and five third-class compartments; with Nos. 6282-85 it meant that one 1st-class compartment had to be downgraded, but with No. 6286 three had to be redone. Seating capacity in each carriage was now 18 1st, 50 3rd, and a new diagram had to be issued

(No. 358A). Sets 736/37/39/41/42, each of which retained its original open driving Third Brake, now had the replacement Composites, which matched the original coaches as to roof profile. The allocations of these five sets in early 1932 were:

736 - Bognor, for Bognor-Barnham shuttle services
737, 741 - Littlehampton; 737 was booked for Ford shuttle services
739 - Horsham
742 - Brighton

By 1934/5 these had changed to:

736, 741 - Bognor
737, 742 - Littlehampton
739 - Horsham

These five sets were withdrawn between 1940 and 1942. One of the Composites, No. 6284, became a service vehicle: it was transferred to Yard Wagon No. 1694S, along with the Third Brake with which it had been paired, in January 1942, and was restricted to Lancing Works yard only. Other Composites were taken off their underframes and grounded at various locations as temporary accommodation.

6282 - body grounded at Lancing Works, October 1942
6283 - body grounded at Newhaven, December 1942
6285 - body grounded at Farnborough, December 1940
6286 - body grounded at Cranleigh, August 1940

No.	Built	Set No.	SR No.	Re-No.	Set No.	Wdn
73	12 06	27	6286	3.27	841, 736 /31	8.40
96	6.07	61	6282	9.25	893, 739 /31	10.42
110	6.07	46	6283	9.24	926, 737 /31	12.42
526	12.07	87, 47, 87	6284	3.27	929, 741 /31	10.41
527	12.07	87	6285	3.27	929, 742 /31	12.40

BOGIE LAVATORY FIRSTS

Nos. 64-66 (SR Nos. 7619-7621)

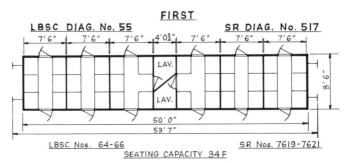

FIRST
LBSC DIAG. No. 55 — SR DIAG. No. 517
LBSC Nos. 64-66 — SR Nos. 7619-7621
SEATING CAPACITY 34 F

Body length: 50 ft Body width: 8 ft 6 in. Bogie centres: 33 ft.
Compartments: Six (7 ft 6 in. between partitions). Two lavatories in centre, each with access from adjacent compartment. Seats: 34.
Tare weight: 24 tons 3 cwt. Diagram No. 55 (SR No. 517). Built 1906.

Three Lavatory Firsts with elliptical roofs were built in 1906; exceptionally they had 50 ft bodies, four feet shorter than standard. Had they been built to the usual length two more lavatories could have been fitted in, and in fact this is exactly what happened with the next batch of Firsts (see following section).

All compartments were generously proportioned and well-stuffed with padding, but only the two central compartments had lavatory access. Whenever passengers complained to the company about the shortage of these facilities they received an official letter recommending them to travel in Pullman cars, in which they would find lavatories and would also be levied a supplementary fare. However, few passengers enjoyed riding in saloon vehicles, much preferring compartments.

No. 64 was formed in Set Train No. 13 (Brighton-Victoria) and No. 65 was in Set No. 4 (Victoria-Brighton) until it was disbanded, after which it was found in the four-coach Victoria portion of Eastbourne Set No. 27. After Grouping, Nos. 64-66, as SR Nos. 7619-21, went to Sets Nos. 934, 926 and 929 respectively; Set 926 was a spare nine-coach formation, Set 929 was an 11-coach spare Boat Train, and Set 934 was a ten-coach train working between Brighton and London Bridge, from which it returned as two five-coach trains.

About 1934 Set 929 was reformed as a first-class-only Race Set and sent to the London West District; No. 7621 remained in it until withdrawal in 1940. No. 7622 was transferred to Set 934 in 1934; this also was reformed as a Race Set with only first-class accommodation and was allocated to the London West District until 1940.

After withdrawal the bodies of Nos. 7619 and 7620 were taken off their frames and grounded as huts at Feltham and Three Bridges respectively. The body of No. 7621 went to Hither Green Loco.

No.	Built	Set No.	SR No.	Re-No.	Set No.	Wdn
64	6.06	13	7619	9.26	934	11.40
65	6.06	4, 27 /21	7620	11.24	926, 934 /34	10.40
66	6.06		7621	10.23	929	6.40

BOGIE LAVATORY FIRSTS

Nos. 62, 70, 71, 153-160 (SR Nos. 7627-7637)

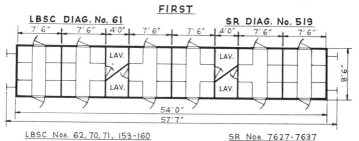

FIRST

LBSC DIAG. No. 61   SR DIAG. No. 519

LBSC Nos. 62, 70, 71, 153-160   SR Nos. 7627-7637

SEATING CAPACITY 32 F

Body length: 54 ft. Body width: 8 ft 6 in. Bogie centres: 37 ft.
Compartments: Six (7 ft 6 in. between partitions). Four lavatories, each with access from one compartment. Seats: 32. Tare weight: 25 tons 13 cwt.
Diagram No. 61 (SR No. 519). Built 1906/7.

Three Lavatory Firsts to standard length were built in 1906, followed by eight more in 1907. The four compartments in the centre had lavatory access, and only the two endmost compartments were without those facilities. Three-a-side seating was provided, although the compartments with lavatories had only five seats each.

All but two of the Firsts were running in set trains by 1917 (see list), although by 1921 Sets 4 and 50 had been disbanded and Firsts Nos. 159 and 160 were loose stock, along with Nos. 62 and 155. Nos. 71 and 157 were both in the six-coach London Bridge portion of Eastbourne Set No. 27 which, with a Pullman car, worked up at 8.33 am and returned from London Bridge at 5.05 pm. It is curious that there should have been two distinct sets both numbered 27, as they do not seem to have run together in the same train at all. In the case of Set 46, First No. 158 was always shown in the lists as being formed outside the set as though it were a loose coach, for no discernible reason.

The Southern renumbered all the Firsts between 1924 and 1927 during routine overhaul at Lancing, and they became Nos. 7627 to 7637. Some were formed in Brighton mainline five-coach sets, all of which ran in traffic with Pullman cars (never numbered as part of the set), and others found their way to the relief boat train sets. All the workings have been detailed in previous sections. From 1934, all the Firsts went to various race sets, in which they lasted until 1940. No. 7631 is believed to have gone from Set 841 to Set 933 in 1934; this was a race set kept on the Central Section and formed mostly of former 'City Limited' stock (see later). Between 1931 and 1934 Nos. 7633/35 ran in four-set No. 840, the coaches of which had come from Set 926; the Firsts were then transferred to Set 934.

After the withdrawal of Set 929, Firsts Nos. 7629/30 had their underframes reused as Yard Wagons at Lancing Works, Nos. 1584S and 1585S, between October and December 1940. The bodies of Nos. 7627 and 7633 were taken off their frames and grounded as huts at Ashford Loco and Norwood Junction Loco respectively; that at Norwood Junction remained there until 1953. Other First bodies were grounded at Crystal Palace (No. 7628), Lancing Works (Nos. 7629/30/32), Ashford Works (No. 7631), Catford (No. 7634), Feltham Loco (No. 7635) and Reading (No. 7636).

LAVATORY FIRSTS (DIAGRAM No. 61)

No.	Built	Set No.	SR No.	Re-No.	Set No.	Wdn
62	12.06		7627	5.27	882, 929 /34	6.40
70	12.06	61	7628	9.26	934	11.40
71	12.06	27	7629	4.25	927, 929 /34	6.40
153	6.07	47	7630	9.25	893, 929 /34	6.40
154	6.07	46	7631	3.27	841, 933? /34	12.40
155	6.07		7632	11.24	881, 929 /34	6.40
156	6.07	46	7633	9.24	926, 840, 934	11.40
157	6.07	27	7634	3.27	929	6.40
158	6.07	46	7635	9.24	926, 840, 934	11.40
159	6.07	50	7636	11.24	879, 926, 934	11.40
160	12.07	4	7637	11.24	880, 929 /34	6.40

BOGIE FIRST BRAKES

Nos. 27-29 (SR Nos. 7772-7774)

Body length: 54 ft. Body width: 8 ft 6 in. Bogie centres 37 ft.
Compartments: Four (7 ft 3 in. between partitions). Seats : 24.
Tare weight: 23 tons 14 cwt. Diagram No. 54 (SR No. 562). Built 1905.

During the second half of 1905, three First Brakes were built at Brighton, each with four compartments but no lavatories. Each compartment could accommodate six passengers. The brake and luggage compartment, which measured 24 ft 2½ in. internally, had two sets of double doors on each side; the guard's doors opened inwards and there were two windows in the body end overlooking the track. No. 28 was fitted with detaching arrangements for working in slip-coach portions, whether from the start or at a later date is not known.

The 1921 carriage workings show a slip Brake First plus a Third formed as a London Bridge portion of the 11.00 am Brighton-Victoria train, returning as the Brighton portion, slipped at Haywards Heath, of the 5.08 pm London Bridge to Angmering. At Haywards Heath the two-coach portion was attached to Set Train No. 9, which had worked up from Brighton at 5.09 pm, and left for Brighton at 6.04 pm if on time. It seems likely that the slip First Brake was No. 28, with perhaps No. 29 acting as relief; neither of these was formed in a numbered set in 1921. No. 27 had been transferred from Set No. 1 to Set No. 61, in replacement of No. 28.

Renumbered 7772-74 by the Southern, the three coaches were dual-braked in 1925/6, although No. 7773 in December 1930 became vacuum-braked only. Initially the Brakes were formed in SR sets Nos. 934, 933 and 879. It is not clear why five-set No. 879 should have had proportionately more first class than the other five-coach sets; it was not a 'business' train, in fact working between Victoria and Eastbourne in the 1920s. Set 933 was the 'Members' Race Train', and comprised former 'City Limited' bogie Firsts. In 1934 No 7773 was transferred from Set 933 to 934, a nine-coach formation now formed of seven Lavatory Firsts and two First Brakes for race traffic.

BOGIE FIRST BRAKES (DIAGRAM No. 54)

No.	Built	Set No.	SR No.	Re-No.	Set No.	Wdn
27	12.05	1, 61	7772	9.26	934	12.40
28	12.05	61, L	7773	7.24	933, 934	11.40
29	12.05	50, L	7774	1.27	879	8.35

BOGIE FIRST BRAKE

No. 26 (SR No. 7771)

Body length: 54 ft. Body width: 8 ft 6 in. Bogie centres: 37 ft.
Compartments: Six (7 ft 6 in. between partitions). Seats: 36.
Tare weight: 24 tons 15 cwt. Diagram No. 56 (SR No. 561). Built 1906.

Only one six-compartment First Brake was built; it emerged in the half-year ending June 1906. Each compartment was designed to seat three passengers each side, and there was a small guard's and luggage compartment at one end with one set of double doors each side and the usual two windows in the coach end.

No. 26 was formed in the six-coach London Bridge portion of Eastbourne Set No. 27; being a 'City' train this required a fairly high proportion of first-class accommodation, although not as much as the more exclusive 'City Limited' which ran between Brighton and London Bridge.

The vehicle was dual-braked in January 1926, and given its Southern number 7771 at Lancing in March 1927; it was formed at one end of nine-set No. 929, one of the relief boat trains. At the other end of the set was First Brake No. 7768, one of two that had been rebuilt from second-class carriages in 1913 for Race Set No. 99. In 1931 five Composites were removed from Set 929 and altered to push-and-pull trailers, leaving only four coaches: First Brakes Nos. 7768/71 and Firsts Nos. 7621/34. This much-reduced set was then berthed at Eardley for special traffic. In about 1934 it was made up to nine coaches again with lavatory Firsts taken from five different sets; the additions were Nos. 7627/29/30/32/37. As a first-class Race Set, No. 929 was then berthed at Brentford, and by 1936 at Barnes, remaining on the London West Division until withdrawal in June 1940. No. 7771 was withdrawn at the same time as the other coaches in the set.

Despite their restricted route availability the Brighton's elliptical-roofed carriages lasted quite well: those for normal services until 1938/9, those for race traffic until 1940, and the push-and-pull conversions until 1942. They were handsome and impressive-looking vehicles whose only fault was that they lacked through corridors.

Of the 8 ft 6 in.-wide 'Balloon' carriages, 102 were built to 20 different designs, between 1905 and 1907. But an even better train, comprising carriages that were 9 ft over body, was built in 1907, and this was for the important 'City Limited' service.

Gas Lamp

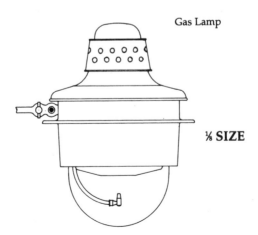

¼ SIZE

Chapter Six

The 'City Limited'

Since Stroudley's time there had been a fast train leaving Brighton for London Bridge at 8.45 am and returning at 5.00 pm, with 1st-class accommodation only and known jocularly as the Stockbrokers' Special. It always had the best carriages allocated to it, including Stroudley's bogie Firsts of 1889. Not only were the 'Stockbrokers' the most important trains on the line, even more so than the famous 'Southern Belle' all-Pullman train, but they were the heaviest.

Albert Panter therefore designed a set of carriages especially for the 'City Limited' that was, apart from the 1897 Royal Train, quite the best on the LB&SC; and these were never to be surpassed during the remainder of that Company's existence. They were built to the maximum permitted width of 9 ft at waist and 8 ft 6 in. at cantrail, and height from rail to top of roof of 12 ft 11 in. These dimensions did restrict the carriages' route availability somewhat: the routes via Redhill and between Victoria and London Bridge via Crystal Palace or Tulse Hill were barred to 9 ft stock, as was Bopeep Tunnel, St Leonards. In emergency the stock could run via Redhill so long as the brake was gently applied (to steady the train) whilst passing through Redhill station, and a speed of 30 mph through Merstham Tunnel was not exceeded.

The new carriages for the 'City Limited', nine in total (Train No. 6) went into service in the summer of 1907. For the up train, the normal formation was six carriages plus two Pullmans in the London Bridge portion, plus a two- or three-coach portion (plus Pullman) for Victoria, slipped at East Croydon. The down train was formed of the London Bridge part only and, being a lighter formation, was timed to do the journey in 60 minutes (the up train was allowed 70). Three of the coaches were gangwayed, allowing access to the Pullman cars .

BOGIE CORRIDOR LAVATORY FIRST

No. 151 (SR No. 7641)

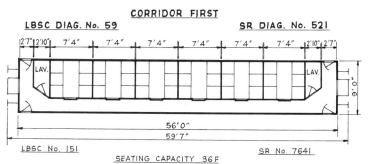

SEATING CAPACITY 36 F

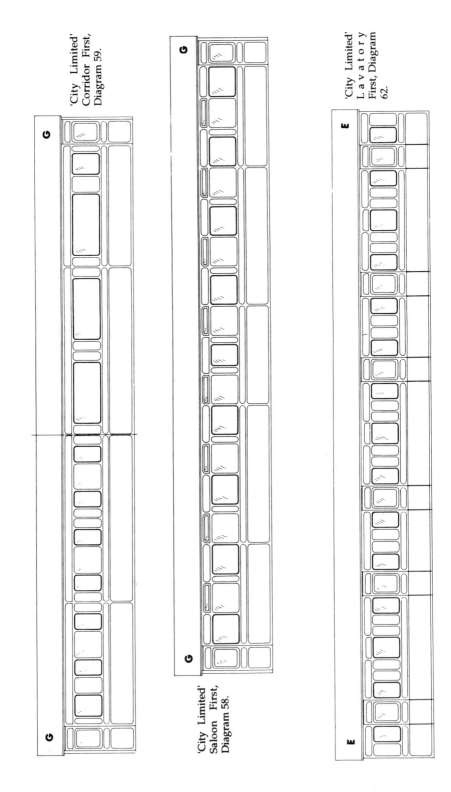

'City Limited'
Corridor First,
Diagram 59.

'City Limited'
Saloon First,
Diagram 58.

'City Limited'
L a v a t o r y
First, Diagram
62.

Body length: 56 ft. Body width: 9 ft. Bogie centres: 39 ft.
Compartments: Six (7 ft 4 in. between partitions). Two lavatories, accessible from all seats. Seats: 36. Tare weight: 25 tons.
Diagram No. 59 (SR No. 521) . Gangwayed both ends.

BOGIE PARLOUR SALOON FIRST

No. 152 (SR No. 7642)

PARLOUR SALOON FIRST

LBSC DIAG. No. 58   **SR DIAG. No. 522**

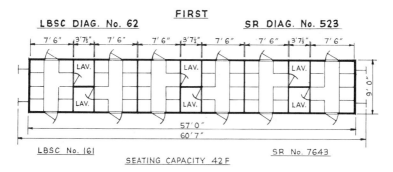

SEATING CAPACITY 40 F

Body length: 56 ft. Body width: 9 ft. Bogie centres: 39 ft.
Compartments: Four saloons (11 ft 10½ in. between partitions). One lavatory in centre, with access from all seats. Seats : 40.
Tare weight: 25 tons. Diagram No. 58 (SR No. 522). Gangwayed both ends.

BOGIE LAVATORY FIRST

No. 161 (SR No. 7643)

FIRST

LBSC DIAG. No. 62   **SR DIAG. No. 523**

SEATING CAPACITY 42 F

Body length: 57 ft. Body width: 9 ft. Bogie wheelbase: 10 ft.
Bogie centres: 39 ft. Compartments: Six (7 ft 6 in. between partitions). Six lavatories, each serving one compartment only. Seats: 42.
Tare weight: 25 tons. Diagram No. 62 (SR No. 523).

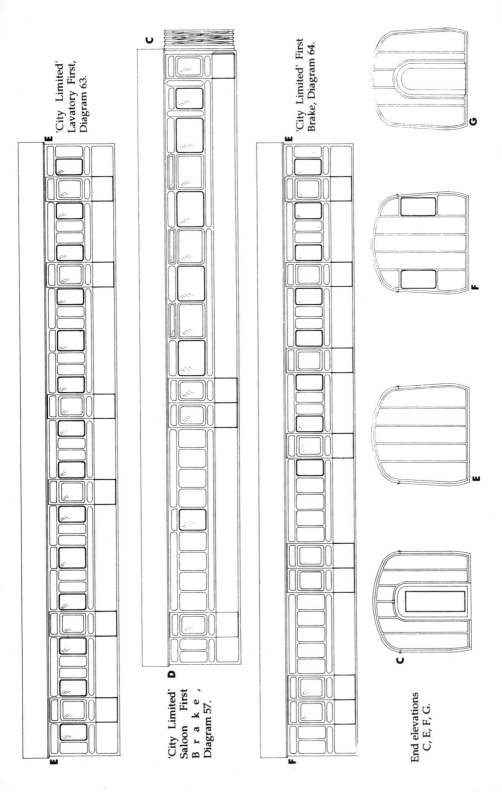

'City Limited' Lavatory First, Diagram 63.

'City Limited' Saloon First Brake, Diagram 57.

'City Limited' First Brake, Diagram 64.

End elevations C, E, F, G.

BOGIE LAVATORY FIRSTS

Nos. 162-164 (SR Nos. 7638-7640)

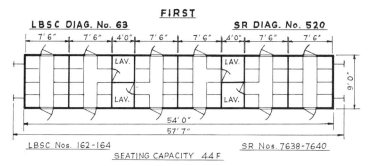

SEATING CAPACITY 44 F

Body length: 54 ft. Body width: 9 ft. Bogie centres: 37 ft.
Compartments: Six (7 ft 6 in. between partitions). Four lavatories, each serving one compartment only. Seats: 44. Tare weight: 24 tons 10 cwt.
Diagram No. 63 (SR No. 520).

BOGIE SALOON FIRST BRAKE

No. 31 (SR No. 7770)

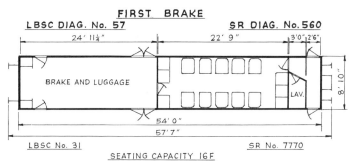

SEATING CAPACITY 16 F

Body length: 54 ft. Body width: 8 ft 10 in. Bogie centres: 37 ft.
One saloon compartment, 22 ft 9 in. between partitions. One lavatory at end, with access from all seats. Seats: 16. Tare weight: 24 tons.
Diagram No. 57 (SR No. 560). Gangwayed one end.

BOGIE FIRST BRAKES

Nos. 165, 166 (SR Nos. 6926, 7775)

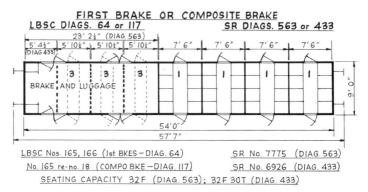

FIRST BRAKE OR COMPOSITE BRAKE

LBSC DIAGS. 64 or 117   SR DIAGS. 563 or 433

LBSC Nos. 165, 166 (1st BKES – DIAG. 64)   SR No. 7775 (DIAG. 563)
No. 165 re-no. 18 (COMPO BKE – DIAG. 117)   SR No. 6926 (DIAG. 433)
SEATING CAPACITY 32F (DIAG. 563); 32F 30T (DIAG. 433)

Body length: 54 ft. Body width: 9 ft. Bogie centres: 37 ft.
Four compartments (7 ft 6 in. between partitions). No lavatories. Seats: 32.
Tare weight: 24 tons 5 cwt. Diagram No. 64 (SR No. 433 and 563).

The Corridor First, No. 151, was for its time a very advanced design, and indeed, 60 years later, British Rail's Mk II vehicles displayed a remarkably similar layout. Each of the six compartments seated six passengers, and the only access to each compartment was from the side corridor by means of a glazed sliding door. Three compartments, designated for smokers, had the seats upholstered in green buffalo hide, but the other three had moquette coverings. Electric lighting was by single lamps and there were additional lamps that could be switched on or off by passengers.

Access to the coach was by inward-opening side doors at each vestibule end and by the gangway connections. Each of the two lavatory compartments was placed between the end vestibule and the end compartment. The coach interior had millboard panels for the sides and ceiling, with lincrusta decorations, the panels being of polished walnut and sycamore. The corridor had a polished walnut dado. Altogether No. 151 was a model of a well-thought-out corridor coach, but no more were built. The Saloon First, No. 152, comprised four saloon compartments in groups of two, each divided by a partition, and in the centre of the carriage a single lavatory compartment was placed. In each saloon were four moveable wickerwork chairs and six fixed seats. Two of the compartments were upholstered in rep and the other two, being for smokers, were upholstered in green buffalo hide. The floor was covered by a special 'Klondyke' carpet; the panels were polished walnut and sycamore; the ceiling was whitewood, painted white enamel; and lighting was provided from central electroliers. As with the Corridor First, entry to the carriage was by inward-opening doors in the end vestibules or through the gangway connections. Each vestibule had a polished walnut dado and polished oak upper panels. There were 16 large windows in each bodyside.

The Saloon First Brake, No. 31, was gangwayed at the non-brake end only, where there was an entrance vestibule (with outward-opening doors) and a lavatory between this and the saloon compartment. Inside there were ten moveable wicker chairs and six fixed seats, all upholstered in Cashmere rep. The floor was covered by a 'Klondyke' carpet, and the interior panels were of polished walnut and sycamore. The ceiling was white-painted whitewood and there were two-lamp electroliers and single ceiling-lamps. Additional lighting was provided along the cantrail moulding projected upwards to illuminate the ceiling. The vestibule had a polished walnut dado and polished oak upper panels.

The brake and luggage compartment, 24 ft 11½ in. long, contained a dynamo and accumulators to supply lighting to No. 31 and to the Pullman cars formed in the train. There was a set of double doors each side giving access to the luggage compartment and the guard had the use of a single inward-opening door each side, near to the end, in which were set two windows overlooking the track.

Nos. 161-6 were more conventional coaches, non-gangwayed with full-width compartments and individual lavatories; the seating was four-a-side in each compartment, there being sufficient room for this as the coaches were 9 ft wide at the waist.

Formation of the 8.45 am from Brighton during 1911/12 was as follows:

London Bridge	48	Bogie 3rd	
	1682	Bogie 3rd	
	165	Bogie 1st brake	Return on 5.00 pm.
	163	Bogie 1st	Return on 5.00 pm.
	161	Bogie 1st	Return on 5.00 pm.
	-	Two Pullmans	Return on 5.00 pm.
	151	Bogie Cor. 1st	Return on 5.00 pm.
	152	Bogie 1st Saloon	Return on 5.00 pm.
	31	Bogie 1st Saloon Bke	Return on 5.00 pm.
Victoria	166	Bogie 1st Bke Slip	
	-	1 Pullman	
	162	Bogie First	
	85	Bogie First	

Note. No. 164 was spare. Thirds Nos. 48 and 1682 were elliptical-roofed stock (Diagram Nos. 185 and 189) and No. 85 was a 48 ft First of 1894 that later went to Set 109.

Formation varied slightly over the years. In July 1908, for example, the full train was eleven coaches: Nos. 165, 163, 164, two Pullmans, 161, 152, 31 (London Bridge) and Nos. 166, one Pullman and 162 (Victoria). Apparently the Corridor First had been temporarily withdrawn. At another stage the two First Brakes had exchanged places, as had Nos. 162/64, and the formation of the up train was now: Nos. 166, 162, 163, 161, Pullman Buffet Car, Pullman Parlour Car, 151, 152, 31 (London Bridge) and Nos. 165, Pullman Parlour Car, 164 (Victoria).

The *Railway Magazine*, writing about the train in 1911 (Vol. 29, p. 433) stated that, while the 'City Limited' was solely for 1st-class passengers on Mondays to Fridays, the Saturday afternoon train, which left London Bridge at 1.20 pm, did admit 'other classes'. The eight-coach down train, weighing about 260 tons, was within the capabilities of Billinton's 4-4-0 locomotives, but the up train, with four extra coaches, was a tougher assignment, weighing about 370 tons. Pullman buffet car *Grosvenor* was able to serve clients a *table d'hôte* breakfast on the 8.45 am up train, and tea in the 5.00 pm down; on Saturdays passengers could 'avail themselves of an excellent luncheon service'.

At a later date the upholstered basket chairs were replaced by less creaky furniture. During World War I Set No. 6 was reduced in length and the Victoria portion was withdrawn, as were the Pullman cars, and the formation in 1917 was shown as First Brake No. 165, Firsts Nos. 163, 161, 151, 152, 164, an unspecified Composite, and a First Brake No. 12, though this was actually part of Set 99, the Members' Race Train.

In February 1921 First Brake No. 165 was rebuilt into a Composite Brake and renumbered 18 (Diagram 117). Three 3rd-class compartments, each 5 ft 10½ in. between partitions, were squeezed into what had been most of the luggage compartment, leaving a very tiny guard's compartment 5 ft 4½ in. long. Seating capacity was thus 32 1st, 30 3rd-class, these being the only 3rd-class seats on the entire train. Apart from this rebuild, formation of the 1921 'City Limited' was the same as it had been in 1917. Neither Pullman cars nor Victoria portion on the up train were restored. The lack of Pullmans is perhaps surprising, as all other fast trains on the main line included them, but it may have been due to the wish to keep the load to eight bogie coaches in order that the fast schedule of 60 minutes down and 65 minutes up could be maintained.

Seven carriages of the original 'City Limited' set were repainted and renumbered by the Southern in July 1924 as SR Set No. 933. Two of the First Brakes - Nos. 31 and 166, which became Nos. 7770 and 7775 in 1927 - were dispersed, and 8 ft 6 in. First Brake No. 28 was transferred to Set 933 and renumbered 7773 in July 1924. Clearly there was growing demand for 3rd-class seating, for two elliptical-roofed 8 ft 6 in. Thirds were also formed into Set 933 in July 1924: Nos. 2339 and 2340. Thus the set was now ten coaches, of which seven were the original 9 ft-wide vehicles. It was dual-braked in July 1925.

Set 933 was replaced on the 'City Limited' service by new Southern-built corridor vehicles early in 1926, after which the ex-LB&SC train was not used in normal traffic again. Instead it was reserved as the 'Members' Race Train'. Meanwhile First Brake No. 7775 had been running with Lavatory Composite No. 6200 as two-set No. 734 since April 1927, regularly as part of the 10.05 am Brighton to London Bridge and as the Brighton slip portion of the 5.08 pm London Bridge to Angmering. This it did until electrification of the Brighton main line.

Set 933 was altered in formation towards the end of 1930. Composite Brake No. 6926 and Lavatory Thirds Nos. 2339/40 were transferred to Set 926 and the Composite Brake was replaced in Set 933 by Saloon First Brake No. 7770 (old No. 31). Now an eight-coach Race Set, No. 933 was altered to vacuum brakes (only) and berthed at Eardley when not in use.

Further alterations were made in 1933 or 1934: First Brake No. 7773 was transferred to Set 934 and replaced by First Brake No. 7775 from Set 734 (which was disbanded). It is believed that 8 ft 6 in. First No. 7631 from Set 841 was also transferred to Set 933, making it up to nine vehicles, all first class. Unlike Race Sets Nos. 929 and 934, which were transferred to the London West District, Set 933 remained on the Central Section, normally berthed at Eardley, working race specials to various places (including Lingfield) when required.

First Brake No. 7775 was withdrawn in May 1936, but the remainder of Set 933 survived until the end of 1940; there is no record of No. 7775 being replaced as all the other elliptical-roofed First Brakes were accounted for in other sets.

Four vehicles were later noted as having become grounded bodies: No. 7641 at Meldon Quarry; No. 7642 at Feltham, observed August 1946; No. 7643 at Ashford, noted January 1944; and No. 7770 at Wembley Hill Trading Estate, May 1948. During the late 1940s No. 7770 was used by Johnson, Matthey & Co. as a Welfare and Rest Room.

'CITY LIMITED' STOCK

No.	Built	Set No.	SR No.	Re-No.	Set No.	Wdn.
151	6.07	6	7641	7.24	933	12.40
152	6.07	6	7642	7.24	933	12.40
161	6.07	6	7643	7.24	933	12.40
162	12.07	6, Spare	7638	7.24	933	12.40
163	12.07	6	7639	7.24	933	12.40
164	12.07	6	7640	7.24	933	12.40
165	12.07	6				
18	12.07	6	6926	7.24	933, 926 /31, Loose /34	9.35
31	6.06	6, Spare	7770	7.27	Loose, 933 /31	12.40
166	12.07	6, Spare	7775	4.27	734, 933 /34	5.36

Chapter Seven

Ambulance Trains

In 1915 several of the elliptical-roofed carriages were converted into Ambulance Train coaches at Lancing. The interiors were stripped and the bodysides received minor alterations; for example a door was blanked off here and an extra window cut in there. Gangways were fitted at the coach ends. The bodies were painted grey, and about halfway along each bodyside appeared a large red cross on a white ground. Seven Third Brakes (Nos. 802, 803, 804, 809, 626, 651 and 1780), plus seven London & North Western carriages and two LB&SC vans were formed into Ambulance Train No. 14, and sixteen LB&SC carriages formed Train No. 25, comprising former Thirds Nos. 6, 7, 87, 634, 737, 750, 759 1682, 1697, 1732 and 1766, and former Third Brakes Nos. 653, 719, 810, 811 and 1736. On each vehicle the Train Number appeared at the ends, and also on each side with a suffix letter (A, B, etc.) to identify the individual carriage.

Train No. 14 was photographed at Lovers Walk sidings, Brighton, shortly after completion. The end coach was one of the four-compartment lavatory Third Brakes, either No. 626 or 651, with an extra window put in between the set of luggage compartment doors and the fourth compartment. The red cross was fitted between this compartment window and the extra window. This individual coach was No. 14H.

Continental Ambulance Train No. 14 was sent to France as seven vehicles but in June 1915 the L&NW was requested to send six carriages - plus a newly built staff car (not L&NW but built at Wolverton) - to strengthen the LB&SC train. The augmented train now had the formation: LBSC Brake Van, Kitchen Car A, Ward Cars B, C, D, E, Pharmacy Car F, Staff Car G, LNW Ward Cars L, M, N, O, P, LBSC Kitchen Car H, LNW Personnel Car R, LBSC Brake Van.

C. Hamilton Ellis recorded that Train No. 25 saw service between Köln Deutz and Calais, and that No. 14 was known as 'Queen Mary's'. Thanks to an enterprising French post card publisher, Editions Arnault, it is known that No. 14 visited Le Tréport during the course of its duties. Coach No. 14D is prominent in the picture, apparently about to unload the wounded into a trio of motor ambulances standing close by. The suffering humanity would have been transferred from these vehicles to a hospital ship.

After World War I the bodies of the Ambulance Coaches were removed from their underframes. Some turned up in the Greenford-Northolt area, beside the Grand Union Canal. At least 13 of the underframes found their way under new carriage bodies constructed in 1922, but it is not known which frames were re-used, or what fate became those frames that did not see further service.

There was also a Home Ambulance Train built by the LB&SC in about 1916, but unlike the Continental Ambulance Trains, which were purchased by the War Office, it remained the property of the LB&SC and ran in original livery. There were 16 carriages: two kitchens, one pharmacy, four ward cars, five sitting, one staff, one personnel and two brake carriages. The actual vehicles forming this train have not been identified, and they are presumed to have reverted to civil use in 1919.

Chapter Eight

Carriage Stock Constructed Between 1907 and 1924

After several of the fine elliptical-roofed carriages had been put into service the LB&SCR seemed to have second thoughts and reverted to its former standards of carriage construction, using the arc roof with its radius of 7 ft and height above rail level of 11 ft 9½ in., and a body width of only 8 ft. It may be argued that the reason for this regression was that the 'Balloon' carriages had a restricted route availability, but this fact must have been known before their construction was embarked upon. After 1907 the design of LB&SCR carriages was, to say the least, unimaginative; money was in short supply and the Company adopted the expedient of rebuilding a very large number of six-wheeled carriages into bogie stock on new standard 54 ft underframes. Relatively few entirely new carriages appeared, and apart from a couple of Saloons they were nothing special; in fact, non-corridor, non-lavatory carriages were still being built for main-line work as late as 1924.

When Marsh resigned in 1911 the Locomotive and Carriage Departments were separated. Lawson Billinton became the locomotive superintendent and Albert Panter became the carriage and wagon superintendent. Carriage construction was transferred from Brighton to a new Works at Lancing about 1909 or 1910. This Works, the construction of which was approved by the Board in 1907, was some years in building: the LB&SCR's half-yearly Report of August 1909 stated that construction was 'making good progress', whilst one year later construction was 'proceeding satisfactorily'. It seems likely that a certain amount of carriage building was undertaken before the Works was completed. But even then the 'Brighton' never had the capacity to build all the carriages it needed and from time to time contractors had to be used.

An important change to LB&SCR carriages was the abolition of second-class accommodation, carried out in two stages: in the suburban area in June 1911 and in main line services in June 1912, except for the Newhaven boat train.

BOGIE THIRDS

Nos. 330, 357, 360, 377, etc. (SR Nos. 9035-59, 9000/02-09/12/15-18, 9019/21/23/24)

Body length: 54 ft. Body width: 8 ft. Bogie centres: 37 ft.
Compartments: Nine, of which five were 5 ft 10¼ in. and four were 5 ft 11 in. between partitions. Seats: 90.
Tare weight: 23 tons approximately. Diagram No. 171 (SR No. 72). Rebuilt 1910/11.

The whole of this series of nine-compartment Thirds, totalling 43 vehicles, was built by mounting the bodies of six-wheel five-compartment Thirds on to new bogie underframes, the work being carried out during 1910 and 1911.

In each rebuilding the complete body of a six-wheeler was used, plus four additional compartments, usually of new construction; in one case, however, the body was made up by using two six-wheelers, Nos. 495 and 558 in 1907. This 'new' bogie vehicle then took the number 495. In all these rebuilds the original gas lighting system was retained, the new compartments also being gas lit to match.

Nos. 460 and 1174 were both found in Set 21 and Nos. 436 and 561 were in Set 37 by 1917, these working between Eastbourne, London and Brighton, some trips being via Oxted. No. 501 in Set 26 and No. 488 in Set 32 worked between Portsmouth and London. By 1921 No. 551 was formed in ten-set No. 40, which worked between Brighton and Victoria.

Only six Thirds received their allocated Southern numbers in the 'steam' series, for in 1925 all 43 vehicles were adapted for use in electric trailer sets, being fitted with electric lighting and jumper cables (these being housed in a somewhat unsightly protruding 'box' at each outer end of the two-coach set). As adapted the coaches were given the SR Diagram Number 724.

The work was carried out at Lancing, and the coaches were allocated to sets randomly, many being paired with nine-compartment Thirds that had been built new in 1911, 1912, 1913 and 1921 (LB&SC Diagram No. 198, SR Diagram No. 723). The trailer sets ran on the Central and Eastern Sections, each set being marshalled between two three-car electric motor units to make an eight-coach train for peak periods; later, they were used on the Western Section also.

Many of the trailer sets were reformed from 1934 onwards. One of the two ex-LB&SC vehicles in each set was replaced by a newly-converted vehicle comprising ex-London & South Western bodywork on a standard SR 62 ft underframe, the displaced coach going to a new series of trailer sets, Nos. 1038 to 1050 and 1195 to 1198, introduced in 1934/5. Each of these was similarly formed of an ex-LB&SC nine-compartment Third and a rebuilt vehicle comprising LSW bodywork. Further trailer sets of similar formation were introduced in February 1937 (Nos. 1118 to 1120), March 1937 (No. 1199) and July 1937 (Nos. 989 to 1000 and 1200).   This left only Sets 1052-54/56-58/60/62/63/65/66/   69/74-77/   79/80/83/88/89/91/94,   1100-02/05-07/09/10/14 still running in their original formations with two ex-LB&SC nine-compartment Thirds each.

However, few of these survived the War. The decision was taken to abolish trailer sets, coaches with standard SR underframes being transferred to the motor units and the remainder being scrapped. Some were damaged by enemy action, the first such being No. 9019 in Set 1120, which was hit by a delayed-action bomb on 7th September, 1940, while working the 5.18 pm Dartford to Charing Cross; the bomb exploded near Plumstead at 10.35 pm causing such damage as to justify breaking-up two days later.

Several of the rebuilt Thirds became grounded bodies after withdrawal, though few were still in place after the War.

9002 to Eastleigh, Aug. 1943
9009 to Folkestone Harbour, Dec. 1943
9023 to Lancing Works, September 1946
9024 to Effingham Junction, Apr. 1943
9038 to Wimbledon, Jan. 1943
9040 to Orpington, Jan. 1943

The centre vehicle in this three-carriage train is a nine-compartment Third with gas lighting, rebuilt in 1910 from a six-wheeled Third. All these Thirds (Diagram No. 171) were converted to D.C. trailer sets in 1925.   *Lens of Sutton*

D.C. Trailer Third No. 9087 in Set 1091 at Hayes. This carriage was built new by Metropolitan RC&W Co. in 1911, LB&SC No. 1359, and was withdrawn in 1948. Originally, smoking compartments had 'tin' ventilators on the doors and non-smoking compartments had louvred ventilators.   *H.C. Hughes*

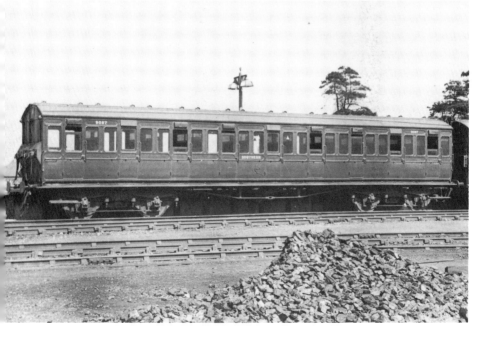

Victoria to Portsmouth Pullman car train between Dorking and Betchworth tunnel, about 1921; class 'B4' locomotive No. 61 heads six-coach Set 75, the leading vehicle of which is a Diagram 168 Third Brake, No. 471, rebuilt in 1908 from six-wheeled Third and Brake Van.

Locomotive Publishing Co.

Victoria to Hastings train near Horley in 1923; class 'B1' locomotive No. 192 heads Set 40, of which the leading coach is a six-compartment Third Brake to LB&SC Diagram No. 201, built in 1916, No. 641. *O.J. Morris*

Third Brake No. 467, formed in three-coach set 60, was rebuilt in 1908 from six-wheel Third No. 467 and six-wheel Brake Van No. 432, retaining gas lighting (LB&SC Diagram No. 168). It was renumbered SR 3926 in 1926. *O.J. Morris*

A close view of the end compartment and luggage section of SR Third Brake No. 3980, of three-set 789, at Kensington Addison Road on 26th August, 1933. The side lookouts have been replaced by steel sheet. *H.C. Casserley*

The next six pictures show some of the varieties of ex-LB&SC Third Brakes as running in the Isle of Wight. Here is No. 4122, originally LB&SC No. 554 and SR No. 4013, built in 1910 and withdrawn in 1959. The bodyside has been plain-panelled. *Lens of Sutton*

No. 4158 was built in 1912 as LB&SC No. 99, later becoming SR No. 4037 ; it has retained most of its original mouldings and lasted until the end of steam operation in the Island. Here shown at Sandown station. *Lens of Sutton*

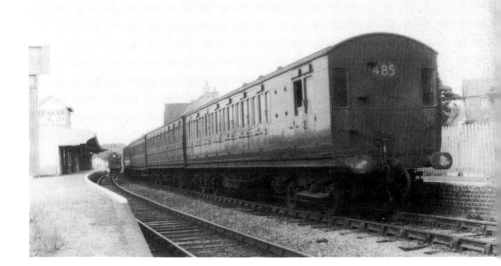

This seven-compartment Third Brake, No. 4161, was built in 1913 as a five-compartment Third Brake, LB&SC No. 890, becoming SR No. 3973 and rebuilt for Island service in 1937. Ryde St Johns, 29th September, 1965.   *J.H. Aston*

Third Brake No. 4163 was built by the LB&SC in 1916 as No. 647, becoming SR No. 4025. It was transferred to the Isle of Wight in 1937, where it was withdrawn in 1966.   *N. Hamshere*

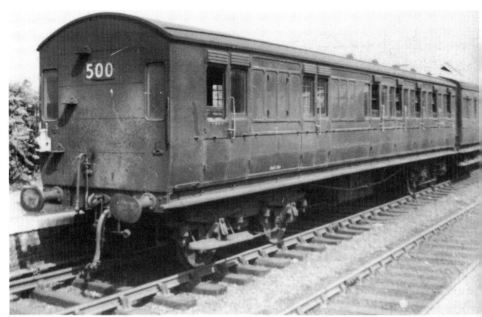

Latterly the only five-compartment Third Brake in the Island, No. 4168 is here shown at Shanklin station, with the set number '500' on a plate screwed into the end. The carriage was built in 1922, originally numbered 93 then SR 3870, and sent to the Island in 1938. *N. Hamshere*

No. 4170 was built in 1907 as LB&SC No. 891, a five-compartment Third Brake which became SR No. 3974. Rebuilt for I.O.W. service with enlarged luggage compartment in 1939, it was formed in Set 490 and withdrawn in 1954. *E.R. Lacey*

Lavatory Composite No. 64, rebuilt in 1910 from six-wheeled Lavatory Composite of 1898.   It became SR No. 6179 in 1925.   *O.J. Morris*

Isle of Wight Composite No. 6354, built in 1924 as SR No. 6165 and transferred in 1936; one of the first-class compartments was reclassified Third.   *J.H. Aston*

LB&SC Family Saloon No. 57 was built in 1916 and became SR No. 7973. In 1934 it was rebuilt as Composite Brake No. 6986 and sent to the Isle of Wight for use in 'The Tourist' limited-stop train. Ryde St Johns, 22nd May, 1937. *H.C. Casserley*

Directors' Inspection Saloon of 1914, LB&SC No. 60, SR No. 291S. This picture shows the vehicle in SR livery; the gangways were fitted in 1934.

British Railways painted the Saloon in crimson and cream livery and it became DS 291; here shown at Clapham Junction, 25th May, 1953.   *J.H. Aston*

DS 291 was obtained by the Bluebell Railway in 1965 and pressed it into service as a refreshment car, even though repainting was nowhere near complete! Here it is formed in the 1.55 pm Sheffield Park to Horsted Keynes in 'patchwork' undercoat, 11th June, 1966.   *D. Gould*

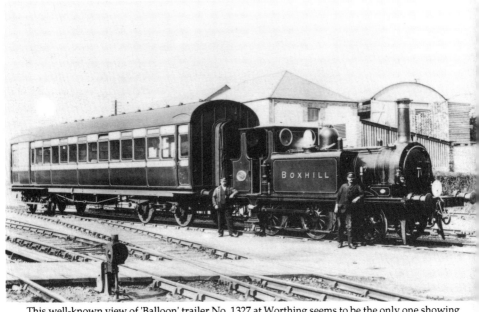

This well-known view of 'Balloon' trailer No. 1327 at Worthing seems to be the only one showing one of the original two cars, which sported corridor connections. No. 1327 was built in 1905 (Diagram No. 179) and became SR No. 3830. *Locomotive Publishing Co.*

Interior of 'Balloon' trailer Third Brake, showing the rattan seat upholstery and ornate LB&SCR monogram. *Lens of Sutton*

LB&SC No. 1329, one of the second batch of 'Balloon' trailers, was built in 1906 (Diagram No. 180) and became SR No. 3832. Here shown at Kemp Town with 'Rooter' No. 643.

D. Cullum Collection

Another 'Balloon' trailer, in charge of 'Rooter' locomotive No. 659   *Lens of Sutton*

'Rooter' No. 681 hauls a 'Balloon' trailer strengthened with an eight-compartment Third between Hassocks and Clayton tunnel *c.* 1921.   *H. Gordon Tidey*

Trailer Third Brake No. 1342, built in 1907 (Diagram No. 181), together with a Composite, has just left Hassocks on a Haywards Heath to Brighton local service, c.1923.   *H. Gordon Tidey*

SR No. 3844, in push-and-pull set 749, was built as LB&SC No. 1341 in 1907. Note the sliding door to the luggage compartment.   *Lens of Sutton*

SR set No. 749 enters Barnham on a Horsham to Bognor Regis service, *c.* 1937. Formation is Third Brake No. 3844 and Composite No. 6275.   *Lens of Sutton*

A typical early formation, with class 'D1' locomotive No. 627 in the curious 'Liver & Bacon' livery, at Brighton, 1909. Driving Trailer Composite Brake No.

A 'sandwich' push-and-pull train comprising two Trailer Composite Brakes, rebuilt in 1909 from six-wheelers, leaves Mitcham on a Sutton-Mitcham Junction-Wimbledon service. *Lens of Sutton*

Push-and-pull set 755 at Bognor in the 1930s. The Composite Brake is No. 6931, formerly LB&SC No. 634, rebuilt in 1909 from a six-wheeled Third. *E. Jackson*

Push-and-pull set 730 at Beckenham Junction on 30th December, 1956. *Top*: Third Brake No. 3827, built 1911 as No. 1345; *Bottom*: Composite No. 6203, built in 1911 as No. 642. The set was withdrawn in 1959. *H.C. Casserley*

9041 to Bricklayers Arms, March 1943
9049 to Wimbledon Park, Aug. 1943
9056 to Fratton, Nov. 1941
9057 to Micheldever, for Social Club, June 1943
9059 to Brighton Top Yard, June 1943

Only one of the rebuilt Thirds became a service vehicle after withdrawal from stock: this was No. 9003, which was fitted out to work as a railcleaning and de-icing trailer, No. 356S, spraying oil fluid on to the conductor rail during icy weather. It was finally withdrawn from these duties in May 1961.

NINE-COMPARTMENT THIRDS (DIAGRAM No. 171)

No.	Built	Reblt.	SR No.	Re-No.	DCE	Re-No.	Set	Wdn	
330	6.95	12.10			9035	10.25	1085	.45	
357	12.95	12.10	2292	3.24	9036	8.25	1071	11.42	Acc. dam. Waterloo
360	6.95	12.10	2293	10.24	9037	10.25	1081	11.40	Enemy action
377	12.95	12.10	2294	2.24	9038	10.25	1086	11.42	Acc. dam. Waterloo
388	12.95	12.10			9039	10.25	1086	11.43	
410	12.93	12.10			9040	12.25	1089	11.42	
413	12.93	6.10			9041	10.25	1089	11.42	
416	12.93	12.10			9042	10.25	1091	.48	
418	12.93	6.10			9043	10.25	1080	4.42	
423	12.93	12.10			9044	10.25	1087	.47	
424	12.93	12.10			9045	12.25	1097	.47	
431	12.93	12.10			9046	12.25	1098	9.44	
436	12.93	12.10	2303	7.24	9047	12.25	1096	8.48	
437	6.95	12.10			9048	5.25	1054	?	
438	6.95	12.10			9049	12.25	1099	4.43	
459	6 95	12.10			9050	12.25	1108	6.42	
460	6.96	12.10			9051	12.25	1101	7.48	
461	6.96	6.10			9052	5.25	1055	.45	
465	6.94	12.10			9053	9.25	1079	.47	
484	6.94	6.10			9054	12.25	1108	.46	
488	12.92	6.10	2311	5.24	9055	12.25	1102	?	
495	12.92	12.07			9056	5.25	1054	10.41	
501	12.91	6.10			9057	12.25	1100	3.43	
502	12.91	6.10			9058	12.25	1104	.45	
503	12.91	6.10			9059	9.25	1077	5.43	
515	6.94	12 10			9000	6.25	1059	10.40	Enemy action
522	6.91	12.10			9002	6.25	1052	3.43	
546	6.95	12.10			9003	6.25	1060	11.45	Re-No. 356S
551	12.92	12.10			9004	6.25	1066	7.43	
555	6.93	12.10			9005	6.25	1058	.48	
557	6.93	6.10			9006	6.25	1057	?	
561	6.93	12.10			9007	6.25	1066	7.43	
562	6.93	12.10			9008	6.25	1057	?	
571	6.93	12.10			9009	6.25	1069	12.43	
1156	6.95	6.10	2325	9.24	9012	7.25	1059	2.44	
1166	6.95	6.10			9015	7.25	1063	11.40	
1167	6.95	6.10			9016	7.25	1063	11.40	
1168	6.95	6.10			9017	7.25	1064	.47	
1169	6.95	6.10			9018	7.25	1072	.45	
1174	6.95	6.10			9019	8.25	1067	9.40	Enemy action
1247	6.97	6.10			9021	8.25	1070	?	
1251	12.97	6.11			9023	9.25	1079	.47	
1253	12.97	6.11			9024	10.25	1084	12.42	

BOGIE THIRDS

Nos. 1,4, etc.; 855-64, 872-4, 879, 880, 883-6, 1351-1400 (SR Nos. 8999, 8949, 9001, 8950-7, 9010/1, 8958, 9013/4, 8959-63, 9020, 8964, 9022, 8965-8, 9027, 8969-74, 9034, 9060-9107, 9025/6/8-33, 9117-20, 9108-16)

Body length: 54 ft. Body width: 8 ft. Bogie centres: 37 ft. Compartments: Nine (5 ft 10½ in. between partitions). Seats: 90.
Tare weight: 24 tons 2 cwt. Diagram No. 198 (SR No. 71). Built between 1910 and 1921.

Construction of what was to become a large series of nine-compartment Thirds totalling 105 vehicles began in 1910. The first 50, Nos. 1351 to 1400, were built by the Metropolitan Amalgamated Railway Carriage & Wagon Co. of Birmingham. They were very similar to the Thirds described in the previous section, but were built new with all compartments of the same dimensions. All 50 were completed during the first half of 1911. Lancing Works turned out a further 25 during 1912/13, and a final batch of 30 was built there during 1921, these being 'renewals' and consequently taking the numbers of recently withdrawn stock. All 105 were equipped with electric lighting, but Nos. 1351 to 1360 did not have dynamos. (The rebuilt nine-compartment Thirds, as mentioned in the previous section, retained gas lighting.)

Six of the Thirds were recorded as formed into sets by 1917. No. 858 was in three-set 22 (Tunbridge Wells-Victoria); No. 1375 in five-set 23 (Brighton-London Bridge); No. 880 in five-set 15; No. 1400 in four-set 28 (Epsom - Victoria); and Nos. 855 and 874 in five-set 109 (London Brighton). Four years later, No. 862 was in seven-set 49 and No. 1376 in 10-set 40.

On coming to the Southern Railway all were allotted a batch of numbers in the 'steam' series (2186 to 2290) but very few of these were painted on. It was quickly decided to use the nine-compartment Thirds in two-coach 'trailer sets' working between two of the D.C. electric motor units. The most recently-built Thirds were the first to be converted, 26 of these being adapted at Lancing, renumbered 8949 to 8974 and formed into trailer sets 1025 to 1037 in pairs and in numerical order during April and May 1925. At first they were employed on the Western Section, for the Guildford and Dorking services, but in later years they were found on all three Sections of the SR. A new diagram was issued for the coaches in this form, being No. 723.

Further vehicles were adapted to work in trailer sets between June 1925 and February 1926, being formed in Sets 1051 to 1110 and 1114. The coaches forming these were not in numerical order, and also included vehicles adapted from the rebuilt nine-compartment Thirds; the complete number range ran from 8999 to 9120, which included both Diagrams 723 and 724. These trailer sets were required for the Eastern Section electrification scheme of 1926 and for the subsequent Central Section scheme; they were not normally observed on the Western Section until the 1930s.

The subsequent history of the nine-compartment Thirds, once they had been formed into trailer sets, is the same as that of the rebuilt Thirds described in the previous section. Several of the sets were reformed from 1934 onwards to include one vehicle with ex-L&SW bodywork and one ex-LB&SC vehicle; few sets survived the War, the last being withdrawn in August 1948; several bodies were grounded at various locations; and a few coaches were converted to de-icing trailers.   Exceptionally, none of Sets 1025-37 was reformed; all were withdrawn between 1946 and 1948 in their original formations.   Despite being less than thirty years old there was no future for them; their bodywork looked outdated and their underframes were non-standard.   Only coaches built on SR standard 62 ft underframes had any life-expectancy in the 1940s.

The following became grounded bodies:

8953 and 8954 to Southampton Docks, noted 5.47
9001 to Wokingham, Aug. 1943
9025 to Redhill locomotive depot, April 1942
9026 to Southampton, May 1942
9027 half to Shalford, half to Tunbridge W. Ctl Goods, May 1942
9029 to Gravesend West Street, May 1943
9062 to Wareham, May 1943
9064 to Tooting Junction, May 1943
9067 to Raynes Park, January 1943
9068 to Bricklayers Arms, April 1944
9072 to Sutton, Sep. 1943
9082 to Brighton Top Yard, June 1943
9084 to Wimbledon Park, April 1943
9085 to Lancing, 1942. In two parts by 9.46.
9090 to Worthing Central, Sep 1943
9093 to Farnham, December 1942
9102 to Eastleigh Works, Sep. 1943
9117 and 9118 to Ashford, June 1943

In November 1945 five of the withdrawn Thirds became de-icing trailers, these being renumbered 351S to 355S (formerly 9010, 9116, 9013, 9069 and 9060 respectively).   A further four were converted in November 1946, Nos. 8957, 8958, 9079 and 9089 becoming 396S to 399S in that order.   They operated as single trailers formed between two motor units.   Finally, in 1947, No. 8951 was altered to 434S, becoming a stores van at Lancing Works.

After 1949 the 'S' suffix to the departmental vehicles was altered on repainting to a 'DS' prefix.   The de-icing trailers were withdrawn as follows: DS 351/5 - December 1956; DS 354 - January 1961; DS 352/3 May 1961.   DS 396-9 are believed to have been withdrawn in 1961, but it is not known how long No. 434S lasted.

NINE-COMPARTMENT THIRDS (DIAGRAM No. 198)

No.	Built	SR No.	Re-No.	DCE	Re-No.	Set	Wdn	
1	6.21			8999	6.25	1051	8.48	
4	6.21			8949	4.25	1025	.47	
5	12.21			9001	6.25	1052	3.43	
6	6.21			8950	4.25	1025	.47	
7	12.21	2190	9.24	8951	4.25	1026	.47	Re-No. 434S.
8	12.21			8952	4.25	1026	.47	
9	12.21	2192	11.24	8953	4.25	1027	.47	

No.	Built	SR No.	Re-No.	DCE	Re-No.	Set	Wdn	
10	6.21	2193	12.24	8954	4.25	1027	.47	
17	12.21			8955	4.25	1028	?	
21	12.21			8956	4.25	1028	?	
22	12.21			8957	4.25	1029	11.46	Re-No. 396S.
26	12.12			9010	6.25	1065	12.45	Re-No. 351S.
31	12.12	2198	10.24	9011	7.25	1056	.48	
32	12.21			8958	4.25	1029	11.46	Re-No. 397S.
36	12.21			9013	6.25	1053	11.45	Re-No. 353S.
38	12.21			9014	6.25	1056	.48	
39	12.21			8959	4.25	1030	.48	
40	12.21			8960	4.25	1030	.48	
42	12.21			8961	5.25	1031	.47	
44	12.21			8962	4.25	1031	.47	
49	12.21			8963	4.25	1032	.48	
51	12.12	2207	4.24	9020	7.25	1072	.47	
54	12.21			8964	4.25	1032	.48	
56	12.12			9022	7.25	1068	.47	
60	12.21			8965	4.25	1033	.47	
64	12.21			8966	5.25	1033	.47	
66	12.21			8967	5.25	1034	.48	
67	12.21	2213	8.24	8968	5.25	1034	.48	
70	12.12			9027	10.25	1087	2.42	
71	12.21			8969	5.25	1035	.47	
73	12.21			8970	4.25	1035	.47	
74	12.21			8971	4.25	1036	.47	
77	12.21			8972	5.25	1036	.47	
78	12.21			8973	4.25	1037	.48	
81	12.21			8974	4.25	1037	.48	
86	12.12	2221	11.24	9034	8.25	1073	.47	
855	12.12			9060	7.25	1060	11.45	Re-No. 355S.
856	12.12			9061	7.25	1065	.45	
857	12.12			9062	7.25	1062	3.43	
858	12.12			9063	7.25	1061	2.44	Enemy Action, Vauxhall
859	12 12			9064	7.25	1062	3.43	
860	12.12			9065	7.25	1061	.45	
861	12.12			9066	7.25	1070	.46	
862	12.12			9067	7.25	1071	9.42	
863	12.12			9068	7.25	1069	12.43	
864	12.12	2231	7.24	9069	5.25	1053	11.45	Re-No. 354S.
872	6.13	2232	12.24	9070	7.25	1067	.46	
873	6.13			9071	7.25	1064	?	
874	6.13			9072	7.25	1073	9.43	
879	6.13			9073	7.25	1074	.48	
880	6.13			9074	10.25	1082	.45	
883	6.13			9075	10.25	1090	1.48	Acc. dam. Selhurst
884	6.13			9076	8.25	1074	.48	
885	6.13			9077	8.25	1068	.46	
886	6.13			9078	9.25	1078	8.35	
1351	12.10			9079	10.25	1083	11.46	Re-No. 398S.
1352	6.11			9080	9.25	1076	.48	
1353	6.11			9081	9.25	1075	7.43	

No.	Built	SR No.	Re-No.	DCE	Re-No.	Set	Wdn	
1354	6.11			9082	9.25	1077	5.43	
1355	6.11			9083	10.25	1088	.47	
1356	6.11			9084	9.25	1082	12.42	
1357	6.11	2247	12.24	9085	9.25	1080	4.42	
1358	6.11			9086	10.25	1090	7.48	
1359	6.11			9087	10.25	1091	.48	
1360	6.11			9088	11.25	1094	9.43	
1361	6.11			9089	10.25	1083	11.46	Re-No. 399S.
1362	6.11			9090	9.25	1075	7.43	
1363	6.11			9091	10.25	1085	8.48	
1364	6.11			9092	9.25	1078	8.48	
1365	6.11			9093	10.25	1092	9.42	
1366	6.11	2256	12.24	9094	9.25	1081	.46	
1367	6.11			9095	10.25	1084	.46	
1368	6.11			9096	10.25	1088	.47	
1369	6.11			9097	10.25	1092	.47	
1370	6.11			9098	11.25	1095	.46	
1371	6.11	2261	9.24	9099	11.25	1095	9.44	
1372	6.11			9100	5.25	1051	9.39	Acc. dam. Horsham
1373	6.11			9101	12.25	1099	.47	
1374	6.11	2264	9.24	9102	11.25	1093	9.43	
1375	6.11			9103	7.25	1058	.48	
1376	6.11	2266	11.24	9104	11.25	1096	.47	
1377	6.11			9105	11.25	1094	9.43	
1378	6.11	2268	9.24	9106	11.25	1093	.44	
1379	6.11	2269	1.25	9107	11.25	1098	.47	
1380	6.11	2270	8.24	9025	1.26	1107	3.42	
1381	6.11	2271	5.25	9026	1.26	1107	3.42	
1382	6.11			9028	12.25	1097	.47	
1383	6.11			9029	12.25	1100	3.43	
1384	6.11			9030	12.25	1103	.46	
1385	6.11			9031	12.25	1102	?	
1386	6.11			9032	1.26	1109	.45	
1387	6.11			9033	1.26	1104	9.44	
1388	6.11	2278	2.24	9117	2.26	1114	3.43	
1389	6.11			9118	2.26	1114	3.43	
1390	6.11			9119	2.26	1110	.47	
1391	6.11			9120	2.26	1110	.47	
1392	6.11	2282	7.24	9108	9.25	1076	.48	
1393	6.11	2283	11.24	9109	12.25	1103	8.48	
1394	6.11			9110	12.25	1101	7.48	
1395	6.11			9111	1.26	1106	8.48	
1396	6.11			9112	1.26	1105	.48	
1397	6.11	2287	8.24	9113	1.26	1105	.48	
1398	6.11			9114	1.26	1106	8.48	
1399	6.11			9115	5.25	1055	11.40	Enemy Action
1400	6.11	2290	5.24	9116	1.26	1109	12.45	Re-No. 352S.

BOGIE THIRD

No. 1676 (SR No. 2334)

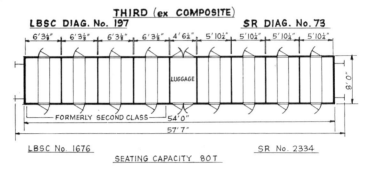

THIRD (ex COMPOSITE)
LBSC DIAG. No. 197   SR DIAG. No. 73

LBSC No. 1676   SR No. 2334

SEATING CAPACITY 80 T

Body length: 54 ft. Body width: 8 ft. Bogie centres: 37 ft.
Compartments: Eight plus luggage. Seats: 80.
Tare weight: 22 tons. Diagram No. 197 (SR No. 73). Rebuilt 1907.

This 'one-off' bogie coach was reconstructed in 1907 as a second/third Composite, No. 305, from the bodies of six-wheel Second No. 231 (built in 1905) and six- wheel Third No. 54 (built in 1894). Four compartments from each of the two bodies were used, the resulting gap of 4 ft 6¼ in in the centre of the reconstructed vehicle being employed as a luggage compartment. The second-class compartments measured 6 ft 3⅛ in. between partitions and the third-class were 5 ft 10¼ in. During the first half of 1912 the coach was reclassified all-Third and renumbered 1676. Electric lighting was fitted.

The Southern renumbered this Third as 2334 in August 1926 at Lancing, at the same time adding vacuum brakes. No details of workings are known, and it appears never to have been formed in a set train. Withdrawal took place as late as July 1940.

BOGIE LAVATORY THIRDS

Nos. 1714 and 1724 (SR Nos. 2335/36)

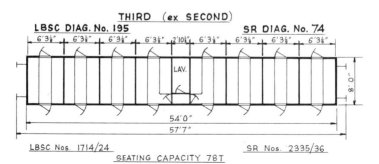

THIRD (ex SECOND)
LBSC DIAG. No. 195   SR DIAG. No. 74

LBSC Nos. 1714/24   SR Nos. 2335/36

SEATING CAPACITY 78 T

Body length: 54 ft. Body width: 8 ft. Bogie centres: 37 ft.
Compartments: Eight (6 ft 3⅛ in. between partitions). Seats : 78.
One lavatory, with access by short corridor from two compartments.
Tare weight: 22 tons 10 cwt. Diagram No. 195 (SR No. 74).

These two coaches, originally Seconds, were also reconstructions from Billinton six-wheel stock; it seems that in each case four compartments of a Second were placed at one end of the new bogie underframe, the other four compartments and the centrally-positioned lavatory being new.

Second-class No. 13, built in 1896, was converted to Bogie Second No. 13 in the first half of 1912 and reclassified as Third No. 1724 in the second half of that year. Second-class No. 57, built in 1898, became bogie Second No. 57 in the first half of 1908 and was reclassified as Third No. 1714 in the first half of 1912. Gas lighting was retained.

Both coaches came to the Southern, who added vacuum brakes in 1926 and stripped out the Westinghouse air brakes in July 1930. Neither coach was formed in a set, and both were withdrawn in 1938.

No.	Built	Rsd	Re-No.	Date	SR No.	Re-No.	Wdn
57	12.98	6.08	1714	6.12	2335	10.26	12.38
13	6.96	6.12	1724	12.12	2336	2.26	3.38

BOGIE LAVATORY THIRD

No. 1669 (SR No. 2337)

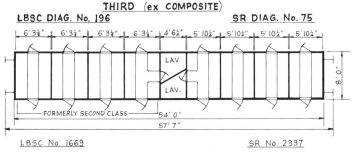

THIRD (ex COMPOSITE)

LBSC DIAG. No. 196   SR DIAG. No. 75

FORMERLY SECOND CLASS — 54' 0"

57' 7"

LBSC No. 1669   SR No. 2337

SEATING CAPACITY 78T

Body length: 54 ft. Body width: 8 ft. Bogie centres: 37 ft.
Compartments: Eight (5 ft 10¼ in or 6 ft 3⅛ in. between partitions).
Lavatories: Two, with access from centre two compartments.
Seats: 78. Tare weight: 22 tons. Diagram No. 196 (SR No. 75). Rebuilt 1907

Yet another solitary specimen, this coach was rebuilt from six-wheel Second No. 192 (built in 1902) and six-wheel Third No. 566 (built in 1893) during the second half of 1907, and was originally classed as Second/Third Composite No. 202. Four compartments from each of the two six-wheelers were mounted at each end of a new underframe, and the resulting gap of 4 ft 6¼ in. in the centre was used to insert two lavatory compartments, one for a second-class and the other for a third-class compartment. Gas lighting was retained. Seating capacity was 39 2nd and 39 3rd class.

In the first half of 1912 the coach was reclassified all-third and renumbered 1669. On coming to the Southern it was renumbered again, as 2337 at Lancing in May 1927; at the same time, vacuum brakes were fitted. In December 1929 it was in works again for the removal of the air brake equipment and replacement of gas lighting by electricity. No set train allocations are known, and the rebuild was finally withdrawn in July 1940.

BOGIE THIRD BRAKES

Nos. 46, 97, 245, 333, etc. (SR Nos. 3865/73/78/79, etc.)

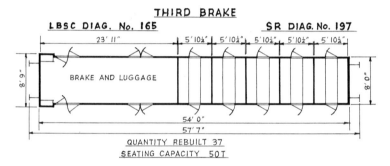

THIRD BRAKE
LBSC DIAG. No. 165   SR DIAG. No. 197

QUANTITY REBUILT 37
SEATING CAPACITY 50 T

Body length: 54 ft . Body width: 8 ft (8 ft 9 in. over duckets).
Bogie centres: 37 ft. Compartments: Five (5 ft 10¼ in. between partitions).
Seats: 50. Tare weight: 23 tons if gaslit, 24 tons if electric-lit.
Diagram No. 165 (SR No. 197). Rebuilt 1906/7.

Right up to 1905 there was scarcely such a thing as a bogie Third Brake carriage on the LB&SCR. However, the Company possessed a large quantity of five-compartment six-wheel Thirds that were not very old, although by then old-fashioned. There was also a large number of six-wheeled passenger brake vans. What happened was that new bogie underframes were built, and the bodies of the Thirds were mounted at one end and the modified bodies of the brake vans mounted at the other end to make well over 100 five-compartment Third Brakes. However, they were not all the same; some had end duckets, some had centre duckets, a few had no duckets at all. The first type of rebuild, with which we are dealing here, was made from a five-compartment Third plus a newly-built guard's and luggage section, with duckets at one end, and they were turned out during 1906 and 1907, mostly being formed in three-coach bogie sets, two per set. Within this particular series were two that incorporated the bodies of six-wheel brake vans (as shown on the list) plus two that appear to have been new construction in 1907 (Nos. 891 and 895). Altogether there were 37 Third Brakes to Diagram No. 165, of which 19 were electrically lit by 1923 (Nos. 97, 245, 354, 365, 378, 386, 397, 402, 412, 417, 422, 452, 453, 458, 497, 500, 547, 891, 895).   Conversion of the remaining gaslit coaches to electric lighting was undertaken by the SR during 1929/30.

Other modifications made by the SR included the conversion from air braking to vacuum and the replacement of the duckets with flat steel to allow the sets to work on to the Eastern Section.   Normally the Southern renumbered all coaches within one diagram as a consecutive group, but, apparently, all the types of five-compartment Third Brake were lumped together in a series running from 3856 to 4004 and only later were they sorted into diagrams; consequently none of the number series for each diagram ran consecutively.

The three-coach sets were dubbed 'Rover Sets' by the Southern, and until the mid 1930s operated all over the Central Section and many parts of the Eastern Section too.   Few remained by 1939. Two coaches (Nos. 3974/75) were modified for use in the Isle of Wight, renumbered 4170/71 and sent over in April 1939. Each now had only four compartments, with a larger luggage compartment, and the mouldings were completely covered with steel sheet.   Formed into three-sets Nos. 490 and 491, Nos. 4170 and 4171 ran in the Island until May 1954.

THIRD BRAKES (END DUCKETS) (DIAGRAM No. 165)

No.	Built	Rsd	Set	SR No.	Re-No.	Set	Wdn	
46	12.94	.07	70	3865	7.24	847	12.36	
97	12.91	.06	120	3873	8.25	774	8.34	
245	12.94	12.06	118	3878	12.26	772	8.36	
333	12.94	12.07	123	3879	?	777	1.36	
354	12.94	12.06	3	3881	3.25	845, 932 /31	3.34	
355	6.95	12.07	70	3882	7.24	847	2.38	
359	12.94	6.07		3883	5.25	845, 932 /31	2.38	
364	12.94	12.07	118	3885	12.26	772	8.36	
365	12.94	6.07	114	3886	12.24	768, 890 /37	7.40	
366	12.94	12.07	117	3887	7.25	771	6.34	
378	12.94	.06	63	3893	6.24	776	9.33	
386	6.94	6.07	114	3896	12.24	768	6.37	Acc. dam. Swanley Jn.
397	6.94	12.06	103	3901	7.25	813	2.40	Re No. 1472S.
402	12.93	6.07	116	3904	9.25	770	11.37	
409	6.94	6.09*		3907	1.27	793	8.37	
412	12.93	6.07	53	3908	5.24	792	5.36	
417	6.95	6.07	53	3909	5.24	792, 828 /36	1.37	
422	6.95	12.06	111	3911	5.25	813	10.38	Re-No. 1264S.
429	12.92	12.07	115	3912	8.26	769, 775 /39	12.40	
449	6.95	12.07	59	3921	4.25	911	1.36	
452	6.95	6.07		3922	4.25	877, 887 /31	7.34	
453	6.95	6.07		3923	4.25	877	7.34	
457	12.93	12.07	123	3924	11.24	777	1.36	
458	6.94	12.06	45	3925	5.27	844	6.36	
497	12.92	12.06	45	3946	5.27	844	9.36	
499	6.94	12.07	115	3947	8.26	769, 890 /37	6.40	
500	6.94	6.07	116	3948	9.25	770	12.40	Re-No. 1651S, 8.41
525	12.91	12.07	117	3954	7.25	771	6.34	
547	12.92	12.06	120	3955	8.25	774	8.34	

No.	Built	Rsd	SetSR No.	Re-No.	Set	Wdn		
556	6.93	6.07	122	3958	5.24	827	11.36	
560	6.93	12 08*	55	3959	12.26	794	5.36	
586	12.99	12.07	71	3964	5.25	848	3.33	
891	6.07		17	3974	5.24	842, 776 /33		Re-No. 4170, 4.39
895	6.07		122	3975	6.24	776		Re-No. 4171, 4.39
1248	6.97	12.07	121	4002	1.27	775	8.40	Re-No. 1434S.
1249	6.97	12.07	121	4003	1.27	775	8.40	Re-No. 1435S.
1252	12.97	12.07	111	4004	4.26	818	1.39	

* No. 409 converted with Brake Van No. 371; No. 560 converted with Brake Van No. 462.

The body of No. 3912 was taken off its underframe after withdrawal of the coach in 1940 and sent to Woking as temporary accommodation; still there in February 1947.

No. 3896 was badly damaged in a collision at Swanley Junction on 27th June, 1937. Two-set 768 (recently reduced from three vehicles), formed of Third Brake No. 3896 and Composite No. 6220, was berthed in the up siding at the London end of the station on that day. It was hit by a late-running train, the 8.17 pm Margate to Victoria, which had been booked to make a special stop at Swanley but whose driver had forgotten this. The train hit some wagons, which were thrown against the two berthed coaches and crushed them. No. 3896 was officially withdrawn six days afterwards.

Five of the Third Brakes were converted to service vehicles after their withdrawal. These were :

3911 to Mess & Tool Van 1264S, October 1938. Breakdown Train Van, Nine Elms Loco.
4002/03 to Mess & Tool Vans 1434/35S, August 1940. Bricklayers Arms Loco.
3901 to Mess & Tool Van 1472S, February 1940. Guildford Loco.
3948 to Mess & Tool Van 1651S, August 1941. Reading Loco.

BOGIE THIRD BRAKES

Nos. 368, 425, 1250 (SR Nos. 4040-4042)

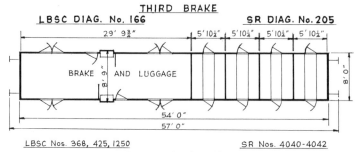

THIRD BRAKE
LBSC DIAG. No. 166   SR DIAG. No. 205

LBSC Nos. 368, 425, 1250   SR Nos. 4040-4042
SEATING CAPACITY 40T

Body length: 54 ft. Body width: 8 ft (8 ft 9 in. over duckets).
Bogie centres: 37 ft. Compartments: Four (5 ft 10¼ in. between partitions).
Seats: 40. Tare weight: 22 tons. Diagram No. 166 (SR No. 205). Rebuilt 1907/8.

The next conversions were these three vehicles, each of which used the whole of a 30 ft brake van body and four compartments of a six-wheel third-class body. They seem to have been 'try-outs', but what was to become virtually the standard rebuild in fact used the whole of a five-compartment Third and a shortened and altered Brake Van body, and no more four-compartment rebuilds were turned out. These three were dated 1907/08.

The luggage portion was practically unaltered, comprising two sets of double doors on each bodyside and an inward-opening guard's door adjacent to a ducket, which had been in the centre of the vehicle.   In the passenger compartments the original gas-lighting was retained.

Nos. 368 and 425 were formed in three-set No. 72, which in 1917 worked between London, Tunbridge Wells and Brighton.   No. 368 was fitted with detaching arrangements so that the whole set could be 'slipped' from the rear of a fast train.   The set became SR No. 801; electric lighting was fitted and Westinghouse brakes removed in February 1930. No. 1250, as SR No. 4042 in nine-set 915, retained gas lighting until at least 1935.

BOGIE THIRD BRAKES (DIAGRAM No. 166)

No.	Built	Rsd	Bke Van	Set	SR No.	Re-No.	Set	Wdn
368	6.95	12.07	50	72	4040	11.26	801	1.35
425	6.95	6.08	184	72	4041	11.26	801	1.35
1250	12.97	12.07	54	74	4042	10.26	915	3.38

BOGIE THIRD BRAKES

Nos. 207, 475, 510/13, 552, 1244 (SR Nos. 4006/08-10/12/32)

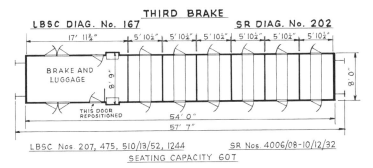

THIRD BRAKE
LBSC DIAG. No. 167   SR DIAG. No. 202

LBSC Nos. 207, 475, 510/13/52, 1244   SR Nos. 4006/08-10/12/32
SEATING CAPACITY 60 T

Body length: 54 ft. Body width: 8 ft (8 ft 9 in. over duckets).
Bogie centres: 37 ft. Compartments: Six (5 ft 10¼ in. between partitions).
Seats: 60. Tare weight: 23 tons. Diagram No. 167 (SR No. 202). Rebuilt 1907-10.

Yet another variation on the 'rebuild' theme, these six Third Brakes each used a five-compartment Third body plus an additional compartment, presumably built new, and a portion of a Brake Van body. The luggage compartment was only 17 ft 11¾ in. long, with one set of double doors each side, and on one side of the coach the guard's door had to be placed to the left of the ducket. Reconstruction was carried out during 1907, 1908 and 1910; all six Third Brakes retained gas lighting.

Nos. 510 and 513 were formed in Set Train No. 77, which in 1917 was booked to work the 9.25 am Portsmouth to Victoria and 4.53 pm return. No. 475 was in three-set 81 for the 12.10 pm Eastbourne to Victoria and the slip portion to Eastbourne of the 5.20 pm Victoria to Hastings. Five-set 77 became SR Set No. 889 in 1923, all the coaches being renumbered in June 1925; its workings in 1928 took in the 10.28 am Portsmouth to Victoria and 4.54 pm (not Saturdays) or 7.30 pm (Saturdays only) return. Set 76, with No. 207, Composite No. 285 and 3rd Slip Brake No. 650, had been formed by 1921 for London, Tunbridge Wells and Brighton services; later it worked between Forest Row and London Bridge.

Electric lighting was fitted to all save No. 1244 (SR No. 4032) in mid-1929. Vacuum brakes were added to all but No. 552 in 1925/6. No. 552 (as SR No. 4012) received them in mid-1929, when the Westinghouse brakes were removed from all except No. 4032.

On withdrawal of No. 4008, part of its body was re-used for Third No. 2404, a nine-compartment vehicle made up from two Third Brake bodies in April 1938 for use in the Isle of Wight, where No. 2404 was placed in Set 490.

BOGIE THIRD BRAKES (DIAGRAM No. 167)

No.	Built	Rsd	Bke Van	Set	SR No.	Re-No.	Set	Wdn
207	12.94	12.07	200	76	4006	7.24	802	6.36
475	6.95	6.10	373	81	4008	3.27	766	2.38
510	6.92	6.08	451	77	4009	6.25	889	12.32
513	6 92	6.08	52	77	4010	6.25	889	12.32
552	6.93	12.07	424		4012	12.25	923	2.34
1244	6.97	12.07	153	73	4032	2.26	849, 915	3.38

BOGIE THIRD BRAKES

Nos. 194, 337, 363, 369, etc. (SR Nos. 3877/80/84/88-92, etc.)

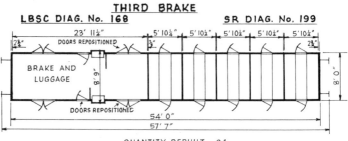

THIRD BRAKE
LBSC DIAG. No. 168   SR DIAG. No. 199

QUANTITY REBUILT   84
SEATING CAPACITY   50 T

Body length: 54 ft. Body width: 8 ft (8 ft 9 in. over duckets).
Bogie centres: 37 ft. Compartments: Five (5 ft 10¼ in. between partitions).
Seats: 50. Tare weight: 23 tons approximately. Diagram No. 168 (SR No. 199). Rebuilt
1908.

By far the most numerous type of rebuilt Third Brake incorporated five
compartments plus Guard's Van with centrally placed duckets, most of this
variety being turned out in 1908 and many being formed in three-coach sets.
On each of the new bogie underframes was placed a 30 ft Third body and a
shortened and modified six-wheel Guard's Van body. This had two sets of
double doors on each bodyside, the innermost set being repositioned; in
addition, on one bodyside the inward-opening guard's door had to be moved
from the right-hand to the left-hand side of the ducket, that on the other side of
the coach body remaining in its original position. Altogether 84 Thirds and
Guard's Vans were converted to five-compartment Third Brakes, and gas
lighting was perpetuated on all of them until 1929/30. The shortened luggage
compartment measured 23 ft 11¼ in. internally.

Some sample workings of set trains including these Third Brakes in 1917
were:

Set 64 - 7.46 am Horsham to London Bridge and 5.00 pm return.
Set 84 - 11.50 am London Bridge to Brighton and 3.53 pm return.
Set 102 - 7.25 am London Bridge to Brighton and 11.30 am return.

Several of the three-coach sets maintained their formations unchanged for
years, and were merely renumbered by the SR; for example LB&SC Set 19
became SR Set 783, LB&SC Set 64 became SR Set 798, LB&SC Set 89 became SR
Set 804, and so on. Others were altered in formation before renumbering.

In most cases the coaches were given vacuum brake equipment in addition to
their original Westinghouse fittings in 1925/6, and the latter were stripped
during 1929/30 at the same time as the gas lighting was replaced by electricity.
Most of the three-sets in SR days became 'general-purpose' in nature, rather
than being allocated to specific train services, and also worked on the Eastern
Section once their side duckets had been removed and replaced by flat steel
sheet - a modification not designed to improve their appearance. From about
1931 some of the sets were reduced to two vehicles (Third Brake and
Composite) and, as the 1930s wore on, several more were so reduced, mainly for
working branch train services on the Eastern Section. By 1935 several more
three-sets were working on the Western Section, as many of their Central
Section duties were being taken over by ex-South Eastern & Chatham three-sets.
Sets Nos. 788/89/97/99, 805/07-10/16 were allocated to Western Section
workings during the mid-1930s.

Of the four-sets running in 1928 and including two Third Brakes of the type
under discussion, No. 853 worked the 9.15 am Victoria to Hastings and 3.45 pm
return, and No. 856 was booked for the 7.30 am Eastbourne to London Bridge
and 12.14 pm return. By today's standards these single out-and-home carriage
workings were not very arduous. However, at least one advantage was that it
gave plenty of time for carriage cleaning.

A curious reformation occurred in the late 1930s, when the Third Brakes of Set 797 (Nos. 3890 and 3989) were marshalled with an ex-SE&C Composite, No. 5220, all being withdrawn early in 1940. There may have been other similar reformations of a temporary nature.

Three Third Brakes, after withdrawal, had part of their bodies re-used to convert other Third Brakes into nine-compartment Thirds for Isle of Wight service. No. 3905 (part) and No. 3967 became Third No. 2406; No. 3914 (part) and No. 3969 became Third No. 2407; and No. 3895 and part of No. 3910 were converted to Third No. 2409. They were sent over in March and April 1937. The new diagram number was 89.

Nos. 3962 and 3986 were reconstructed as seven-compartment Third Brakes with shorter luggage compartments, renumbered 4174/75, and sent over to the Isle of Wight in April 1939 where they were formed in Sets 491 and 492. The bodywork of the coaches was entirely covered with galvanised steel sheets to update them to some extent; in the long term not a good idea, for water would get behind the steel panels and gradually rot the timber. Perhaps this is why the coaches so rebuilt were withdrawn after only about 18 years in the Island, whilst many of the unmodified examples lasted until the end of steam operation.

On withdrawal of No. 3915 in June 1934, its underframe was transferred as a replacement for that of First No. 7627, an elliptical-roofed coach of 1906. The underframe of No. 3992 was re-used for Isle of Wight Third Brake No. 4170 (formerly 3974) in April 1939.

Six of the coaches became service vehicles shortly after being withdrawn. These were:

3897 to Mess & Tool Van 1263S, October 1938. Breakdown Train Van, Nine Elms Loco.
3993 to Mess & Tool Van 1470S, April 1940. Feltham Loco.
3934 to Mess & Tool Van 1471S, April 1940. Feltham Loco.
3966 to Mess & Tool Van 1473S, February 1940. Guildford Loco.
3929 to Mess & Tool Van 1541S, April 1940. Exmouth Junction Loco.
3987 to Mess & Tool Van 1652S, August 1941. Loco Running Dept., Staines.

And finally, two became grounded bodies: No. 3926 at Sittingbourne in February 1941 and No. 4000 at Dartford c.1941.

BOGIE THIRD BRAKES (DIAGRAM No. 168)

No.	Built	Rsd	Bke Van	Set	SR No.	Re-No.	Set	Wdn
194	12.94	6.08	179		3877	2.25	788	3.40
337	12.94	6.08	14	64	3880	?	798	11.37
363	12.94	12.08	468	101	3884	3.26	812	5.38
369	12.94	12.08	94	98	3888	7.24	809	11.38
370	12.94	12.08	412	106	3889	10.25	815	3.35
372	12.94	12.08	108	63	3890	7.24	797	3.40
375	12.94	6.08	14	10	3891	1.25	784	8.35
376	6.95	6.08	6	7	3892	7.24	791	7.34
379	12.95	6.08	30	49	3894	4.26	855	9.33
382	12.94	12.08	470	82	3895	2.24	873	Re-No. 2409, 4.37
389	6.95	12.08	461	97	3897	3.27	808	Re-No. 1263S, 10.38

No.	Built	Rsd	Bke Van	Set	SR No.	Re-No.	Set	Wdn
390	12.95	12.08	429	105	3898	6.24	858	3.39
391	6.94	12.08	415	106	3899	10.25	815	3.35
395	6.94	6.08	444		3900	11.26	790	8.35
398	12.95	6.08	431	88	3902	9.26	855	9.33
401	12.93	6.08	185	91	3903	12.26	806	12.37
403	12.93	12.08	386		3905	7.24	791	12.36
407	6.95	6.08	76	96	3906	10.26	807	4.38
420	6.94	6.08	61		3910	1.27	793	10.36
434	6.95	12.08	89	86	3913	6.26	854	5.38
435	12.93	6.08	170	90	3914	2.27	805	2.37
440	12.93	6.08	360	34	3915	2.25	787	6.34
441	12.93	6.08	35	100	3916	10.26	811	1.35
442	12.93	6.08	91	104	3917	7.25	814	7.36
444	6.96	6.08	77	80	3918	7.24	803	8.35
445	12.93	6.08	90	90	3919	2.27	805	9.36
446	12.93	6.08	56	89	3920	7.26	804	4.33
467	6.96	6.08	432	51	3926	11.26	795	2.40
469	6.95	6.08	161		3927	12.26	846	1.32
470	6.95	6.08	352	112	3928	12.26	819	5.33
471	6.94	6.08	346	75	3929	6.26	851	Re-No. 1541S, 4.40
472	6.95	12.08	31	100	3930	11.26	811	1.37
473	6.96	6.08	92	64	3931	12.26	798	6.38
474	6.94	6.08	401	94	3932	10.24	856, 804	4.35
476	6.95	6.08	65	96	3933	10.26	807	10.37
477	6.95	12.08	21	113	3934	1.26	820	Re-No. 1471S, 4.40
478	6.96	12.08	469	11	3935	2.25	785	9.34
479	6.95	12.08	190	7	3936	9.24	796	6.37
481	6.94	12.07	361	74	3937	4.26	818	4.38
482	6.96	6.08	382	84	3938	3.27	891	3.39
483	6.94	6.08	459	92	3939	12.26	874	7.38
486	6.94	12.08	355	14	3940	4.27	799	4.36
490	12.92	12.08	413	80	3941	7.24	803	8.35
491	12.92	12.08	396	82	3942	2 24	873	12.36
492	12 92	6.08	304	104	3943	7.25	814, 815	1.39
493	12.92	6.08	78	119	3944	9.24	796	6.37
496	12.92	6.08	?	102	3945	3.24	876, 857	7.36
504	12.91	6.08	41	94	3949	10.24	856	7.34
505	6.92	12.08	98		3950	4.27	799	4.36
506	6.92	6.08	487	51	3951	12.26	846	3.39
512	6.92	6.08	95	86	3952	6.26	854, 853	12.35
516	6.94	12.08	416	85	3953	9.26	853	12.35
548	12.92	6.08	198		3956	3.26	790	9.33
549	12.92	6.08	72	11	3957	2.25	785	10.37
564	6.93	12.08	63	97	3960	3.27	808	9.36
565	6.93	12.08	445	105	3961	6.24	858	3.39
568	6.93	12.08	55	107	3962	8.24	816	Re-No. 4174, 4.39
582	6.99	12.08	68	102	3963	3.24	876	9.35
591	6.99	6.08	347	85	3965	9.26	853	9.33
593	6.99	6.08	372	73	3966	11.25	849	Re No. 1473S, 2.40
1140	6.95	12.08	186	89	3978	10.26	804	4.35
1141	6.95	6.08	471		3979	3.26	812	7.35
1145	6.95	6.08	461		3980	5.24	789	2.36

No.	Built	Rsd	Bke Van	Set	SR No.	Re-No.	Set	Wdn
1147	6.95	6.09	15	34	3981	2.25	787	10.36
1150	6.95	6.09	173	14	3982	12.25	810	5.37
1151	6.95	6.08	17	98	3983	7.24	809	9.36
1153	6.95	12.08	395	10	3984	1.25	784	10.34
1154	6.95	12.08	178	93	3985	6.25	875	12.35
1155	6.95	6.08	397	107	3986	8.24	816	Re-No. 4175, 4.39
1159	6.95	12.08	44	112	3987	11.26	819, 770	Re-No. 1652S, 8.41
1165	6.95	6.08	381	91	3988	12.26	806	9.36
1172	6.95	6.08	376	103	3989	7.24	797	4.40
1175	6.95	12.08	359		3990	5.24	789	2.36
1176	6.95	12.08	481		3991	2.25	788	3.40
1178	6.95	6.08	70	19	3992	10.26	783	12.38
1179	6.95	12.08	393	113	3993	1.26	820	Re-No. 1470S, 4.40
1181	6.95	12.08	419	19	3994	11.26	783, 786	4.36
1182	6.95	6.08	145		3995	12.25	810	5.37
1183	6.95	6.08	158	84	3996	3.27	891	3.39
1185	6.95	6.09	99	101	3997	6.27	800	5.34
1191	12.96	6.08	353	93	3998	6.25	875	12.35
1242	6.97	6.08	182	55	3999	12.26	794	12.37
1243	6.97	6.08	10	92	4000	11.26	874	6.40
1245	6.97	6.08	388		4001	6.27	800	7.34

After withdrawal from traffic in 1940, Nos. 3926 and 4000 had their bodies removed from the underframes and were sent to Sittingbourne and Dartford respectively to do further duty as huts.

Note: Isle of Wight Third No. 2409 was withdrawn in March 1959 and Isle of Wight Third Brakes Nos. 4174 and 4175 were withdrawn in February 1956 and May 1954 respectively.

BOGIE LAVATORY THIRD BRAKES

Nos. 468 and 550 (SR Nos. 3803/04)

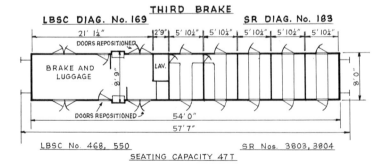

Body length: 54 ft. Body width: 8 ft (8 ft 9 in. over duckets). Bogie centres: 37 ft. Compartments: Five (5 ft 10¼ in. between partitions). One lavatory, with access by short corridor from two inner compartments. Seats: 47. Tare weight: 23 tons approximately. Diagram No. 169 (SR No. 183). Rebuilt 1908.

At the same time as the five-compartment Third Brakes were being turned out, the decision was made to reconstruct two as Lavatory Third Brakes. As usual, a five-compartment Third body and most of a six-wheel Guard's Van body were used in the rebuild, but in addition a small lavatory was shoehorned rather awkwardly into part of the luggage space, between the innermost compartment and one of the sets of double doors. The lavatory, 2 ft 9 in. wide, had access from this compartment by means of an 'open' side corridor, which led directly into the compartment adjacent.

Nos. 468 and 550, originally built in 1895 and 1892 respectively, were rebuilt in the first half of 1908 with Guard's Vans Nos. 453 and 390. The vans were modified in the usual way: the innermost set of double doors were moved close to the duckets, and the inward-opening guard's door on one side was moved so as to be opposite its fellow on the other side of the coach. The coaches were fitted with both Westinghouse and vacuum brakes, but remained lighted by gas.

By 1917 the two Lavatory Third Brakes were formed in four-set No. 95, which regularly worked the 10.45 am Tunbridge Wells to London Bridge, 4.44 pm London Bridge to East Croydon and 7.25 thence to East Grinstead. By 1921 Set 95 was on the 9.45 am Victoria to Eastbourne and 5.10 pm return. The set was not perpetuated by the Southern however, for No. 468 went to three-set No. 778 and No. 550 was placed in three-set 857, a 'Rover' set. The coaches were renumbered 3803 and 3804. Set 778 in 1928 was booked for the 8.33 am Seaford to London Bridge and the Seaford portion of the 5.20 pm from Victoria.

Westinghouse brakes were removed from and electric lighting was installed in No. 3803 in July 1929, and No. 3804 in April 1930. About 1931 No. 3804 was transferred from Set 857 to six-set No. 923 as replacement for No. 3767, but was itself withdrawn in February 1933, its underframe later being re-used for Third No. 2405 on the Isle of Wight. Set 778 was re-formed about February 1933, and its Third Brake, No. 3803, lasted until April 1936.

BOGIE LAVATORY THIRD BRAKES (DIAGRAM No. 169)

No.	Built	Reblt	Bke Van	Set	SR No.	Re-No.	Set	Wdn
468	6.95	6.08	453	95	3803	11.24	778	4.36
550	12.92	6.08	390	95	3804	12.26	857, 923	2.33

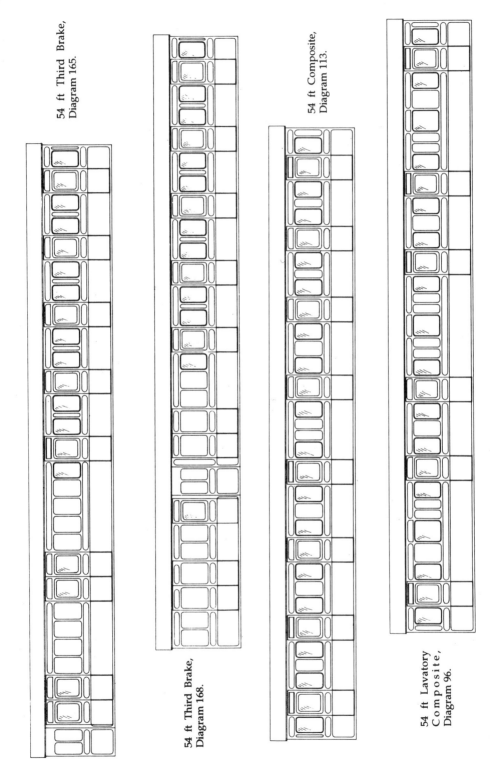

54 ft Third Brake, Diagram 165.

54 ft Third Brake, Diagram 168.

54 ft Composite, Diagram 113.

54 ft Lavatory Composite, Diagram 96.

BOGIE THIRD BRAKES (SLIP-FITTED)

Nos. 59, 367, 514, 554 and 1246 (SR Nos. 4005/07/11/13/33)

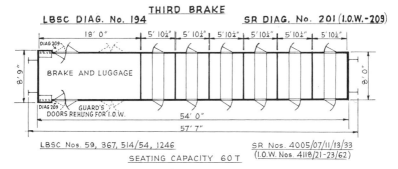

THIRD BRAKE

LBSC DIAG. No. 194   SR DIAG. No. 201 (I.O.W. -209)

LBSC Nos. 59, 367, 514/54, 1246   SR Nos. 4005/07/11/13/33
SEATING CAPACITY 60 T   (I.O.W. Nos. 4118/21-23/62)

Body length: 54 ft. Body width: 8 ft (8 ft 9 in. over duckets).
Bogie centres: 37 ft. Compartmer.ts: Six (5 ft 10¼ in. between partitions).
Seats: 60. Tare weight: 23 tons approximately. Diagram No. 194 (SR No. 201).
Rebuilt 1910.

During 1910 the last five Third Brakes rebuilt from six-wheeled bodies emerged from Lancing Works. Each of these was made up from part of a double-ended Guard's Van and a five-compartment Third plus one additional compartment, presumably newly-built. The van had duckets at the outer end (so these coaches differed from Diagram No. 167, whose duckets were towards the centre) and the luggage compartment was about 18 ft long. All the coaches were gaslit, and all had detaching arrangements for slip-coach working. They were formed into three- or four-coach sets, some of which had a slip brake at one end and others a slip brake at both ends.

By 1917 Nos. 59 and 514 were formed in three-set No. 16, which worked between London and Hastings; No. 1246 was in four-set No. 71 (8.25 am Hastings to Victoria and 3.20 pm return); and No. 367 was at one end of three-set No. 81, working between Eastbourne and Victoria. No. 554 was not allocated to a set. In 1921 Set 16 was booked for the 6.15 am Brighton to London Bridge, 5.56 pm London Bridge to Eastbourne, 9.28 pm Eastbourne to Haywards Heath and 11.5 pm thence to Brighton. Set 81 was on the 8.15 am Hastings to London Bridge and 5.20 pm Victoria to Hastings.

These sets were not perpetuated by the Southern Railway, who removed the slip fittings from all except Nos. 59 and 514 in the 1920s. No. 59 as SR No. 4005 was in three-set 781, working alternate days in the 8.27 am Forest Row to Victoria and 5.05 pm London Bridge to Forest Row, slipped at Horley. No. 514 as SR No. 4011 was formed in three-set 761, a 'Rover' set; the other three Brake Thirds also were in 'Rover' sets.

Nos. 4007/13/33 received vacuum brake equipment in 1925, losing their Westinghouse brakes four years later. Nos. 4005/11 went straight from air to vacuum brakes in 1927. Gas lighting was replaced by electric lighting in 1929 for Nos. 4005/07/13/33 and in 1930 for No. 4011. It is curious to note that, although the slip coaches were able to be worked using vacuum brakes, one of the reasons given by the SR for the abolition of slip coaches in 1932 was the changeover from air to vacuum brakes.

Four of the coaches were sent to the Isle of Wight in June 1934, the fifth following in March 1937. Alterations were minor: the coaches needed converting back to Westinghouse air brakes, the duckets were removed and the bodywork was covered with steel sheets. The guard's doors were rehung to open outwards. A new diagram was issued: No. 209.

The 1934 transfers were Nos. 4005/07/13/33, which were renumbered in the Isle of Wight series to 4118/21-23 and placed two each in Sets 498 and 499. (Nos. 4119/20 were already occupied by two ex-London, Chatham & Dover 30 ft Third Brakes that had been sent over in 1926.) No. 4011, sent over in 1937 as Isle of Wight No. 4162, completed the transfer of all five Third Brakes and was placed in Set 500.

Ex-LB&SCR coaches in the Isle of Wight lasted far longer in service than those remaining on the Mainland, although none of these five Third Brakes survived until the end of steam working in December 1966. They had been withdrawn in the 1950s after certain lines in the Island had been closed, resulting in a surplus of carriages.

BOGIE THIRD BRAKES (DIAGRAM No. 194)

No.	Built	Reblt	Bke Van	Set	SR No.	Re-No.	Set	IOW No.	Re-No.	Wdn
59	12.91	6.10	?	16	4005	8.24	781	4118	6.34	5.54
367	12.94	6.10	373	81	4007	3.27	766	4121	6.34	3.59
514	6.92	12.10	?	16	4011	5.25	761	4162	3.37	3.59
554	6.93	6.10	148		4013	7.24	802	4122	6.34	3.59
1246	6.97	6.10	146	71, 40	4033	5.24	827	4123	6.34	3.59

BOGIE THIRD BRAKES, formerly SECOND BRAKES

Nos. 1663/80/89, 1723/39/53/71/72/76 (SR Nos. 3856-64)

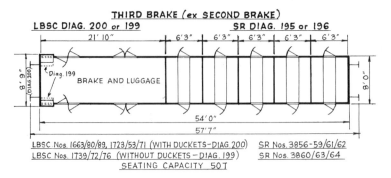

THIRD BRAKE (ex SECOND BRAKE)
LBSC DIAG. 200 or 199   SR DIAG. 195 or 196

LBSC Nos. 1663/80/89, 1723/53/71 (WITH DUCKETS—DIAG.200)   SR Nos. 3856-59/61/62
LBSC Nos. 1739/72/76 (WITHOUT DUCKETS—DIAG. 199)   SR Nos. 3860/63/64
SEATING CAPACITY 50 T

Body length: 54 ft. Body width: 8 ft. (8 ft 9 in. over duckets).
Bogie centres: 37 ft. Compartments: Five (6 ft 3 in. between partitions).
Seats: 50. Tare weight: 23 tons if gaslit, 24 tons if electric lit.
Diagram No. 200 (SR No. 195) with duckets; 199 (SR No. 196) without duckets. Rebuilt
between 1907 and 1909.

These nine vehicles started life as 32 ft six-wheel Seconds, three of which -
Nos. 106, 155 and 158 - were rebuilt in 1907 as bogie Second Brakes without
duckets; and six of which - Nos.14, 38, 75, 96, 111 and 185 - were rebuilt in
1907/09 as bogie Second Brakes with duckets at the outer end. The brake and
luggage compartment, which was 21 ft 10 in. long internally, appears to have
been new construction, as were the bogie underframes.

Following the abolition of second class, Nos. 38, 96, 111, 14 , 185 and 75 were
renumbered 1663/80/89, 1723/53/71 and Nos. 106, 155 and 158 became Nos.
1739/72/76 in the third class series in 1912. Nos. 1723, 1739 , 1772 and 1776
were electrically-lit in LB&SC days, though the others retained gas lighting until
1929/30.

No. 1689 (which was slip-fitted) was formed in spare four-set No. 3 by 1917;
as SR No. 3858 this coach was in three-set No. 782 which alternated with Set 781
on the 5.05 pm London Bridge to Forest Row slip working in the 1920s. No.
1723 was in five-set No. 17, working between Brighton and Victoria. No. 1680
worked in the 6.45 am Hastings to London Bridge and 4.05 pm return formed
in four-set No. 38, and was also slip-fitted. Five-set No. 62 included both Nos.
1739 and 1772, and worked in the 9.45 am Eastbourne to Victoria and 3.20 pm
return. Nos. 1663, 1753 and 1776 had been allotted to set trains by 1921.

All nine coaches received SR numbers between 1924 and 1926 at Lancing.
Nos. 3856/62 were given vacuum brake equipment in 1925 and Nos. 3859-
61/63/64 in 1926. Apart from No. 3864 they lost their Westinghouse braking in
1930. Nos. 3857/58 went straight from air to vacuum brakes in 1929, when they
also had their gas lighting replaced by electricity; Nos. 3856/61/62 were
similarly converted in 1930.

Four of the coaches in LB&SC Set 17 became part of SR five-set 842, which
was spare in 1928. Three coaches from Set 38 went to SR Set 843, whose booked
workings included the 9.30 am Portsmouth to Victoria and 4.20 pm return in
1928. Five-set 888 contained elements of LB&SC Set 62, and in 1928 worked the
9.20 am Eastbourne to Victoria and 5.20 pm return. Third Brake No. 3861 was
formed in four-set 851, for the 3.35 pm Victoria to Brighton and 8.35 pm return,
while No. 3856 in four-set 911 worked between Bognor and Victoria, with a run
to Brighton and back in the middle of the day. Set 911 was withdrawn at the
end of 1931 and Third Brake No. 3856 was reformed in two-set No. 765 for the
Allhallows branch about 1934/5. Set 843 was withdrawn about 1931 and No.
3857 went to Set 924 for a while before going to two-set 780 about 1934 for the
Maidstone West branch.

In the early 1930s the guard's duckets were removed and replaced with a flat
sheet of steel to permit unrestricted use of the vehicles on the Southern. Most
of the carriages were withdrawn in the 1930s, only two lasting until 1940. No .
3861 was altered to Mess & Tool Van No. 1544S in April 1940, for the

Locomotive Running Department at Eastleigh, and was withdrawn in May 1957.

No.	Built	Reblt	Re-No.	Date	Set	SR No.	Re-No.	Set	Wdn
38	6. 98	6.09	1663	6.12	59	3856	4.25	911, 765	10.36
96	6.00	6.09	1680	6.12	38	3857	10.25	843 ,924 ,780	9.35
111	12.00	6.09	1689	6.12	3	3858	12.26	782	7.36
14	6.96	6.07	1723	6.12	17	3859	5.24	842	10.33
106	6.00	6.07	1739	6.12	62	3860	2 25	888	8.35
185	12.01	.08	1753	6.12	75	3861	7.26	851	4.40
75	6.00	6.08	1771	12.12		3862	10.26	795	12.40
155	12.99	6.07	1772	12.12	62	3863	2.25	888	12.32
158	12.99	6.07	1776	12.12	49	3864	10.24	922, 828	1.38

The body of No. 3862 was grounded at West Croydon, observed there in September 1943.

BOGIE THIRD BRAKES (SLIP-FITTED)

Nos. 88, 89, 99, 105 and 109 (SR Nos. 4035-4039)

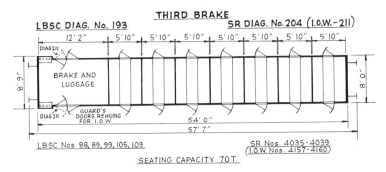

Body length; 54 ft. Body width: 8 ft (8 ft 9 in. over duckets).
Bogie centres: 37 ft. Compartments: Seven (5 ft 10 in. between partitions).
Seats: 70. Tare weight: 24 tons approx. Diagram No. 193 (SR No. 204). Built 1912.

These were the first Third Brakes to have been built new since the decision was made, after the appearance of the recent elliptical stock, to revert to the plain arc roof for all further construction. Five seven-compartment Third Brakes were turned out by Lancing during the half-year ending June 1912, all being fitted with slip apparatus. To the casual observer they looked no different from the rebuilt bogie coaches, and showed no advance in design; the only way they could be distinguished was that at the brake end there were two small windows with an additional small window in the centre, whereas the rebuilds with end duckets had four large windows overlooking the track. All five vehicles were electrically lit, in contrast to the rebuilds, almost all of which retained gas lighting as a reminder of their origin as six-wheelers. Electric lighting was standard for all new construction.

None of the coaches was formed in a set, according to the 1917 lists. However the Southern placed them in five different sets, of which Nos. 821, 860 and 861 included a slip Third Brake at each end. Nos. 821 and 861 were three-coach 'Rover' sets and included SR Nos. 4039 and 4037 respectively. Set 860 was five coaches, with No. 4036 at one end, and in 1928 was booked to work in the 1.55 pm Littlehampton to Victoria and 6.40 pm return. No. 4038 was in seven-set No. 922, which worked in the 8.10 am Bognor to London Bridge and 1.20 pm (Saturdays) or 5.50 pm (not Saturdays) return. Finally No. 4035 was placed in a three-coach 'Rover' set, No. 767. Only No. 4036 still retained slip apparatus in 1931.

No. 4035 became dual-braked in February 1925 and No. 4038 did so exactly a year later. Nos. 4036/37/39 were converted from Westinghouse to vacuum brakes around mid-1927, and the Westinghouse brakes were taken off No. 4035 in December 1930. Set 922 was withdrawn about March 1931, but its Third Brake and two other coaches went to Set 828, which ran until 1936.

In May 1936 Nos. 4035/37-39 were transferred to the Isle of Wight and renumbered 4157-60, in the same order. Modifications included the refitting of Westinghouse brakes, the removal of duckets and reducing the width of the windows at the brake end, and the rehanging of the guard's doors to open outwards instead of inwards. Each of the coaches was formed, one per set, in Set Nos. 485-88 in numerical order; these sets were maintained until after the War. All four coaches lasted until the 1960s, Nos. 4158/59 surviving until the end of steam working.

No.	Built	SR No.	Re-No.	Set	IOW No.	Re-No.	Wdn
88	6.12	4035	1.27	767	4157	5.36	1 66
89	6.12	4036	5.24	860	-	-	9 36
99	6.12	4037	6.27	861	4158	5.36	1.67
105	6 12	4038	10.24	922, 828	4159	5.36	1.67
109	6.12	4039	8.24	821	4160	5.36	1.66

BOGIE THIRD BRAKES

Nos. 636-50, 851-53 (SR Nos. 4014-31)

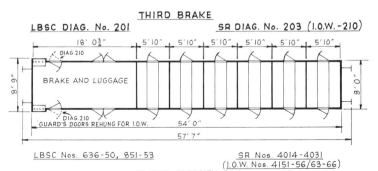

THIRD BRAKE
LBSC DIAG. No. 201   SR DIAG. No. 203 (I.O.W.-210)

LBSC Nos. 636-50, 851-53   SR Nos. 4014-4031
                                  (I.O.W. Nos. 4151-56/63-66)
                    SEATING CAPACITY 60T

Body length: 54 ft. Body width: 8 ft (8 ft 9 in. over duckets).
Bogie centres: 37 ft. Compartments: Six (5 ft 10 in. between partitions).
Seats: 60. Tare weight: 24 tons 1 cwt. Diagram No. 201 (SR No. 203). Built 1912.

Three six-compartment Third Brakes with end duckets were constructed at Lancing in 1912 and a further batch of 15, fitted with slip apparatus, came out during 1916. Each brake-end was fitted with two small windows overlooking the track, and there was an inward-opening door for the guard immediately adjacent to each side ducket. The luggage compartment, which measured 18 ft 0¾ in. internally, had one set of double doors on each bodyside.

All three of the 1912-built coaches were in sets by 1917. No. 853 went to the three-coach London Bridge portion of Set No. 17, which worked the 5.05 pm Brighton to Victoria, the London Bridge portion being detached at East Croydon. It then returned to Brighton in the 7.20 pm from London Bridge. Three-set No. 30 included No. 852 and worked the 7.10 am Tunbridge Wells to London Bridge, returning thence at 12.25 pm on Saturdays or 5.22 pm Mondays to Fridays. Third Brake No. 851, in four-set No. 35, was booked to work the 7.03 am Brighton to London Bridge, the 1.25 pm London Bridge to Tunbridge Wells and the 9.30 pm thence to Brighton.

Of the slip-fitted batch, Nos. 636-50, only No. 645 was recorded in 1917 as running in a set train, this being three-coach No. 119. This ran in the 11.40 am Victoria to West Worthing, 2.05 pm Worthing to Brighton, and 7.30 pm Brighton to Victoria. By 1921, No. 639 was in four-set No. 38 and No. 641 in 10-set No. 40.

As SR Nos. 4014-31, all the coaches found their way into sets, mostly three-coach 'Rovers'. The only ones to retain their slip apparatus up to 1928 were Nos. 4019 (Set 861), 4020 (Set 860), 4022 (Set 763) and 4028 (Set 821). Nos. 4020/22 were still so-fitted in 1932.

Four-set No. 850 contained two of the six-compartment Third Brakes, Nos. 4015/18, and in 1928 worked the 6.53 am West Worthing to London Bridge and 3.35 pm return. No. 4017 was in four-set 843, working between Portsmouth Harbour and Victoria; it was transferred to Set 924 about 1931. Six-set No. 916, berthed at Dorking North, included Third Brake No. 4029, and worked an intensive daily diagram that took in Victoria, Brighton, London Bridge, Tunbridge Wells and Victoria. No. 4031 was formed in six-set 915 for the 6.15 am Eastbourne to Victoria and 7.20 pm return.

Dual brake gear was fitted to Nos. 4014/15/16/18/21-25/27/29/30 during 1925-27. Vacuum brakes were fitted to and air brakes removed from Nos. 4019/20/28 in 1927, and Nos. 4017/26/31 in 1929. Westinghouse brakes were taken off Nos. 4015/16/18/21/24/30 during 1930, and about this time the side duckets were removed and replaced by flat steel sheets.

Most of the coaches were transferred for further service in the Isle of Wight in May 1936 and March 1937. Six of them were rebuilt as nine-compartment Thirds, three additional compartments being built into what had been the luggage compartment; the new numbers were 2412-17 (Diagram No. 90). Ten of those remaining were retained as six-compartment Third Brakes with only minor alterations such as outward-opening guard's doors and the refitting of air brakes (Diagram No. 210). Six vehicles went over in May 1936, these becoming

Nos. 4151-56, and the remaining four, Nos. 4163-66, followed in March 1937. All were formed into sets in the Island, one each of Nos. 4151-54 in Sets 485-488 and two each in numerical pairs of Nos. 4155/56/63-66 in Sets 489, 506 and 507. Of the rebuilt Thirds, No. 2412 was in Set 492, 2414 in Set 488, and 2415-17 in Sets 485-487. The sets were not maintained after about 1948, and the Thirds tended to be used as summer-only strengthening vehicles when six-coach trains were required on the Ryde to Ventnor line. Some years after the arrival in the Island of converted ex-SE&C Third Brakes, trains were normally formed with an ex-LB&SC Third Brake at the south end and an ex-SE&C Third Brake at the Ryde end. Most of the ten six-compartment Third Brakes and six nine-compartment Thirds lasted in service until 1966. No. 4165 had its bodywork covered with steel sheeting and, latterly, several coaches were given rubber-lined cushions in their compartments to improve passengers' comfort.

No.	Built	Set	SR No.	Re-No.	Set	IOW No.	Re-No.	Wdn
636	6.16		4014	12.25	773	2412	5.36	5.54
637	6.16		4015	3.26	850	2413	5.36	5.54
638	6.16		4016	12.24	762	2414	5.36	1.67
639	6.16	38	4017	6.25	843, 924			5.35
640	6.16		4018	4.26	850	2415	5.36	1.67
641	6.16	40	4019	6.27	861	2416	5.36	1.67
642	6.16		4020	4.24	860			4.36
643	6.16		4021	1.27	767	2417	5.36	1.67
644	6.16		4022	6.24	763	4151	5.36	1.66
645	6.16	119	4023	11.26	773	4152	5.36	9.66
646	6.16		4024	6.26	764	4153	5.36	12.66
647	6.16		4025	1.27	826	4163	3.37	12.66
648	12.16		4026	5.25	848, 829	4164	3.37	1.66
649	12.16		4027	3.27	763	4154	5.36	1.66
650	12.16	76	4028	8.24	821	4155	5.36	1.66
851	12.12	35	4029	8.24	916	4165	3.37	1.67
852	12.12	30	4030	4.27	786, 762	4156	5.36	1.67
853	12.12	17	4031	10.26	915, 849	4166	3.37	1.66

After its withdrawal from BR traffic, nine-compartment Third No. 2416 was acquired by the Wight Locomotive Society and repainted in SR malachite green. From 1978 it ran regular services with other vintage carriages on the Isle of Wight Steam Railway between Havenstreet and Wootton. The rebuilt end faced Wootton, and during restoration the lettering 'Test the Brake' was found still to be on the green-painted wall, behind the seats and picture-frames, of the end compartment.

BOGIE THIRD BRAKES

Nos. 865/67/69/71/87/88/90/96, 900 (SR Nos. 3967-73/76/77)

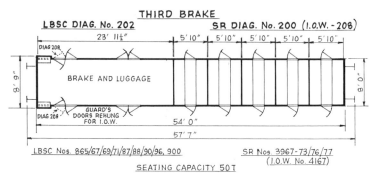

Body length: 54 ft. Body width: 8 ft (8 ft 9 in. over duckets).
Bogie centres: 37 ft. Compartments: Five (5 ft 10 in. between partitions).
Seats: 50. Tare weight: 22 tons approximately.
Diagram No. 202 (SR No. 200). Built 1913.

Built by Lancing during 1913, these nine Third Brakes were very similar in appearance to the five-compartment rebuilds, but they were fitted with electric lighting, and in the brake-end there were only two small windows overlooking the track instead of the four large windows found in the older vehicles. There were duckets at the end, and two sets of double doors in each bodyside giving access to the luggage compartment, whose internal length was 23 ft 11½ in. The guard's door, adjacent to each ducket, opened inwards.

Nos. 865/67/69/71 were placed, two each and in order, in four-sets 78 and 79. These worked two-day cyclic diagrams as follows: 6.35 am Brighton to London Bridge and 9.50 am London Bridge to Hastings; 11.45 am Hastings to London Bridge and 5.10 pm London Bridge to Brighton. Nos. 887 and 896 were formed into four-set 83, for the 10.20 am Hastings to Victoria and 1.25 pm return. Nos. 888 and 890 went to three-set No. 124, which worked in the 7.10 am Eastbourne to London Bridge and 4.05 pm return. No. 900 was in the three-coach London Bridge portion of Set 17.

All nine coaches received Southern numbers and became dual-braked during 1925/26. The Southern sets did not bear much resemblance to the LB&SC ones. Four-set 852 contained Third Brakes 3971/76, and was spare in 1928. Three-set 859, with Third Brakes 3972/73, was a 'Rover'. Four-set 885 was booked to work the 10.20 am Bognor to Victoria and 1.30 pm (Saturdays) or 4.20 pm (not Saturdays) return; its Third Brakes were Nos. 3970/77. Seven-set 890 included Third Brakes 3967/69 and in 1928 ran 201 miles each day, taking in the 10.05 am Brighton to London Bridge and 11.48 am return and the 4.08 pm Brighton to London Bridge and 6.18 pm return. No. 3968 was in three-set No. 826.

Westinghouse brake equipment was removed from Nos. 3970/77 in June

1929. By 1931 four-set 885 was on the Eastern Section, working in the 8.42 am Ashford to Charing Cross and 11.53 am return, on Saturdays leaving Cannon Street for Ashford at 11.33 am.

Set 852 was withdrawn in January 1936; its Third Brakes had lasted only 23 years. The other sets were soon disbanded as most of the remaining Third Brakes were required for service in the Isle of Wight. In March and April 1937 Nos. 3967, 3969 and 3972 were rebuilt as nine-compartment Thirds Nos. 2406 to 2408; part of the body of No. 3970 was used to make up the four extra compartments on No. 2408 (Nos. 2406/07 also used part of the bodies of Third Brakes 3905/14 - SR Diagram No. 199). The rebuilt Thirds were given Diagram No. 89. Nos. 2406/07 were allotted to Set No. 500, while No. 2408 was in Set 506 from 1937.

Also in March 1937, one Third Brake was rebuilt with two additional compartments, which reduced the luggage compartment to a length of 12 ft 2 in., and was sent to the Island. This was No. 3973, which was renumbered 4161 and formed in Set No. 500. Duckets had been removed, and the small luggage compartment now had only one set of double doors on each side. As a seven-compartment Third Brake this vehicle was given a new Diagram No. 211. No. 3977 was not rebuilt and was sent over as No. 4167 for Set 500 in March 1937; minor alterations to the body resulted in the issuing of a new diagram No. 208.

No. 4167 was damaged during shunting operations in wartime blackout at Ryde St Johns on 7th April, 1940. The brake-end was badly crushed, and the coach was subsequently condemned. No. 4161, at the other end of Set 500, was as a result transferred to Set 494, whilst Set 500 received No. 4162. The bodywork of No. 4161 was later covered with steel sheets.

Only No. 3968 now remains to be dealt with. In December 1937 its body was placed on the underframe of Brake Composite No. 6939, a push-and-pull driving trailer that had been withdrawn four months previously. The body of No. 3968 was then reconstructed as a nine-compartment electric trailer Third, renumbered 9140, and placed in trailer set No. 1152 in May 1938. The original vehicle numbered 9140 in this set had been an eight-compartment ex-SE&CR Third, but this had been condemned following accident damage at Epsom Downs on 13th August, 1937. The 'new' No. 9140 ran in Set 1152 until August 1948.

BOGIE THIRD BRAKES (DIAGRAM No. 202)

No.	Built	Set	SR No.	Re-No.	Set	IOW No.	Re-No.	Wdn
865	6.13	78	3967	8.25	890	2406	4.37	5.54
867	6.13	78	3968	1.27	826			12.37
869	6.13	79	3969	8.25	890	2407	4.37	12.66
871	6.13	79	3970	9.26	885			2.37
887	12.13	83	3971	4.27	852			1.36
888	12.13	124	3972	4.27	859	2408	3.37	5.54
890	12.13	124	3973	4.27	859	4161	3.37	1.66
896	12.13	83	3976	4.27	852			1.36
900	12.13	17	3977	7.26	885	4167	3.37	.47

BOGIE THIRD BRAKES

Nos. 82, 85, 87, 90, 93-95, 104, 107, 112 (SR Nos. 3866-72/74-76)

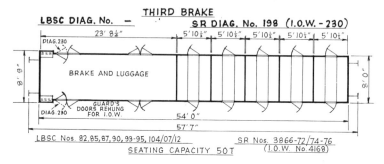

Body length: 54 ft. Body width: 8 ft (8 ft 9 in. over duckets).
Bogie centres: 37 ft. Compartments: Five (5 ft 10½ in. between partitions). Seats: 50.
Tare weight: 22 tons approximately.
No LB&SC Diagram No. given. SR Diagram No. 198. Built 1922.

These ten vehicles, ordered from Lancing in 1920, were new bodies mounted on underframes salvaged from the Ambulance Train No. 25 and sent into traffic in 1922. The original bodies on these frames had been elliptical-roofed coaches of 1905. The new bodies were virtually indistinguishable from those of Diagram No. 202, built in 1913; the compartments were half an inch wider and the luggage compartment about three inches shorter. As before, there were two small windows in the brake end, end duckets, and two sets of double doors in each side of the luggage compartment. The LB&SC just did not seem to be interested in improving its carriage stock with such features as corridors, lavatories, or exterior steel panelling, as its two neighbours were doing; these carriages of 1922 displayed full mouldings on their bodies in exactly the same style as the carriages of the 1890s did.

They did not remain in LB&SC brown livery for long; Southern green was applied to four in 1924, two in 1926 and the remaining four in 1927. Eight were formed into three-sets Nos. 131 to 134, which became SR Nos. 822 to 825; and Nos. 3866/67 (LB&SC Nos. 82/5) went to four-set No. 862, which in 1928 was the regular set on the 8.50 am Victoria to Portsmouth and 4.30 pm return. In 1931 Set 862 worked the 8.03 am London Bridge to Brighton via East Grinstead, returning on the 11.30 am up via Redhill.

Westinghouse brakes were retained for a few years, vacuum brakes being added during 1925/6; Nos. 3875/76 became vacuum-only in June 1929 and No. 3866 in September 1930. No. 3870 was transferred from Set 825 to Set 819 in about 1933, replacing No. 3928 which was withdrawn.

Five of these Third Brakes were transferred to the Isle of Wight in the late 1930s. Two from Set 824 - Nos. 3869/71 -were rebuilt as nine-compartment Thirds Nos. 2404/05, the four extra compartments in each reconstruction having been taken from the bodies of Third Brake No. 4008 and Third No. 2189 respectively. In addition, the body of No. 2405 was mounted on the underframe of Third Brake No. 3804. The rebuilds were sent to the Island in April 1938, No. 2405 being placed in Set 490 and No. 2405 in Set 491. The new Diagram number was 89.

No. 3870 was renumbered 4168 and sent to the Island in April 1938 still as a five-compartment Third Brake. It originally ran in Set 502 and was destined to be the last remaining five-compartment brake in the Isle of Wight, running in service on the final day of steam working, 31st December, 1966. It was acquired by the Wight Locomotive Society and is now one of the three ex-LB&SC bogie carriages running on the Isle of Wight Steam Railway, repainted in SR malachite green livery (Diagram No. 230).

Nos. 3872/74, taken from Set 823, were extensively reconstructed for further use in the Isle of Wight in April 1939. No. 3872 became a four-compartment Third Brake with extended luggage compartment and, renumbered 4172, was placed in Set 492. No. 3874 became a seven-compartment Third Brake, renumbered 4173, and this went to Set 490. Both vehicles were completely repanelled with galvanised steel sheets in an effort to 'modernise' them. However, in this form they lasted only another 20 years or so.

BOGIE THIRD BRAKES (SR DIAGRAM No. 198)

No.	Built	Set	SR No.	Re-No.	Set	IOW No.	Re-No.	Wdn
82	6.22		3866	3.26	862			10.35
85	6.22		3867	3.26	862			4.33
87	6.22		3868	5.24	825			10.36
90	6.22		3869	7.24	824	2404	4.38	2.56
93	6.22		3870	5.24	825, 819	4168	4.38	1.67
94	6.22		3871	7.24	824	2405	4.38	2.56
95	6.22		3872	3.27	823	4172	4.39	3.59
104	6.22		3874	3.27	823	4173	4.39	2-56
107	6.22		3875	4.27	822			6.34
112	6.22		3876	4.27	822			6.34

BOGIE TRI-COMPOSITES

Nos. 26, 238-49/52/53/56-59/73-76/78-96, 442-61/68-71 (SR Nos. 6096-6160, 6235)

Body length: 54 ft. Body width: 8 ft. Bogie centres: 37 ft.
Compartments: Two 1st class (7 ft 4½ in. between partitions), two 2nd class (one of which was 7 ft 4½ in. and the other 6 ft 3¾ in. between partitions) and four 3rd class (of which one was 5 ft 9 in. and three were 6 ft 2⅝ in. between partitions). Seats: 12 1st, 20 2nd and 40 3rd class. Tare weight: 23 tons. Diagram No. 92 or 113 (SR Nos. 335 or 348). Rebuilt 1909/10.

At the same time as several six-wheeled Thirds and Guard's Vans were being rebuilt into bogie Brake Thirds on new 54 ft underframes, 66 six-wheeled tri-Composites were converted to bogie tri-Composites by placing them on new frames and building on extra compartments to make up the increased length. Many of these rebuilt Composites were formed with two rebuilt Third Brakes to run as three-coach sets.

The work of rebuilding was carried out in 1909 and 1910 at Brighton and later Lancing Carriage Works. The basis of the rebuilds was a series of 33 ft 6 in. tri-Composites, originally built between 1891 and 1898, with the compartment layout 3, 1, 2, 1, 3. Each of these was mounted at one end of a new frame, the 3rd-class compartment that ended up in the middle being removed and replaced by a new 1st-class compartment, with three new 3rd-class compartments being added at the other end of the new frame. This meant that the compartment layout was now 3, 2 (formerly 1), 2, 1, 1, 3, 3, 3. The original 3rd-class compartment measured 5 ft 9 in. between partitions, but the newly-grafted 'thirds' were each 6 ft 2⅝ in. across.

A rather noticeable omission in all these rebuilds was that of a lavatory compartment, but it would seem that the 'Brighton' did not believe in providing such accommodation too generously. As it was, the majority of the newly-formed three-coach bogie sets were minus sanitation, despite being used on long-distance runs.

Upon the abolition of second class in 1912, the coaches were divided into two groups, each of which had different proportions of 1st- and 3rd-class accommodation. Diagram No. 92 had the two second-class compartments upgraded to first, so that there were now four 1st-class and four 3rd-class compartments, viz.: 3, 1, 1,1, 1, 3, 3, 3. Diagram No. 113, in contrast, had its former second class downgraded to third, so that the make-up was now 3, 3, 3, 1, 1, 3, 3, 3. However, within the next four years, all but one of Diagram No. 113 were again re-upholstered to conform to Diagram No. 92, the solitary exception being No. 273.

Vehicles originally altered to Diagram 92:

26,238-40/42/45-49/52/53/56/57/79/83/84/86/87/89/93/95, 443/46/47/49/52/53/55/57/59-61/70.

Vehicles altered to Diagram 113 and later 92:

258/76/81/82/91/92/94/96, 442/50/51/54/56/58/68 in 1913. 241/44/59/74/75/78/80/85/88/90, 444/45/48/69/71 in 1914.
243 only in 1916.

Although No. 273 was stated to have been converted to Diagram No. 92 in 1915, it seems to have come to the Southern as the sole example of Diagram 113 - that is to say, with two 1st-class and six 3rd-class compartments - and as such received the SR Diagram No. 348 and vehicle No. 6235. All the others came to the Southern as Diagram No. 92 (four 1sts and four 3rds), becoming SR Diagram No. 335, vehicle Nos. 6096-6160. Later, No. 6235 was also altered to seat 24 1st class and 40 3rd class in four 1st-class and four 3rd-class compartments.

Just over half the series of rebuilt Composites were formed into sets by 1917, mostly three-coach but some four-coach. Three-sets Nos. 10 and 11, with centre coaches Nos. 257 and 446 respectively, worked two-day Oxted line diagrams, alternating with each other. Day One took in the 8.07 am London Bridge to Brighton via Oxted; working back from East Grinstead to London Bridge it finished with the 7.38 pm thence to East Grinstead. Day Two started with the

6.54 am East Grinstead to Lewes, included local trips between Brighton and Haywards Heath, and concluded with the 7.45 pm from Brighton to London Bridge.

Three-set No. 63 included Composite No. 246 and worked in the 2.25 pm Eastbourne to London Bridge and 9.13 pm return. Three-set No. 64 was booked for the 7.46 am Horsham to London Bridge and 5.00 pm return; it included Composite No. 470. Three-set No. 111 (Composite No. 461) had a 'three-leg' diagram taking in the 1.25 pm Brighton to Portsmouth, 7.10 pm Portsmouth to Victoria and 12.05 am Victoria to Brighton. All the other three-sets worked between London, Tunbridge Wells and Brighton: Nos. 19, 30, 72, 80, 89, 96 to 98, 100 to 104, 106, 107, 112 and 113.

Two Composites were formed in five-set No. 62 for the 9.45 am Eastbourne to Victoria and 3.20 pm return in 1917, these being Nos. 469 and 283. Another Eastbourne five-set, No. 70, included Composite No. 449 and worked the 9.00 am Victoria to Eastbourne and 2.25 pm return.

Of the three-sets that were unchanged in formation at Grouping, the following were renumbered to SR sets: Nos. 10/11 to 784/5, 19 to 783, 30 to 786, 64 to 798, 72 to 801, 80/9 to 803/4, 96-8 to 807-9, 100 to 811, and 104/6/7 to 814-6. The other sets suffered minor or major alterations and so could not be said to have been renumbered directly from ex-LB&SC to SR.

Three of the rebuilt Composites were dual-braked before Grouping, these being Nos. 286, 293 and 450. As for lighting, all except one retained gas illumination after rebuilding, only No. 283 being electrically lit. From 1925 most coaches were fitted with vacuum brakes in addition to Westinghouse, and any that had not been so modified by 1929 simply had their Westinghouse equipment stripped and replaced by vacuum brakes only. In 1929/30 gas lighting was replaced by electricity on all but Nos. 6104 and 6135.

Virtually all the three-sets were classified 'Rover' in SR days and worked mostly local train services on the Central and Eastern Sections. Other sets in 1928 had the following workings:

Four-set 847 (Compo. 6144) - 9.15 am Victoria to Eastbourne and 4.20 pm return.
Four-set 876 (Compo. 6113) - 7.27 am Horsham to London Bridge and 6.08 pm return.
Four-set 877 (Compos. 6133/45) - 7.40 am Tunbridge Wells West to London Bridge and 8.00 pm return.
Four-set 874 (Compo. 6157) - 10.20 am Eastbourne to Victoria and 1.00 pm (Saturdays) or 1.20 pm (not Saturdays) return.
Four-set 885 (Compo 6120) - 10.20 am Bognor to Victoria and 1.30 pm (Saturdays) or 4.20 pm (not Saturdays) return.
Six-set 891 (Compo. 6101) - 2.55 pm London Bridge to Oxted and 3.59 pm return; 5.11 pm London Bridge to Brighton and 9.00 pm return.

In 1931, 13 ten-coach Central Section special traffic sets, numbered 863-72, 878, 886 and 892 were formed; each one included two of the rebuilt Composites. All were withdrawn about 1933.

From about 1931 a start was made to reduce some of the three-sets to two vehicles by removing one of the Third Brakes. Nos. 783, 784 and 785 were the first, but No. 786 was a complete reformation, using Third Brake No. 3994 left over from Set 783 and Composite No. 6109, formerly 'loose'. Set 876, with Composite No. 6113, was originally a four-coach set. All worked branch-line services in the Tonbridge, Maidstone and Ashford areas.

By 1934 there were 17 two-coach sets, allocated as follows:

Allhallows Branch	765	Polegate	791, 911
Bexhill West Branch	784, 876	Strood	786
Gillingham	787	Swanley	782
Hastings	829	Tonbridge	783, 790
Hawkhurst Branch	857	Relief Sets	802, 814, 815
Maidstone West	780, 785		

Each of these included a rebuilt Composite, several of which had had their 1st-class seating altered from three-a-side to four-a-side, Nos. 6110/28/50/53 being among the first recorded, c. 1930.

By 1934 several three-sets had been allocated to local workings on the Western Section, these being Nos. 788, 797, 799, 807-10, 816, 875 and 885. Two years later, withdrawals had reduced these to Nos. 788, 797, 799, 810, 816 and 885 only, but some of the others had been reduced to two-sets and remained on the Western Section until withdrawal: Nos. 806, 807, 808 and 809.

Three underframes were retained after their bodies had been withdrawn, and reused as replacement frames for other ex-LB&SC coaches. The frame of No. 6139 went to Third Brake No. 3894 in September 1932; and in February 1939 the frames of Nos. 6103/56 passed to Third Brakes Nos. 3975 and 3841 respectively.

Four Composites were transferred to the Isle of Wight, one in April 1938 and three exactly one year later. All received Westinghouse air brakes once again, and the seating was altered so that there were now three 1st-class compartments (the three wide ones), seating four-a-side, and five 3rd class. Thus the make-up was now 3, 1, 3, 1, 1, 3, 3, 3. The first to be sent over, No. 6347 (formerly 6111), was placed in Set No. 502. The 1939 trio, Nos. 6344-46 (formerly 6119/32/42), were entirely steel-panelled and were formed as the centre coaches of Sets 490-492. These Isle of Wight coaches long outlasted their mainland sisters, but were surplus after line closures in 1955 so did not last until the end of steam operation, all being withdrawn between 1955 and 1959. Incidentally their Isle of Wight Diagram Number was 375.

Three Composites to Diagram No. 335 became service vehicles upon withdrawal. The underframe of No. 6105 was used as Yard Wagon No. 1369S at Redbridge from December 1938; No. 6120 was transferred to Mess & Tool Van No. 1547S for the Locomotive Running Department at St Leonards in May 1940; and No. 6155 became Stores Van No. 1957S at New Cross in April 1944. All were scrapped after 1946.

Three other vehicles, after withdrawal, were recorded as having become grounded bodies: No. 6096 at St Leonards West Marina, and Nos. 6128 and 6135 at Angerstein Wharf (noted July 1947).

BOGIE COMPOSITES (DIAGRAM No. 92)

No.	Built	Rebuilt	Set	SR No.	Re-No.	Set	IOW No.	Re-No.	Wdn
26	12 98	12.09		6096	6.24	884, 849			12.40
238	12.91	6.09		6097	6.24	781, 849			12.40
239	12.91	12 09	108	6098	9.25	935, L			2.38
240	12.91	6.10	97	6099	3.27	808			9.36
241	12.91	12.09	35	6100	8.24				5.32
242	12.91	12.09	75	6101	3.27	891, L			12.40
243	12.91	12.09		6102	2.26	L, 911 /34			1.36
244	6.92	12.09	19	6103	10.26	783			12.38
245	6.92	6.09		6104	2.26	L, 924 /29			9.34
246	6.92	12.09	63	6105	7.24	797			11.38
247	6.92	12.09	104	6106	7.25	814			7.36
248	12.92	6.10		6107	12.26	782			7.36
249	12.92	12.09	91	6108	12.26	806			9.36
252	12.92	12.09	103	6109	10.26	L, 786 /31			5.36
253	12.92	6.09		6110	8.26	L, 765 /34			10.36
256	6.93	12.09		6111	9.24	L, 890 /34	6347	4.38	3.59
257	6.93	6.10	10	6112	1.25	784			8.35
258	6.93	12.09	102	6113	3.24	876, 857			6.36
259	6.93	.10		6114	3.25				5.38
274	12.93	6.09		6115	11.26	790			8.35
275	12.93	12.09		6116	10.24				6.32
276	12.93	12.09	93	6117	6.25	875			12.35
278	6.94	6.09		6118	7.24	791			11.36
279	6.94	6.09		6119	2.25	788	6344	4.39	12.55
280	6.94	6.09		6120	9.26	885, L			5.40
281	12.94	6.09	98	6121	7.24	809			9.36
282	12.94	6.10	30	6122	4.27	786, 891			2.39
283	12.94	12.09	62, 59	6123	2.25				10.36
284	12.94	12.09		6124	4.27	799			5.36
285	6.95	6.09	76	6125	7.24	802			6.36
286	6.95	12.09		6126	5.27	L, 780 /34			9.35
287	6.95	12.09		6127	9.24	796			6.37
288	6.95	6.09	82	6128	2.24	873, L			4.39
289	6.95	6.09	96	6129	11.26	807			1.37
290	6.95	6.09		6130	2.25				9.34
291	6.95	6 09	106	6131	10.25	815, L			11.37
292	6.95	6.09	107	6132	8.24	816	6345	4.39	2.56
293	6.95	6.09		6133	4.25	877			7.34
294	6.95	6.09		6134	4.27	852			1.36
295	6.95	6.09	113	6135	10.26	L, 924 /31			12.38
296	6.95	12.09	89	6136	8.26	804			4.35
442	12.95	6 09		6137	2 25	787			10.36
443	12.95	12 09		6138	3.27	L, 924 /36?			1.38
444	12.95	6.10	9	6139	3.26	812			9.32
445	12.95	6.09		6140	12.25	810			5.37
446	12.95	6.09	11	6141	2 25	785			10.37
447	12.95	6.09	100	6142	10.26	811, 849	6346	4.39	3.59
448	12.95	6.09	112	6143	5.27				2.39
449	12.95	12.09	70	6144	7.24	847			4.33
450	12.95	12.09	95	6145	4.25	877, 887 /31			7.34

No.	Built	Rebuilt	Set	SR No.	Re-No.	Set	IOW No.	Re-No.	Wdn
451	12.95	6.09		6146	1.27	793			10.37
452	12.95	12.09	80	6147	7.24	803			8.35
453	12.95	6.09		6148	6.27	800			5.34
454	6.96	6.09	72	6149	11.26	801			1.35
455	6.96	12.09	105	6150	10.25				9.34
456	6.96	12.09	78	6151	8.25	L, 891 /32			7.35
457	6.96	6.09		6152	5.24	789			2.36
458	6.96	12 09		6153	2.27	805			9.36
459	6.96	12.09		6154	10.26				7.32
460	6.96	6.09	101	6155	5.24	827, 849			12.40
461	6.96	12.09	111	6156	4.26	818			2.39
468	6.97	6.09	92	6157	11.26	874, 829			2.39
469	6.97	12.09	62, 40	6158	11.26	794			5.36
470	6.97	6 09	64	6159	6.26	798			6.38
471	6.97	6.09		6160	6.27	L, 876 /34			9.35

BOGIE COMPOSITE (DIAGRAM No. 113)

No.	Built	Rebuilt	Set	SR No.	Re-No.	Set	Wdn
273	12.93	12.09		6235	11.25	L, 815 /34	1.39

BOGIE COMPOSITE

No. 181 (SR No. 6161)

COMPOSITE

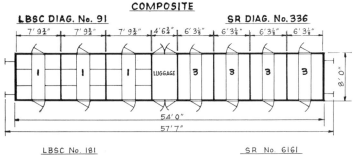

SEATING CAPACITY 18F 40T

Body length: 54 ft. Body width: 8 ft. Bogie centres: 37 ft.
Compartments: Three 1st class (7 ft 9¾ in. between partitions), one luggage compartment and four 3rd class (6 ft 3⅛ in. between partitions). Seats: 18 1st and 40 3rd class. Tare weight: 22 tons 18 cwt. Diagram No. 91 (SR No. 336). Rebuilt 1909.

In 1909 a rather odd bogie Composite was sent into traffic. This one-off vehicle was assembled with three compartments of six-wheeled four-compartment First No. 36 of 1892 and four compartments of six-wheeled five-compartment Second No. 198 of 1902. Each portion was mounted at one end of a new 54 ft underframe, but the result was not a perfect fit as there was a gap of 4 ft 6¾ in. between them; this was made good by building a new section of roof, putting in two sets of double doors on each bodyside and using the space as a luggage compartment. The carriage was illuminated by gas.

No. 181 eventually found its way into four-set No. 73, with Third Brakes 593 and 1244 and Lavatory Composite No. 12, but in 1917 this train had no booked workings. Set 73 was renumbered by the SR as Set 849, with an extra Lavatory Composite, No. 6176, added; in 1928 its workings included the 6.37 am Tunbridge Wells to Victoria and 4.05 pm return via Three Bridges and East Grinstead.

The carriage was given vacuum brake equipment in addition to its existing Westinghouse gear at overhaul and renumbering to SR No. 6161 at Lancing Works in November 1925.

By 1931 No. 6161 had been transferred from Set 849 to reformed five-set No. 884, which included two bogie Thirds and two six-wheeled Guard's Vans; this worked local train services in the Brighton/Worthing area.

It was withdrawn about 1933, the Composite being condemned in September; however, although the body was scrapped the newer underframe was salvaged with typical Southern economy for re-use on Composite No. 6270 in April 1934. This coach, originally Third Class No. 2339, was adapted as a push-and-pull trailer in Set 735, running in this wise until October 1941.

BOGIE LAVATORY TRI-COMPOSITES

No. 254 (SR No. 6172)

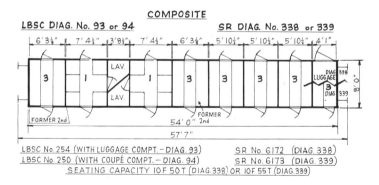

Body length: 54 ft. Body width: 8 ft. Bogie centres: 37 ft.
Compartments: Two 1st class (7 ft 4½ in. between partitions), two 2nd class (6 ft 3½ in. between partitions) and three 3rd class (5 ft 10½ in. between partitions). Two lavatories with access from 1st-class compartments only. Luggage compartment. Seats; 10 1st, 20 2nd class and 30 3rd class. Tare weight: 22 tons 10 cwt. Diagram No. 93 (SR No. 338). Rebuilt 1910.

.No. 250 (SR No. 6173)

Details as above except that instead of the luggage compartment there was a 3rd-class coupé, seating five passengers, at one end. Diagram No. 94 (SR No. 339). Rebuilt 1910.

After completion of the scheme to rebuild six-wheeled Composites into bogie vehicles, attention was next turned to similar conversion of a small range of six-wheeled Lavatory Composites, of which 17 had been built between 1892 and 1898. Fourteen of these were rebuilt as tri-Composites with the addition of two extra compartments and two additional lavatories, but the other three were rebuilt, perhaps experimentally, as three individual and unique coaches, all during 1910 at Lancing Works.

As built these six-wheelers had 32 ft bodies with the makeup 2, 1, Lavs, 1, 2. The first rebuild, that of No. 254, had the body placed at one end of a new 54 ft underframe, with three new 3rd-class compartments and a luggage compartment 4 ft 1 in. between partitions at the other end. The second rebuild, that of No. 250, was very similar but in place of the luggage compartment there was a half-compartment (coupé) of the same dimensions. In the body end were two small windows so that passengers could view the track - or, more probably, the end of the adjacent carriage.

Gas lighting was retained in both vehicles.

In 1912 the second class was downgraded to third, so that the seating capacity was now 10 1st and 50 3rd in No. 254, and 10 1st and 55 3rd in No. 250.

Both coaches received their Southern numbers in 1926, and in May 1929 both had their Westinghouse brakes replaced by vacuum and their gas lighting by electricity. So far as is known, neither coach was formed in a set until 1931, when No. 6173 replaced Lavatory Composite No. 6017 in four-set No. 873. It remained in this set until withdrawal in 1936. No. 6172, still a 'loose' coach, was withdrawn in 1933.

No.	Built	Rebuilt	SR No.	Re-No.	Set	Wdn
254	6.93	6.10	6172	2.26		6.33
250	12.92	6 10	6173	11.26	873	12.36

BOGIE LAVATORY TRI-COMPOSITE

No. 2 (SR No. 6174)

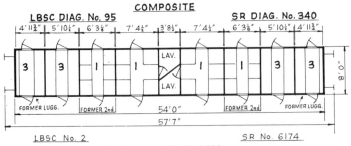

SEATING CAPACITY 22F 30T

Body length: 54 ft. Body width: 8 ft. Bogie centres: 37 ft.
Compartments: Two 1st class (7 ft 4½ in. between partitions), two 2nd class (6 ft 3¼ in. between partitions) and two 3rd class (5 ft 10½ in. between partitions). Two lavatories with access from 1st-class compartments only. Two luggage compartments, one at each end. Seats: 10 1st, 20 2nd, 20 3rd class. Tare weight: 23 tons approximately. Diagram No. 95 (SR No. 340). Rebuilt 1910.

The next rebuild of a six-wheeled Lavatory Composite produced a very different vehicle from Nos. 250 and 254 previously described. The body of No. 2 was mounted in the *centre* of a new bogie underframe and the additional compartments were built on at each end, these being a 3rd-class and luggage compartment at one end, and another 3rd-class and luggage compartment at the other end. Each luggage compartment measured 4 ft 11¾ in. between partitions. The reconstruction was carried out at Lancing during 1910. Gas lighting was retained.

In 1912, on the abolition of second-class accommodation, the 'seconds' were upgraded to 'firsts', so that there were now four 1st-class compartments seating a total of 22 passengers. Later still, the two luggage compartments were altered to 3rd class coupés (half-compartments) each with five seats, so that the total 3rd class accommodation was increased to 30. Small windows were included at each end, as in No. 250.

No. 2 was renumbered SR No. 6174 at Lancing in February 1924, and was formed in six-set No. 915, which in 1928 was booked to work the 6.15 am Eastbourne to Victoria and 7.20 pm return train services. This set, which suffered several reformations, seems to have been withdrawn about 1933 and certainly before 1935, but Composite No. 6174 was not itself withdrawn until March 1938 so presumably it must have found some other employment in those last three years.

No.	Built	Rebuilt	SR No.	Re-No.	Set	Wdn
2	6.98	12.10	6174	2.24	915, L	3.38

BOGIE LAVATORY TRI-COMPOSITES

Nos. 1, 8, 12, 63-65, 251/55, 462-67 (SR Nos. 6175-6188)

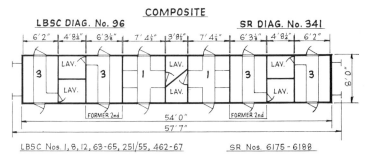

COMPOSITE

LBSC DIAG. No. 96   SR DIAG. No. 341

LBSC Nos. 1, 8, 12, 63-65, 251/55, 462-67   SR Nos. 6175-6188

SEATING CAPACITY 10F 36T

Body length: 54 ft. Body width: 8 ft. Bogie centres: 37 ft.
Compartments: Two 1st class (7 ft 4½ in. between partitions), two 2nd class (6 ft 3⅛ in. between partitions) and two 3rd class (6 ft 2 in. between partitions). Six lavatories - one per compartment. Seats: 10 1st, 18 2nd and 18 3rd class. Tare weight: 23 tons 5 cwt. Diagram No. 96 (SR No. 341). Rebuilt 1910.

These 14 Lavatory tri-Composites were rebuilt from the balance of the six-wheeled Lavatory Composites at Lancing during 1910. Again, the original body was mounted in the centre of the new bogie underframe and new compartments fabricated at each end but, instead of luggage compartments, two additional lavatory compartments were fitted in between the original 2nd-class compartment and a new 3rd-class compartment at each end. Thus the new make-up was 3, Lavs, 2, 1, Lavs, 1, 2, Lavs, 3.

In 1912 the second-class compartments were downgraded to third class so that there were now 36 such seats in each of the carriages.

No. 255, in four-set No. 95, was dual-braked and worked on the Oxted line. No. 462 was in four-set No. 24 (two bogies and two 6-wheeled vans) which worked the 5.20 am London Bridge to Brighton, a trip to Hastings and back, and the 8.50 pm Brighton to London Bridge. No. 65, in four-set No. 71, was booked for the 8.25 am Hastings to Victoria and 3.20 pm return; Set No. 73, which included Lavatory Composite No. 12, was spare in 1917. Five-set No. 23, with Composite No. 465, worked the 7.40 am Brighton to London Bridge and 4.10 pm return, whilst five-set No. 25, which included Composite No. 64, two other Composites and two six-wheeled vans, worked between Hastings and Brighton. A photograph of No. 64, with the wording 'Set Train 25' clearly visible on the solebar, appeared in G.M. Kichenside's *Railway Carriage Album* (Ian Allan, 1966). There was certainly nothing to show that the carriage was a rebuild, for the newer section matched the older perfectly.

All 14 carriages were still gaslit when they became Southern property, and electric lighting was not fitted until 1929/30. SR numbers were painted on between 1924 and 1927 at Lancing. Nos. 6178/81/84/85/87/88 became dual braked in 1926, but the remainder were altered from Westinghouse to vacuum braking (only), three years later. All the coaches were formed into sets.

Four-set No. 844 included Composite No. 6184 and ran between Portsmouth and London in 1928; four-sets 845/48 had Composites 6178/80; and five-set No. 849 included two, Nos. 6176/77, for working between Tunbridge Wells and London. No. 6183 ran in four-set No. 873 between Portsmouth and London, and No. 6185 was formed in six-set No. 891, whose workings were described in a previous section. Nos. 6175/79 were used to strengthen three-sets Nos. 803 and 804 to four vehicles by 1931 and their workings in that year took in Brighton-Gillingham and Sheerness-Brighton through services.

The first Lavatory Composite to be withdrawn was No. 6184, in October 1931; the body was broken up but the underframe was re-used on Composite No. 6243 (push-and-pull set 987) and lasted until 1948. Another underframe, that of No. 6185, became a Yard Wagon for internal use at Redbridge in December 1938, numbered in the Service Vehicles list 1370S.

LAVATORY COMPOSITES (DIAGRAM No. 96)

No.	Built	Rebuilt	Set	SR No.	Re-No.	Set	Wdn
1	6.98	12.10		6175	11.25	L, 803	8.35
8	6.98	6.10	108	6176	9.25	935, 849	10.38
12	6.98	6.10	73	6177	11.25	849	2.39
63	12.98	12.10		6178	5.25	845	2.34
64	12.98	12.10	25	6179	8.25	L, 804	4.35
65	12.98	12.10	71	6180	5.25	848, 853	10.35
251	12.92	12.10		6181	11.26	917, L /31	3.38
255	6.93	6.10	95	6182	11.24	778, 890	10.38
462	12.96	6.10	24	6183	10.26	873	12.36
463	12.96	12.10		6184	3.26	844	10.31
464	12.96	12.10	84	6185	3.27	891	11.38
465	6.97	12.10	23	6186	3.26	923	11.32
466	6.97	12.10		6187	10.27	L, 852 /31	1.36
467	6.97	12.10		6188	12.24	829	9.32

Nos. 462-467 were originally built by the Birmingham Railway Carriage and Wagon Company.

LAVATORY COMPOSITES

Nos. 119/21/25/26/28/37/52/54/55/60, 588-97 in 1912/13 and Nos. 72, 75, 76, 85, 88, 91, 95, 98, 105/20 in 1923/24 (SR Nos. 6205-34)

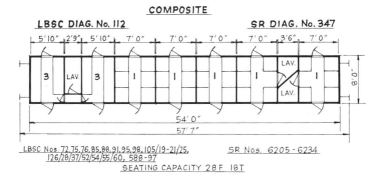

COMPOSITE
LBSC DIAG. No. 112   SR DIAG. No. 347

LBSC Nos. 72,75,76,85,88,91,95,98,105/19-21/25,   SR Nos. 6205 - 6234
126/28/37/52/54/55/60, 588-97
SEATING CAPACITY 28F 18T

Body length: 54 ft. Body width: 8 ft. Bogie centres: 37 ft.
Compartments: Five 1st class (7 ft between partitions) and two 3rd class (5 ft 10 in. between partitions). Three lavatories, two with access from two 1st-class and one with access from both 3rd-class compartments. Seats: 28 1st and 18 3rd class passengers. Tare weight: 26 tons 1 cwt. Diagram No. 112 (SR No. 347). Built between 1912 and 1924.

These carriages, although newly-built, featured the arc roof favoured by the LB&SC and whose appearance must have been viewed by discerning passengers as a retrograde step after the brief proliferation of the magnificent elliptical-roofed coaches. There is nothing especially noteworthy about their construction, except for the lavatory shared by both 3rd-class compartments by means of a short corridor linking them - an arrangement often found on the 'Brighton'. Twenty of these Lavatory Composites were built in 1912/13, eleven of them being formed as the centre coach of three-coach sets mainly intended for use in London and Portsmouth train services, on which the distance involved demanded at least some lavatory facilities. The Portsmouth sets were Nos. 114 to 118 and 120 to 123, each having two rebuilt Third Brakes to Diagram No. 165. Set 119 differed in including a Slip Third Brake and worked between London, Worthing and Brighton, while three-set No. 124 was entirely new in 1913 and ran in the 7.10 am Eastbourne to London Bridge and 4.05 pm return.

Five of the other Lavatory Composites were formed in four-coach sets. Set 45, which included No. 591, was berthed at Portsmouth and divided each morning, one two-coach portion working in the 6. 58 am to London Bridge and the second portion following in the 9.25 am Up. At London Bridge the portions were reunited and the four-coach train returned to Portsmouth as the 1.50 pm Down. Set 83 comprised two Lavatory Composites, Nos. 593 and 595, and two new Third Brakes built in 1913, and worked between Hastings and Victoria. Sets 78 and 79 also comprised two 1913-built Third Brakes and one new Composite each; both sets worked between London Bridge and Brighton/Hastings. Set 74 included Composite No. 119 and a Slip Third Brake, and was found working between Victoria and Brighton during 1917.

No. 592 was placed in a five-coach set, No. 70, and this worked in the 9.00 am Victoria to Eastbourne and 2.25 pm return.

Ten more Lavatory Composites, to the same design as the 1912 series, were authorised in December 1922 to be built by Lancing Works. Construction was slow, owing to the shortage of skilled men at the Works, and the first four vehicles did not appear until December 1923, the remaining six entering traffic during 1924. Although all were built after the LB&SC had become part of the Southern Railway, they still appeared in LB&SC umber but by 1927 all had been renumbered and repainted in Southern colours as Nos. 6225-34. The earlier twenty were renumbered as they entered Lancing Works for overhaul, although not in the same order as the 'Brighton' numbers, becoming Nos. 6205-24. All ten of the SR-built Composites were formed into three-coach sets with existing ex-LB&SC Third Brakes. These, along with the other three- and four-coach sets, ran until the mid-1930s.

Vacuum brake equipment was fitted to all except No. 6211 during 1925 and 1926, and the Westinghouse air brakes were removed from Nos. 6207-11, 6215/16/18/21-23/26/27/30 during 1929 and 1930. No. 6211 became vacuum-braked in March 1929.

Set No. 768, which included Lavatory Composite No. 6220, was reduced to two coaches in about 1936 or 1937, and was involved in the Swanley Junction collision on 27th June, 1937 (see page 106). The resultant damage caused the set to be withdrawn almost at once.

Here are some of the workings of sets that included Lavatory Composites, as shown in the September 1931 carriage working notice:

3-set 763: 6.18 am Bognor to London Bridge, 9.05 pm Victoria to Bognor.
3-set 761: 9.30 am Eastbourne to Victoria, 6.10 pm (N.S.) Victoria to Heathfield, 8.21 pm (N.S.) Heathfield to Eastbourne or 9.05 pm (S.O) Victoria to Eastbourne.
4-set 847: 6.31 am Reigate to London Bridge, 8.00 am London Bridge to Reading and 12.05 pm return; 3.17 pm (S.O.) or 4.44 pm (N.S.) London Bridge to Reading and 7.28 pm Reading to Redhill.
4 set 850: 8.24 am Horsham to London Bridge, 10.10 am London Bridge to Portsmouth, 7.00 pm Portsmouth to Victoria, 11.45 pm Victoria to Horsham.
4-set 851: 8.32 am (N.S.) or 8.40 am (S.O.) Tunbridge Wells to London Bridge, 10.40 am return, 1.08 pm Tunbridge Wells to London Bridge and 8.00 pm (N.S.) London Bridge to Tunbridge Wells.
4-set 874: 6.15 am Eastbourne to London Bridge and 12.14 pm return.

Four of the Lavatory Composites, on withdrawal from service, were given a further term of life as Mess & Tool vans during the 1940s. These were :

6233 to 1542S, April 1940. Locomotive Running Dept., Exmouth Junction.
6217 to 1545S, May 1940. Locomotive Running Dept., Bournemouth.
6228 to 1562S, December 1940. Locomotive Running Dept., Tonbridge.
6231 to 1563S, December 1940. Locomotive Running Dept., Tonbridge.

The underframe of No. 6211 was re-used as a Yard Wagon No. 1372S for internal use at Redbridge in August 1939.

No.	Built	Set	SR No.	Re-No.	Set	Wdn	
72	12.23		6225	11.26	795	12.40	
75	12.23		6226	1.27	767, L /36	12.40	
76	12.23		6227	12.24	762, L /36	12.40	
85	12.23		6228	3.27	763, L /36	12.40	Re-No. 1562S.
88	6.24		6229	6.27	861, L /36	12.40	
91	6.24		6230	8.24	821, L /36	12.40	
95	12.24		6231	3.27	766, 849	12.40	Re-No. 1563S.
98	12.24		6232	1.27	826, L	12.40	
105	6 24		6233	5.25	761, L /37	4.40	Re-No. 1542S.
120	6.24		6234	3.27	823, L /39	7.40	
119	6.12	74	6216	6.26	850, L /36	12.36	
121	6.12	75	6217	7.26	851	5.40	Re-No. 1545S.
125	6.12	116	6218	9.25	770	12.40	
126	6.12	117	6219	7.25	771	6.34	
128	6.12	114	6220	12.24	768	7.37	Acc. dam. Swanley Jn.
137	6.12	115	6211	8.26	769	5.39	Re-No. 1372S.
152	6.12	120	6221	8.25	774	8.34	
154	6.12	59	6222	11.26	819, L /38	12.40	
155	6 12	118	6223	4.26	772	8.36	
160	6.12	119	6224	3.26	773, L /36	12.40	
588	12.12	121	6205	1.27	775	8.39	
589	12 12	122	6206	6.24	776, L/39	7.40	
590	12.12	123	6207	11.24	777	4.36	
591	12.12	45	6208	9.26	874	6.40	
592	12.12	70	6209	7.24	847	12.36	
593	6.13	83	6210	1.26	820	12.40	
594	6.13	124	6212	4.27	859, L /37	12.40	
595	6.13	83	6213	10.24	922, 828,L	7.40	
596	6.13	78	6214	8.25	890	9.33	
597	6.13	79	6215	6.26		4.36	

After withdrawal, the bodies of eight Composites were taken off their frames and grounded at various locations noted by observers:

6205	Hoo Junction	6213	Lewes, noted 7.43
6206	Sherborne, noted 10.46	6218	Earlswood, noted 9.46
6208	Eardley, noted 2.48	6225	Durnsford Rd, noted 6.47
6212	Eastleigh Loco, noted 8.46	6226	Fratton

BOGIE COMPOSITES

SR Nos. 6162-6171

Body length: 54 ft. Body width: 8 ft. Bogie centres : 37 ft.
Compartments: Four 1st class (7 ft 2 in. between partitions) and four 3rd class (6 ft 1 in. between partitions). No lavatories. Seats: 24 1st and 40 3rd class. Tare weight: 26 tons. SR Diagram No. 337. Built 1924.

Although these ten Composites did not appear until early 1924 their 'Brighton' pedigree is indisputable. Plans were made in mid-1920 for a design of non-lavatory Composite with four centrally placed 1st-class compartments, and in December 1922 the carriages were authorised to be built at Lancing. As with the Lavatory Composites described in the previous section, construction was slow and the first appeared in January 1924, the other nine following in February. Although the Southern had standardised on the automatic vacuum brake in 1923, the Westinghouse brake was still in use on the former LB&SC lines and so all ten of these outdated vehicles entered service equipped with air brakes, becoming dual-braked during the next couple of years.

The carriages were electrically lit, each compartment having a single lamp. They were also steam heated with a radiator in each compartment. Roof ventilators were of the 'torpedo' type, two to each compartment.

Although LB&SC numbers were allocated in the carriage register, the vehicles never carried them. Instead they entered service with Southern numbers and in Southern green livery. Similarly, no LB&SC diagram number was given. Six of the Composites were formed as the centre vehicle in three-coach sets Nos. 761, 764, 813, 822, 824 and 825, whilst No. 6165 was placed in five-set No. 860, which in 1928 worked the 1.55 pm Littlehampton to Victoria and 6.40 pm return. About 1933 No. 6165 was transferred to six-set No. 890, in which it remained until early 1936. Around the same time 'loose' coach No. 6169 was placed in four-set 852, along with Composite No. 5942, to strengthen it to six coaches until withdrawal in January 1936.

'Loose' coach No. 6170 was running on the Western Section by 1933; on 25th May of that year it formed part of a Waterloo to Southampton train that ran into a Waterloo to Alton train at Raynes Park and was very badly damaged, being withdrawn officially in June 1933.

By 1934 Sets Nos. 813 and 824 were allocated to the Western Section, on which they ran until 1936/37. Sets 764 and 825 were each reduced to two coaches by removing one of the Third Brakes, and in 1934/35 were allocated to the Eastern Section for branch-line working in the Tonbridge and Ashford areas respectively.

In May 1936 four of the surviving nine Composites were withdrawn from their sets and altered for use in the Isle of Wight: one of the 1st-class compartments was downgraded to 3rd class (total seating capacity now being 24 1st and 50 3rd class) and the braking system converted back to Westinghouse air. The Composites - now to Diagram No. 373 - were renumbered from 6163/65/66/69 to 6353-56 in the Isle of Wight series. In March 1937 the remaining five were similarly altered and sent to the Island, these being Nos. 6162/64/67/68/71 which became Nos. 6348-52. Originally, the newcomers to the Island were formed in basic three-coach sets, which often were strengthened during the summer season. Nos. 6353-56 went to Sets 485 to 488, one per set and in numerical order; Nos. 6348/49 were in Set No. 500, Nos. 6350/51 in Sets 506 and 507, and No. 6352 was placed in Set No. 494. After 1948 there were many changes in formation, but all nine of these Composites did in fact last until the very end of steam operation in the Isle of Wight, being withdrawn at the end of 1966.

Over the years the bodywork was modified, steel panelling being added to cover over defective timber panelling here and there. Nos. 6348/51/53 were completely repanelled with steel sheets on one side only. A few torpedo roof ventilators were removed from various coaches, with the result that no two vehicles were alike.

Latterly it proved impossible to maintain set formations in the Island because of the frequency that coaches needed to be withdrawn for maintenance. However, in the early 1960s seven of the nine Composites were booked to be formed in Ryde-Ventnor sets Nos. 490 to 494, 497 and 500.

After withdrawal, No. 6349 (formerly 6164) was acquired by the Wight Locomotive Society for preservation. Fortunately this coach was still displaying its full complement of wooden mouldings. When the section of line between Havenstreet and Wootton reopened in the late 1970s No. 6349 formed part of the Society's vintage train and was the only carriage still more-or-less in original condition, the other two ex-LB&SC carriages being rebuilds.

No.	Built	Set	IOW No.	Re-No.	Wdn	
6162	2.24	813	6348	3.37	12.66	
6163	1.24		6353	5.36	12.66	
6164	2.24	822	6349	3.37	12.66	To Wight Loco Society
6165	2.24	860,890	6354	5.36	12.66	
6166	2.24	764	6355	5.36	12.66	
6167	2.24	761	6350	3.37	12.66	
6168	2.24	825	6351	3.37	12.66	
6169	2.24	L, 852	6356	5.36	12.66	
6170	2.24				6.33	Acc. dam. Raynes Park.
6171	2.24	824	6352	3.37	12.66	

BOGIE TRI-COMPOSITE BRAKES (SLIP-FITTED)

Nos. 403, 405 (SR Nos. 6937, 6938)

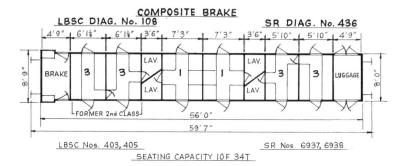

Body length: 56 ft. Body width: 8 ft (8 ft 9 in. over duckets). Bogie centres: 39 ft. Bogie wheelbase: 10 ft. Compartments: Two 1st class (7 ft 3 in. between partitions), two 2nd class (6 ft 1⅛ in. between partitions) and two 3rd class (5 ft 10 in. between partitions). Four lavatories - one to each 1st class compartment, one to both 2nd-class and one to both 3rd-class compartments. Luggage compt. Seats: 10 1st, 17 2nd and 17 3rd class. Tare weight: 25 tons approx. Diagram No. 108 (SR No. 436). Built 1908.

Built at Brighton in 1908, these two Tri-Composite Brakes had some unusual features: their bodies were two feet longer than the current standard, they had a guard's compartment at one end and a luggage compartment at the other, and they were dual-braked for through working on to other companies' lines. The guard's compartment featured duckets at the extreme end and a single inward-opening door each side. For some passengers, access to the lavatories was far from direct, and they must have felt they were negotiating Hampton Court Maze.

The second-class compartments were downgraded to third class in 1912, and the seating capacity of each coach was now 10 1st and 34 3rd class.

Both carriages were always 'loose stock', and even the Southern, which renumbered them 6937/38, never formed them into sets.

In 1931 No. 6937 was booked to work in the 7.51 am Eastbourne to Victoria via Eridge and the 3.45 pm return, whilst No. 6938 was based at Paddock Wood for Hawkhurst branch workings. By 1935 No. 6938 was a spare vehicle berthed at Eardley carriage sidings.

No.	Built	SR No.	Re-No.	Wdn
403	6.08	6937	10.26	1.37
405	6.08	6938	6.26	6.36

DIRECTORS' SALOON

No. 60 (SR No. 291S).

Body length: 60 ft. Body width: 8 ft 6 in.
Two saloon compartments, kitchen and pantry, One lavatory, with access from all seats. Seats: 22. Tare weight: 38 tons 8 cwt.
Diagram No. 67 (SR No. 1851). Built 1914.

During the half year ending June 1914 Lancing Works built a magnificent twelve-wheeled saloon for the use of the directors on their inspection trips. It had a lounge and a large dining saloon, these being joined by a short corridor off which was the kitchen and pantry, and also a lavatory.

Each end of the vehicle was bowed, and fitted with three large windows for observation. No. 60 had an elliptical roof, not as high as the 'balloon' roof but higher than the standard arc roof. The Saloon was steam-heated.

External livery was umber brown with lining-out in gold. The LB&SCR coat of arms appeared twice on each bodyside, with the number 60 in the waist panels above it. The roof was white. This vehicle and the King's Saloon were the only twelve-wheeled bogie vehicles ever built by the 'Brighton'. The overall length and width were 63 ft 8 in. by 8 ft 11 in.

The larger of the two compartments, the dining saloon, was 26 ft long internally, and there were two tables with moveable chairs. The smaller saloon, at the other end of the carriage, was 12 ft long. Between them, connected by a corridor, were the kitchen and a lavatory. The interior finish was in mahogany and satinwood.

According to a retired LB&SC coach finisher, writing in 1966, No. 60 was laid aside during World War I, only partly finished inside. In 1918 he began work on the vehicle at Preston Park shops, fitting the woodwork below the windows and completing other tasks.

No. 60 normally worked with a six-wheeled brake van, No. 380, from it which was not detached. This van was always to be returned to Brighton with the Saloon, which was berthed there when not in use.

Although No. 60 was numbered in the First Class list, the Southern Railway did not regard this vehicle as a passenger carriage and so it was placed in the Service Vehicles list from the very start, taking the number 291S. Green livery was applied. At an unknown date all the windows were altered, with large sliding ventilators replacing the original toplights. Six new roof ventilators, rather resembling smoke-ducts, were installed, four over the large saloon and two over the smaller. A handbrake was fitted, operated by a brake wheel placed just underneath the solebar each side. In July 1934 a further modification came in the shape of gangway connectors, which were fitted at each end, rather spoiling the appearance although they did not block the view through the end windows.

No. 291S was kept at Stewarts Lane for occasional use by SR officers. As Southern Region No. DS 291 it was repainted crimson and cream and, because the coach saw relatively little use and was kept indoors, this livery lasted a long

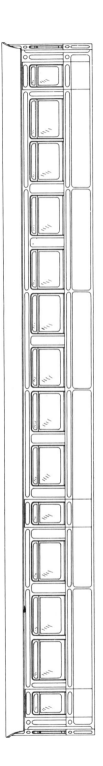
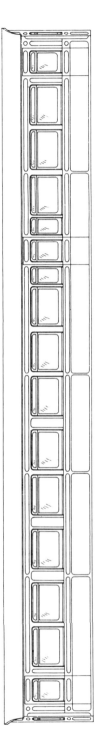

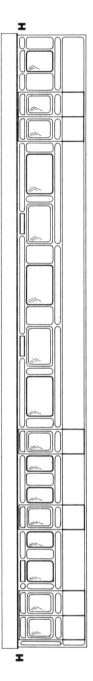

Above: Side elevations of Directors' Saloon, Diagram 67.
Right: End elevation of Directors' Saloon, Diagram 67.
Below: Invalid Saloon, Diagram 68.

time. In November 1962 unlined green was applied, and electric heaters were installed, thus making the vehicle dual heated.

DS 291 was withdrawn in early 1965 and, because of its uniqueness and perhaps the fact that it was the last ex-LB&SCR vehicle to remain in use on the mainland, it was offered to the Curator of Historical Relics, BRB, for preservation. However, he turned it down and the Bluebell Railway stepped in and negotiated its purchase. The Saloon was sent to Haywards Heath in June 1965, whence it was taken by road to Sheffield Park on 4th August. Each of the six-wheeled bogies had to be transported separately, after they had been detached from the body, which then made the third load. On arrival the body was reunited with its bogies, with the assistance of tower-jacks and blocks of timber. Four days later the Saloon made its first journey by rail under Bluebell auspices, complete with silver platters and trays and even a packet of cornflakes still in the pantry, left over from its last journey on BR.

Its first Bluebell trip was as a tea car, and the riding of the six-wheeled bogies was found to be exemplary. Subsequently the coach was fairly regularly used on Sundays in 1966, 1967 and 1968 as a light refreshment car, being attached at the south end of the scheduled train from mid-afternoon onwards. During 1966/7 it was repainted in umber, although without lining or crests; repainting was a protracted operation because of the railway's habit of pressing the Saloon into service whilst still in a patchwork of undercoat! By March 1967 the corridor connections had been removed. Frequent use of the Saloon took its toll; and after 1968 it ran on rare occasions only and after 1978 it was withdrawn. It has been out of service ever since, but at least is kept under cover. The intention is eventually to restore No. 60 to 1914 condition.

INVALID OR FAMILY SALOON

No. 57 (SR No. 7973)

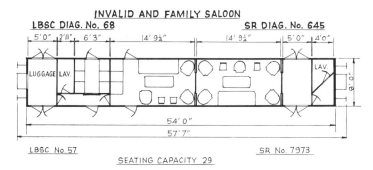

Body length: 54 ft. Body width: 8 ft. Bogie centres: 37 ft.
Compartments: Two saloons, one servants' compartment. Two lavatories, one accessible from the saloons, one from servants' compartment. Luggage compartment.
Seats: 29 (11 in one saloon, 12 in the other, six in the servants' compartment).
Tare weight: 26 tons 14 cwt. Diagram No. 68 (SR No. 645). Built 1916.

Built at the surprisingly late date of 1916, at a time when one would have thought there was little requirement for either invalid or family saloons, this rather splendid carriage was one of the few to be put into service during World War I. The make-up, viewed from one end, consisted of a luggage compartment, a lavatory and servants' or nurses' compartment past which ran a short side corridor, two saloons each 14 ft 9¼ in. between partitions and connected by a sliding door, an entrance lobby with double doors so as to admit stretcher cases, and another lavatory. The vehicle had gangways at both ends, was dual braked, electrically lit and steam heated. Each of the couches in the saloons could be adapted to form a bed. Most of the remaining seating accommodation was in the shape of individual chairs, and there was a fixed table in each saloon.

As the Saloon was fitted with chain communication operating brakes it was not allowed to be formed in trains from which carriages were slipped.

Shortly after being taken into Southern stock the vehicle was rebuilt internally. The luggage compartment and servants' lavatory were done away with, and in their place an additional small saloon was installed. Seating capacity was now increased to a total of 44. These alterations were completed in November 1925 at Lancing, and the Saloon emerged in Southern green as No. 7973.

In August 1930 the Westinghouse brakes were taken off and the Saloon was thus vacuum only. Further structural modifications were made in 1934 when the coach was adapted as a Composite Brake for service in the Isle of Wight. There were now two 1st-class and two 3rd-class compartments, seating 12 and 36 passengers respectively, and the lavatory was retained: the only lavatory ever found in an Island carriage. Westinghouse air brake equipment was refitted, and the coach was sent across the Solent in June 1934. Its new SR Diagram Number was 438, vehicle number 6986.

The coach was used as an observation saloon in a newly-instigated train, 'The Tourist', which worked between Ventnor and Freshwater via Sandown and Newport. The 1st-class observation compartment, with big windows overlooking the track, was extremely popular with passengers. Third-class passengers had the use of a large open section with wide observation windows. Leaving Ventnor at 9.55 am, 'The Tourist' called at Wroxall, Shanklin, Sandown and Newport, where engines were changed; the train then ran non-stop to Freshwater, where it was due at 11.12 am. The return train departed at 5.20 pm and it was due back at Ventnor at 6.46 pm. The train was formed of four ordinary compartment coaches plus an Isle of Wight Central Third Brake and the LB&SC Composite Brake No. 6986. During one week in summer 1934 2,700 passengers rode in 'The Tourist' 'between Ventnor and Freshwater. (*Railway Magazine* Vol. 75 p. 465).

As rebuilt, the layout of the carriage was odd indeed. At the observation end was a first-class compartment with three individual chairs overlooking the track, and three fixed seats where the lavatory had been. The six-seat 1st-class compartment with short side corridor was retained from Invalid Saloon days. The two former saloon compartments were done up as 3rd-class saloons, mainly with longitudinal seating, 16 in each section. Four additional transverse seats were placed in what had been the entrance lobby; one of the two entrance

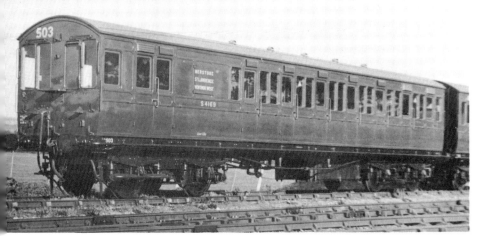

Modified push-and-pull set 503 for Isle of Wight service, at Merstone, on 18th March, 1949. Built as LB&SC No. 1346 in 1911, the Third Brake became SR No. 3828 and, its sliding doors replaced by swing doors in the luggage compartment, it was renumbered 4169 and sent to the Island in 1938. The Trailer Composite, No. 6367, was also built in 1911 and originally numbered 643 and SR 6204.
(Both) J.H. Aston

This eight-compartment Trailer Third Brake, No. 3821 of Set 726, was built in 1912 as LB&SC No. 1347 (Diagram No. 183); here shown at Tonbridge on 18th September, 1948.   *D. Cullum*

Trailer Third Brake No. 3848, of Set 716, also had eight compartments but all were equally-spaced. It was built in 1921 as LB&SC No. 1403 (Diagram No. 187).   *Lens of Sutton*

Trailer Composite No. 6242 in Set 719 at Brighton, 10th June, 1950. As LB&SC No. 650 (Diagram No. 120) this was introduced in 1922, the underframe of 1905 being taken from an Ambulance coach.   *H.C. Casserley*

Push-and-pull set 723 at Colyton, on the Seaton branch, on 28th June, 1948. LB&SC No. 1410 was built in 1922 (Diagram No. 204) and the Southern renumbered this six-compartment Third Brake to 3855.   *J.H. Aston*

Driving Trailer Composite Brake No. 6940, rebuilt in 1931 from Composite No. 6261 of 1921. Although nominally allocated to the Eastern Section, Set 650 is here shown at Guildford on a Horsham line working in the 1930s. *E. Jackson*

Push-and-pull set 650 enters Appledore on a Hastings to Ashford service, 18th June, 1958.
H.C. Casserley

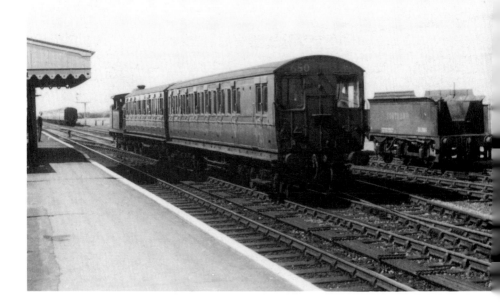

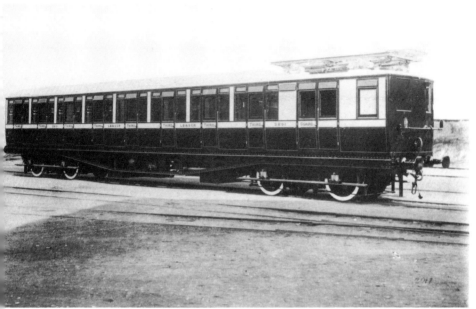

'South London' Motor Third Brake No. 3201, built by Metro in 1909 (LB&SC Diagram No. 280). It became SR No. 8601. *Official photo*

A 'South London' two-car formation at Peckham Rye in March 1927. Original Motor Third Brake No. 3204, built by Metro in 1909, and later Driving Trailer Composite No. 4057, converted from Bogie Block Third Brake. It became SR No. 9817 in 1927. *O.J. Morris*

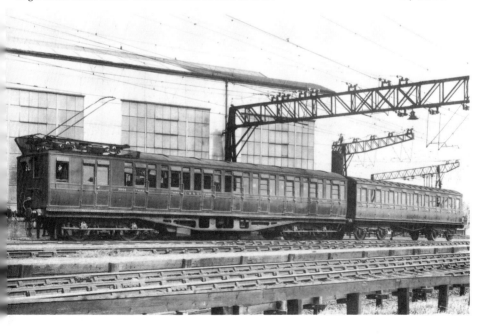

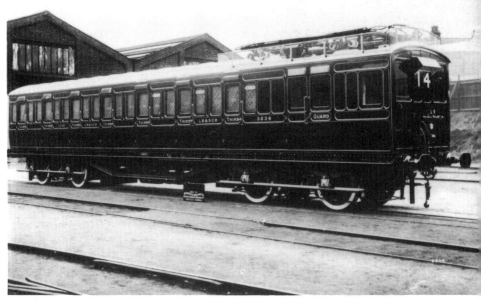

'Crystal Palace' Motor Third Brake No. 3236, built by Metro in 1911. (LB&SCR Diagram No. 282). It became SR No. 8572. *Official photo*

A complete 'Crystal Palace' six-car train, posed probably at Saltley and conveying a headcode never actually used by A.C. trains. Motor Third Brake No. 3234 (Diagram No. 282) is nearest the camera; it later became SR No. 8570. *Official photo*

Inauguration of the Victoria to Sutton via Selhurst A.C. electrification, 1st April, 1925; 'Coulsdon/Wallington' five-car unit at the former Beeches Halt, then being rebuilt as Carshalton Beeches.

'Coulsdon/Wallington' Driving Trailer Third No. 3285, built at Lancing in 1924, leads a ten-car Coulsdon North train.

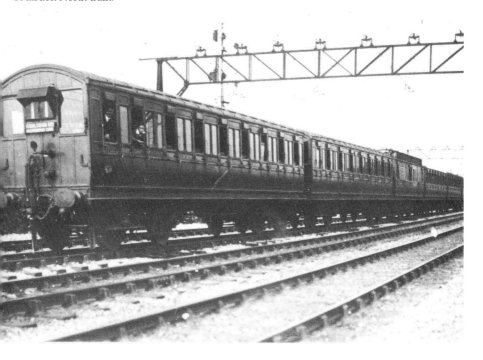

'Coulsdon/Wallington' five-car train at Coulsdon North, July 1928. Driving Trailer Third No. 3275, built at Lancing in 1923, is the leading vehicle.

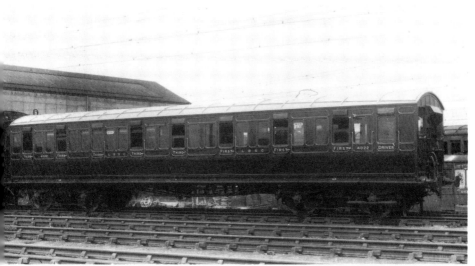

'Crystal Palace' Driving Trailer Composite No. 4022, built by Metro in 1911; at Peckham Rye about 1927 still in LB&SC livery.   *O.J. Morris*

Typical 'Crystal Palace' three-car formation with motor brake in centre. Nearest vehicle is Driving Trailer Composite No. 4056 (seemingly revarnished though still in LB&SC livery), which was built at Lancing in 1911.   *O.J. Morris*

Above: Interior of 'South London' Motor Third Brake, clearly showing the 'open' side corridor.
LB&SCR photo

Opposite: Later view of the corridor of a 'South London' Motor Third Brake, looking towards the guard's compartment; the ornate ironwork bracket was still intact.
J.L. Smith

'Coulsdon/Wallington' Motor Luggage Van No. 10112, built by Metro in 1924 (SR Diagram No. 830). It appears to have had a revarnish only two years after construction. *O.J. Morris*

SR Motor Third Brake No. 8702 in D.C. unit No. 1733 (later 4534). It was converted from 'CW' Driving Trailer Third No. 3270 in 1929, using all eight original compartments plus new driving and luggage compartments. *H.C. Hughes*

Brake Van No. 438 built in 1900 (LB&SC Diagram No. 226). It has guard's lookouts without mouldings, the extreme width over body of which was 9 ft 2 in., and is fitted with oil lighting. The van became SR No. 919.   *Lens of Sutton.*

Mail Van No. 351, built in 1897; it was converted in 1921 to a Guard's Van, the sliding doors being replaced by swing doors, and renumbered 3. Later it became SR No. 928.

D. Cullum Collection

R. L. Van Nice, 101, built in 1907 (Diagram No. 230). Formed in the Newhaven boat train, which included four Lavatory Composites

One of the D.C. Trailer Thirds that was converted to a de-icing trailer: No. 9089 (built by Metro in 1911) became 399S in 1946 and is here shown as DS 399.   *J.L. Smith*

Many former LB&SC carriages ended up as grounded bodies in the 1940s. Here is Lavatory Composite No. 6218 in Earlswood goods yard on 21st September, 1946. It was built in 1912 as No. 125 and withdrawn in 1940. The windows have been modified, and a stove-pipe protrudes through the roof.   *D. Cullum*

'City Limited' 9 ft-wide Lavatory First No. 7640 at Ashford Works, 7th May, 1949. It was built in 1907 as LB&SC No. 164.   *D. Cullum*

'City Limited' 9 ft-wide Corridor First No. 7641 at Meldon Quarry, its appearance not improved by the addition of a protective corrugated-iron roof. Originally LB&SC No. 151 of 1907, the carriage was withdrawn in 1940.   *J.H. Aston*

doors each side was retained, but the other two were fixed. The lavatory at the opposite end of the coach was retained, and beside it was a handbrake and an amazingly cramped accommodation for the guard. Both end gangways had been removed at the time of conversion.

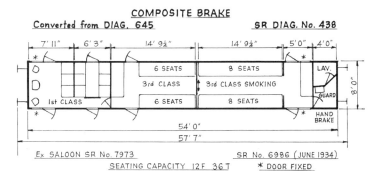

COMPOSITE BRAKE
Converted from DIAG. 645   SR DIAG. No. 438

Ex SALOON SR No. 7973   SR No. 6986 (JUNE 1934)
SEATING CAPACITY 12F 36T   * DOOR FIXED

No. 6986 remained in use until 1959, sometimes being appropriated as an inspection saloon; in September 1959 it was transferred to the Service Vehicles list as DS 70008. In its new capacity as a breakdown van for the Motive Power Department at Ryde St Johns it was kept until the end of steam operation in the Isle of Wight, being finally withdrawn in April 1967. It was not preserved, although undoubtedly it was worthy of retention.

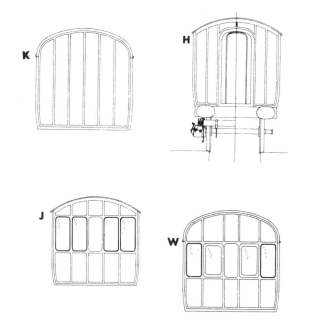

Chapter Nine

'Motor' Trains

At the turn of the century, many lines on the LB&SCR system were being operated at a loss, partly because of the high cost of locomotive coal and partly because of dwindling traffic. The railway sought ways of reducing costs and at the same time stimulating traffic by opening new unstaffed halts. Competition from tramways was severe in Brighton itself, and to some extent in Hastings, Portsmouth and parts of South London. What was needed was a service of cheap trains, each comprising a single coach with the guard issuing tickets and hauled or propelled by a small tank engine which would stay attached to the carriage all day. Before these became general, however, the 'Brighton' experimented with two petrol-electric cars, which from September 1905 worked the Eastbourne to Hastings local service, and two steam railmotors, which replaced the petrol cars from January 1906, these going to the Kemp Town branch for a short time.

The separate auto-train trailers, worked initially by Class A1 tank locomotives and later by Class D1 engines, were much more successful. Of the high-roofed variety there were three designs, although all were very similar in appearance, and they were introduced in 1905-7.

TRAILER THIRD BRAKES

Nos. 1326, 1327 (SR Nos. 3829, 3830)

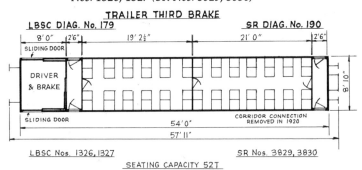

Body length: 54 ft. Body width: 8 ft 10 in. Bogie centres: 37 ft.
Two saloon compartments, 21 ft and 19 ft 2½ in. between partitions. Driver and brake compartment. Seats: 52. Tare weight: 24 tons 5 cwt. Diagram No. 179 (SR No. 190). Built 1905.

TRAILER THIRD BRAKES

Nos. 1328 to 1333 (SR Nos. 3831 to 3836)

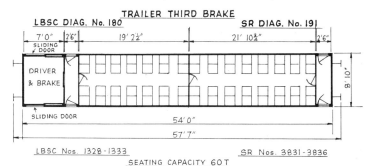

Body length: 54 ft. Body width: 8 ft 10 in. Bogie centres: 37 ft.
Two saloon compartments, 21 ft 10¾ in. and 19 ft 2¼ in. between partitions. Driver and brake compartment. Seats: 60. Tare weight: 24 tons 5 cwt. if gaslit, 25 tons approx. if electrically lit. Diagram No. 180 (SR No. 191). Built 1906.

TRAILER THIRD BRAKES

Nos. 1334 to 1342 (SR Nos. 3837 to 3845)

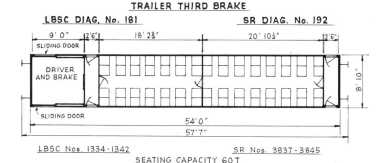

Body length: 54 ft. Body width: 8 ft 10 in. Bogie centres 37 ft.
Two saloon compartments, 20 ft 10¼ in. and 18 ft 2¾ in. between partitions. Driver and brake compartment. Seats: 60. Tare weight: 25 tons approximately.
Diagram No. 181 (SR No. 192). Built 1907.

All three types had entry vestibules with inward-opening doors, and large sliding doors to the driver's compartment. The seating, upholstered in rattan, was of the tramcar type with reversible seat-backs, although seats against bulkheads had fixed backs. All 17 vehicles measured 9 ft 6 in. over stepboards and 12 ft 11 in. from rail to top of roof. At the drive-end were four windows in groups of two, those nearest the centre-line being droplights.

The differences between the three batches included the following: Nos. 1326/27 had 13 windows each side, six being droplights (each alternate window) and Nos. 1328-42 had 15 windows each side, seven being droplights. Nos. 1326/27 sported a corridor connection at the inner end, the others had none; it never served any purpose as no other gangwayed vehicles ran with them, and the gangways were removed from both carriages in August 1920. Nos. 1326/27, also Nos. 1331-33, surprisingly were lit by gas; all the others had electric lighting. The internal length of the brake compartment differed in all three batches: 8 ft on Nos. 1326/27, 7 ft on Nos. 1328-33 (which had larger saloons with eight extra seats) and 9 ft on Nos. 1334-42 (which as a result had smaller saloons but still managed to cram in 60 seats).

Livery when new was umber with white upper panels, the mouldings being umber lined out in yellow. At the first repaint, the cars became all-over brown.

Originally the cars had mechanical linkage controls; the driver could thus operate the regulator from his compartment when the carriage was being propelled and he could operate the brakes. The fireman remained on the locomotive. Mechanical control was not altogether satisfactory and was replaced by air-pressure control after 1909. This required the coupling-up of four hoses: main train pipe, back pressure pipe, main storage pipe and regulator pipe.

Nos. 1326/27 were placed on Brighton to Worthing local services from 3rd September, 1905; on the same day new halts were opened, served only by the trailers: Holland Road (closed 7th May, 1956), Dyke Junction (renamed Aldrington 17th June, 1932), Fishersgate, and Ham Bridge (renamed East Worthing 23rd May, 1949). By 1917 the two cars were working the Brighton-Dyke service, but four years later they were shown in lists as spare cars.

Of the next batch of six cars, some were placed on the Chichester to Portsmouth local service from 1st April, 1906, and another based at Brighton worked a complex daily diagram from July 1906 that took in Brighton-Lewes-Seaford-Sheffield Park-East Grinstead-Three Bridges-Lewes-Uckfield-Brighton. Motor halts at Fishbourne, Nutbourne, Southbourne and Bedhampton were all opened on 1st April, 1906, for passengers using the Chichester to Portsmouth cars. On 11th June, 1906, a car began working between West Croydon and Belmont. Allocations of these six cars in 1917 and 1921, as shown in official lists, were:

	October 1917	*February 1921*
1328	Brighton-Haywards Heath.	Brighton-Seaford.
1329	Horsham-Guildford.	Brighton-Seaford.
1330	Spare, London area	Brighton-East Grinstead.
1331	Brighton-Kemp Town.	Brighton-Dyke.
1332	Spare.	Spare.
1333	Brighton-Uckfield.	Spare.

Of the final batch, some worked in the London area, particularly around Croydon, Sutton and Epsom Downs. Of the rural services, two new 'motor' diagrams were introduced in June 1907, one based at Horsham taking in Three Bridges and Tunbridge Wells, the other based at Tunbridge Wells for Oxted services. Halts at Ifield, Littlehaven and Roffey Road on the Three Bridges-Horsham section, and Hurst Green, Monks Lane and High Rocks on the Tunbridge Wells-Oxted section, were all opened on 1st June, 1907, being served only by the motor cars. Not all these halts proved successful in generating traffic, and Roffey Road closed on 3rd January, 1937, Monks Lane on 11th November, 1939, and High Rocks on 5th May, 1952. From July 1907 an additional motor diagram began operating from Tunbridge Wells, covering mainly the service to Crowborough. The cars moved around over the years, as a comparison between the 1917 and 1921 allocations will show;

	October 1917	February 1921
1334	Spare.	Tunbridge Wells-Crowborough.
1335	Tunbridge Wells-Oxted.	Portsmouth-Emsworth
1336	Brighton-Seaford.	Tunbridge Wells-Oxted.
1337	Coulsdon-Crystal Palace.	Coulsdon-Crystal Palace.
1338	Tunbridge Wells-Crowborough.	Brighton-Dyke.
1339	West Croydon-Banstead.	Brighton-Kemp Town
1340	Horsham-Three Bridges.	Horsham-Three Bridges.
1341	Streatham-Croydon	Spare.
1342	Bognor Branch.	W. Croydon, Sutton, Crystal Palace.

There is photographic confirmation that No. 1331 worked the Kemp Town branch c.1920 and No. 1336 was on Tunbridge Wells-East Grinstead-Oxted services c.1921. No. 1342, however, later moved to Brighton and on one occasion was photographed at Hassocks working the Haywards Heath to Brighton local service, strengthened by an eight-compartment Third.

All services operated by the elliptical roof 'Balloon' trailers were third-class only. Generally each car operated singly, although sometimes two were coupled; and in later years two or three ordinary carriages with first-class accommodation were through-piped in order to work with the trailers as strengthening vehicles. Nine-compartment Third No. 1734 (a former 'Bogie Block' carriage that later became SR No. 2166) was specially allotted in 1917 to work with trailer No. 1339 on the West Croydon-Sutton services.

After Grouping the trailer Third Brakes began running as permanent two-coach formations, each being paired with a through-piped vehicle; 48 ft Composites Nos. 533 to 545 were formed in numerical order with Nos. 1328 to 1340 and 50 ft former 'Bogie Block' Composites Nos. 548/49 ran with Third Brakes Nos. 1341/42. No. 1326 ran with the Third already mentioned, No. 1734. Between 1924 and 1927 Sets 736 to 750, as they now were, were repainted in Southern sage green livery, the Third Brakes becoming Nos. 3831-45 and the Composites Nos. 6033-45/56/57. The set including Nos. 1326 and 1734 was non-standard, being 3rd-class only, and was numbered 979 (vehicles 3829 and 2166). Set 980 officially included Third Brake No. 3830 (formerly 1327) and eight-compartment Third No. 2063 (adapted as a trailer in November 1925), but usually No. 3830 ran as a single coach, mainly on Brighton-Kemp Town services.

Gas lighting was replaced by electricity on Nos. 3834-36 in November 1929, on No. 3829 in March 1930 and on No. 3830 in May 1930. Westinghouse brakes were replaced by vacuum on Nos. 3831/34/35-39/42-45 in November or December 1929, Nos. 3832/33/41 in January 1930, and on the remainder in spring 1930.

Apart from Set 980, which was disbanded by 1928, Sets 736-750 and 979 ran until late 1931 with their 1924 formations. The arc-roof vehicles, nearly one foot narrower and over one foot lower than the 'Balloons', looked ridiculous coupled with the much larger driving trailers and so, when the opportunity arose to replace them with something that matched the outline a good deal better, it was taken. Some main-line Composites were withdrawn and adapted as trailers, their lavatory compartments being removed and the frosted glass replaced by panelling. From September 1931 these trailer Composites were paired with the 'Balloons' in Sets 736, 737, 739 to 750, and similarly adapted nine-compartment trailer Thirds (Nos. 2179/80) went to Sets 979 and 738. The Composites were of four different types, some with 54 ft and some with 56 ft bodies, some with 8 ft and others with 10 ft-wheelbase bogies; they were not allotted to the sets in numerical order.

Below are shown official allocations in three separate years.

	1931	1935	1939
736	Bognor-Barnham.	Bognor.	Pulborough.
737	Littlehampton-Ford.	Littlehampton.	Horsham.
738	Relief.	Brighton-Dyke.	Petersfield.
739	Horsham.	Horsham.	Steyning.
740	Horsham.	Horsham.	Horsham.
741	Littlehampton.	Bognor.	Hailsham.
742	Brighton.	Littlehampton.	Brighton.
743	Brighton.	Brighton.	?
744	Relief.	Bognor.	?
745	Relief.	Bognor.	?
746	Relief.	Eastbourne.	?
747	Horsham.	Relief.	?
748	Relief.	Horsham.	?
749	Horsham.	Horsham.	?
750	Horsham.	Horsham.	?
979	Brighton-Dyke.	Relief.	Midhurst (as Set 733)
3830	Brighton-Kemp Town.	Arundel.	

Set 979 was renumbered 733 in about 1936 or 1937. The single coach of this set (No. 3829) ran on the Dyke Branch latterly; Set 740 was photographed at Horsham on the Guildford service in October 1937; Set 741 also was at Horsham in July 1938; and Set 749 was photographed on a Horsham to Bognor service shortly before electrification of these lines.

Two 'Balloon' push-and-pull sets (a 'sandwich' formation with the locomotive in the centre) ran on the West Coast line in August 1936 and no doubt at other times too.

'Loose' Third Brake No. 3830 was the first of the 'Balloons' to be withdrawn, in February 1936 after accidental damage at Littlehampton. The 16 sets were withdrawn between 1938 and 1943. When No. 3845 in Set 750 was withdrawn in 1941 its place was taken by No. 3841 ex-Set 746 and the reformed Set 750 was the very last to remain in traffic, being withdrawn in January 1943.

The only wartime allocations known are those of Sets 733 and 738, which in 1941 were reserved for Pulborough-Petersfield services, normally working as single Third Brakes, their trailer Thirds standing spare.

Four trailer Third Brakes, after withdrawal from passenger service, were retained as service vehicles, all becoming Yard Wagons at Lancing Works. These were:

1645S, ex-3833 in June 1941. Withdrawn April 1946; cut up at New Cross Gate in October 1946.
1693S, ex-3836 in October 1941. Withdrawn November 1941. Body grounded at Lancing Works, noted September 1946.
1715S, ex-3844 in January 1942. Withdrawn August 1945. Body grounded at Lancing Works, noted September 1946.
1796S, ex-3841 in January 1943. Remained at Lancing Works, on wheels, until February 1964, when it was broken up.

No. 1796S is of interest in that it was last 'Balloon' trailer to remain in existence; in 1963 it was officially a Mobile Stores Van (fitted with dumb buffers), although in fact not very mobile. The Bluebell Railway had hoped to acquire it, but on examination it was found to be in too poor a condition for restoration. (*Bluebell News*, June 1963 and December 1963.) Several other elliptical-roofed bodies were found by the Bluebell team at Lancing on 21st September, 1963, including Third Brake No. 3836, but all were in such a terrible state that they would have disintegrated had any attempt been made to move them.

Six other Third Brakes after withdrawal were grounded as huts at various places. These were:

3829	Lymington Junction	3834	Lancing Works
3831	Aldershot, noted 5.44	3842	Hounslow
3832	Farnborough, noted 4.44	3845	Gomshall, noted 6.48

No.	Built	SR No.	Re-No.	Set No.	Wdn
1326	12.05	3829	11.25	979, 733	9.42
1327	12.05	3830	5.25	980, L	2.36
1328	6.06	3831	3.24	736	8.40
1329	6.06	3832	5.24	737	12.42
1330	6.06	3833	2.26	738	6.41
1331	6.06	3834	2.25	739	10.42
1332	6.06	3835	5.27	740	12.40
1333	6.06	3836	4.26	741	10.41
1334	6.07	3837	9.26	742	6.40
1335	6.07	3838	8 27	743	10.38
1336	6.07	3839	?	744	8.38
1337	6.07	3840	?	745	8.38
1338	12.07	3841	2.27	746, 750	1.43
1339	12.07	3842	6.27	747	11.42
1340	12.07	3843	4.25	748	2.39
1341	12.07	3844	8.25	749	1.42
1342	12.07	3845	8.27	750	7 41

For details of the Composites that ran with the 'Balloon' trailers, see pages 26, 47, 72, 73, 78 and 80.

TRAILER COMPOSITE BRAKES

Nos. 630 to 633 (SR Nos. 6927 to 6930)

Body length: 54 ft. Body width: 8 ft. Bogie centres: 37 ft.
Compartments: Four 3rd class (5 ft 10¼ in. between partitions) and three 1st class, of which one was 5 ft 10¼ in. and two were 6 ft 10½ in. between partitions. Driver and brake compartment. Seats : 24 1st and 40 3rd class.
Tare weight : 25 tons approximately. Diagram No. 109 (SR No. 434). Rebuilt 1909.

Nos. 634 to 639 (SR Nos. 6931 to 6936)

Body length: 54 ft. Body width: 8 ft. Bogie centres: 37 ft.
Compartments: Five 3rd class (5 ft 10¼ in. between partitions) and two 1st class (6 ft 10½ in. between partitions). Driver and brake compartment. Seats: 16 1st and 50 3rd class.
Tare weight: 25 tons approximately. Diagram No. 111 (SR No. 435). Rebuilt 1909/11.

For the suburban area there was a desire to provide motor train services on some of the lighter-used routes, but as the stations were all staffed there was no need to include through corridors for the guard to sell tickets. Also, some first-class accommodation, which the 'Balloon' trailers did not have, was desirable. Thus, ten Composite driving trailers of ordinary compartment type were knocked up cheaply by using former six-wheel five-compartment Third bodies, mounted on new 54 ft underframes, with two additional compartments plus driver's compartment built on at one end.

The first four cars had one of the former 3rd-class compartments re-upholstered as 1st class, so that in these vehicles there were three 1st-class compartments and four Thirds; but in subsequent rebuilds all five 3rd-class compartments were retained as such and there were only two Firsts. Oddly enough, the early four cars were never altered to match the later six, but the bodywork in all ten was the same. Nos. 630-35 were completed at Lancing during the second half of 1909, but the final four did not appear until early 1911.

The driver's compartment measured 10 ft 0⅛ in. and access to it was by a large sliding door each side, as in the 'Balloon' trailers. The driver's seat was on the left-hand side facing the track; there were four windows in groups of two in the driving end, which was fully panelled. The LB&SC's air-control system was used, probably from the start, and each carriage was fitted with a whistle worked by compressed air.

Livery was umber and white, but possibly the last four cars, Nos. 636-39, appeared in the new plain umber livery with yellow lining-out.

The first of these trailers appeared on the Epsom Downs branch in October 1909, presumably in replacement of the 'Balloon' trailer that had begun operating the service in June 1906. Usually, two-car trains were run, with one car each side of a 'D1' class 0-4-2 tank locomotive. One unit was based at West Croydon, the other at Sutton. Other services operated included Streatham to

Wimbledon, West Croydon to Wimbledon, and West Croydon-Crystal Palace-Coulsdon North.

Allocations of cars in 1917 were: 630/33 - Streatham and Wimbledon (suspended during the War); 631/32 - West Croydon and Wimbledon; 634/35 - Epsom Downs and Sutton; and 636-39 - West Croydon, Crystal Palace and Coulsdon. By February 1921 the only changes were that No. 632 had been transferred to Coulsdon-Crystal Palace services and No. 633 worked between Sutton, West Croydon and Crystal Palace.

The *Railway Magazine* noted (Vol. 43 p. 423 (1918)) that since 1st November, 1918, the West Croydon and Wimbledon branch had been worked by motor trains (which presumably had been withdrawn temporarily). Morden station (the present Morden Road) had been re-opened as a motor halt, and both Beddington Lane and Merton Park were also motor halts dealing only with passengers.

First of the Composite Brakes to be renumbered and repainted in SR green was No. 636, which became SR 6933 in April 1924. In 1925 it was decided to adapt ten eight-compartment Thirds to run as trailers with the driving trailer Composite Brakes and number the two-coach trains as sets 751 to 760. This was done between November 1925 and January 1926, and the Thirds were allotted to the sets in the order 2061, 2039, 2002, 2038, 2007, 1995, 1967, 1963, 2110 and 2048. At the same time the Composite Brakes in Sets 751/53-56/58/59 were renumbered to 6927/29-32/34/35. No. 6933 had already been reliveried in 1924, and was formed in Set 757. Because Nos. 6928/36 did not receive their new numbers until early 1927, Sets 752 and 760 ran for about a year with the Composite Brakes in LB&SC brown and the trailer Thirds in SR green.

It was one of this type of push-and-pull set, No. 754, that was employed in trials during 1928/9 to decide on the best control system to be used for motor trains throughout the Southern Railway. A report dated 25th October, 1927, stated that the London & South Western push-and-pull train control, using wires, was unsatisfactory; the wires needed constant adjustment, and in fact drivers usually employed whistle signals to the fireman to start the train. The report found that the South Eastern & Chatham through rod control was fairly satisfactory; it consisted of shafting running under the coaches and connected to the driving gear by means of bell cranks and rods, but was a bit 'hit-and-miss' in operation. The LB&SC air-control system was clearly the best, but as the SR was standardising on the vacuum brake and rejecting the Westinghouse air brake the two systems had somehow to be combined on push-and-pull locomotives and carriages. During August 1928 'D1' class 0-4-2T No. B234 was fitted with vacuum ejectors and brake combination valves. It now had vacuum brake control for the coaches in addition to Westinghouse air control apparatus for the push-and-pull working. Set 754 also now had vacuum brakes, though still retaining its Westinghouse air control (and air braking, until December 1929).

This locomotive and train then did the rounds of SR branches. From 28th November, 1928, it worked the Gravesend West Street branch, then from 4th December the Gravesend Central to Port Victoria service.

From 11th to 14th December the Ash Junction to Aldershot service was

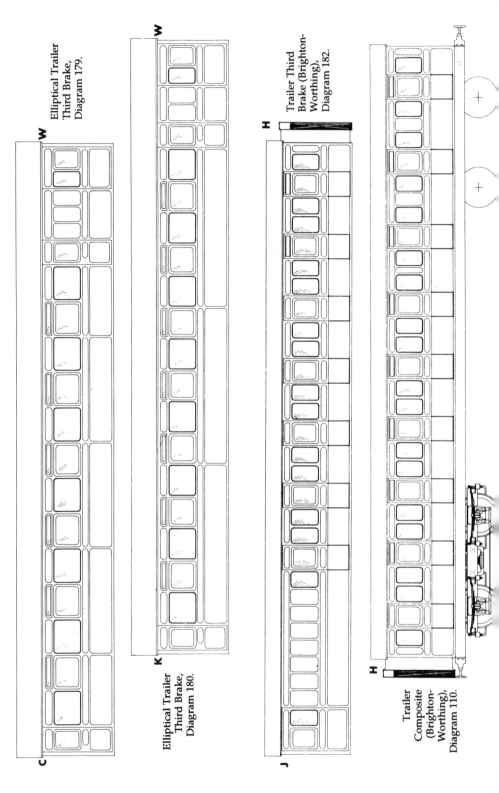

Elliptical Trailer Third Brake, Diagram 179.

Elliptical Trailer Third Brake, Diagram 180.

Trailer Third Brake (Brighton-Worthing), Diagram 182.

Trailer Composite (Brighton-Worthing), Diagram 110.

covered, and the following week the Bentley to Bordon branch saw the trial train. Further west, Set 754 and locomotive No. B234 did a tour of the Yeovil and Seaton branches during the last two weeks of January 1929. In March 1929 the Rolling Stock Committee recommended that the compressed-air regulator control be fitted on ex-LSW and ex-SEC locomotives and that both the wire and rod systems be abolished. The LB&SC system had won the day!

Some of the LB&SC push-and-pull sets were semi-permanently allocated to the Eastern Section, and some later types even went on to the Western. Set 755 was noted working the Sevenoaks-Swanley Junction service in November 1930, though in August that year Set 751 was based at Eastbourne, 753 at Brighton, 752/56 at Horsham and 754 at Tunbridge Wells West.

The braking system was changed from Westinghouse to vacuum on the following dates: December 1929 - Sets 757/58; January 1930 - Sets 752/53/56/60; February 1930 - Sets 755/59; and March 1930 Set 751. To facilitate coupling up all the various hoses used in connection with air-control apparatus, they were colour-coded. The regulator control hose pipe was blue, the main storage hose pipe was green, the back pressure hose pipe was yellow. In addition there was a cable with three-pin coupler containing the regulator indicator and bell wires for bell communication between the driving compartment and the locomotive.

Allocations of sets shown in the September 1931 Carriage Working Notice were:

751	Eastbourne.	756,757	Relief.
752	Horsham.	758	Sevenoaks, for Westerham branch.
753	Cranleigh.	759	Littlehampton.
754, 755	Tunbridge Wells West.		

Set 760 was disbanded on the withdrawal of its Third, No. 2048, in April 1931; Composite Brake No. 6936 became a loose trailer once again, although it now had no booked workings, being a spare vehicle. It was withdrawn in March 1936.

From late 1931 to early 1932 the eight-compartment Thirds were removed from the sets and withdrawn (see page 14), being replaced by 54 ft vehicles that had been built as A.C. driving trailer Composites - with four 1st-class and four 3rd-class compartments, or three 1st-class and five 3rd-class compartments - but since 1924 had run as steam-hauled Composites, the driver's compartment having been converted to a luggage compartment, still with windows in the end. Composites Nos. 6252-55/58/62/64 were altered to push-and-pull trailer Thirds Nos. 2186-90/91/92, whilst Composites Nos. 6268/69 (which had three Firsts and five Thirds) became all-Third trailers Nos. 2193/94 during spring 1932. Each seated 80 passengers, and the luggage compartment was retained. These Thirds were allocated to Sets 751-759 in the order 2194/92/91/89/88/86/90/87/93 between October 1931 and May 1932. Possibly at this time the driving ends of the Composite Brakes were given steel panels which covered the old wooden mouldings.

By 1935 seven of the sets were working on the Eastern Section, only two still being allocated to the former LB&SCR. Set 758 had worked the Ford-Littlehampton branch for a time, before going to the Eastern Section.

751	Gillingham (Relief).	755	Relief, Eastern.
752	Horsham.	756	Paddock Wood.
753	Cranleigh.	757-59	Gillingham.
754	Ashford.		

Sets 751, 752 and 754 were withdrawn before the decade was out, and Set 756 went in 1944. The remaining five sets, however, outlasted their fellows by several years, not being scrapped until the late 1950s.

Allocations in 1941 were shown as 753 - Central, and 755 to 759 - Eastern; by 1944 all save Set 755 were back on the Central. From then until withdrawal the allocations remained constant, Set 755 being on the Eastern Section, usually based at Ashford for Hastings or New Romney services, and Sets 753/57-59 being on the Central Section. Set 759 was withdrawn in July 1954; Composite Brake No. 6935 was broken up and Third No. 2193 was sent to push-and-pull set No. 37 in replacement of ex-L&SW Third No. 608. This change failed to be notified to the printers of the London Central/London East Appendix to Carriage Working Notices, and so the June 1955 issue of this still showed Set 759 with its original coaches; the correction was made in the June 1956 issue, almost two years late!

TRAILER COMPOSITE BRAKES (DIAGRAM No. 109)

No.	Old No.	Built	Rebuilt	SR No.	Re-No.	Set No.	Wdn
630	433	1895	12.09	6927	12.25	751	12.39
631	508	1892	12.09	6928	3.27	752	12.39
632	524	1891	12.09	6929	3.26	753	4.59
633	498	1894	12.09	6930	12.25	754	1.38

TRAILER COMPOSITE BRAKES (DIAGRAM No. 111)

No.	Old No.	Built	Rebuilt	SR No.	Re-No.	Set No.	Wdn
634	406	1893	12.09	6931	4.26	755	12.58
635	464	1896	12.09	6932	12.25	756	7.44
636	381	12.94	6.11	6933	4.24	757	8.59
637	511	6.92	6.11	6934	1.26	758	8.58
638	1170	6.95	6.11	6935	1.26	759	7.54
639	1188	6.95	6.11	6936	2.27	760, L	3.36

Note. Five-compartment Thirds Nos. 1170 and 1188 were originally built by the Lancaster Railway Carriage & Wagon Co.

TRAILER THIRD BRAKES

Nos. 1343 to 1346 (SR Nos. 3825 to 3828)

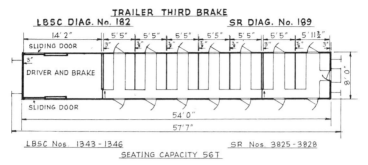

LBSC Nos. 1343-1346   SR Nos. 3825-3828

SEATING CAPACITY 56 T

Body length: 54 ft. Body width: 8 ft (7 ft 6 in. over sliding doors). Bogie centres: 37 ft. Compartments: Seven, of which six were 5 ft 5 in. and one was 5 ft 11¾ in. between partitions. Driver and brake compartment. Seats: 56. Tare weight: 25 tons approximately. Gangway at non-driving end. Diagram No. 182 (SR No. 189). Built 1911.

TRAILER COMPOSITES

Nos. 640 to 643 (SR Nos. 6201 to 6204)

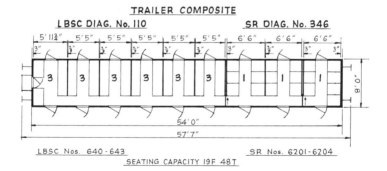

LBSC Nos. 640-643   SR Nos. 6201-6204

SEATING CAPACITY 19F 48T

Body length: 54 ft. Body width: 8 ft. Bogie centres: 37 ft.
Compartments: Three 1st class (6 ft 6 in. between partitions) and six 3rd class, of which five were 5 ft 5 in. and one was 5 ft 11¾ in. between partitions. Seats: 19 1st and 48 3rd class. Tare weight: 23 tons approximately. Gangway at 3rd-class end only. Diagram No. 110 (SR No. 346). Built 1911.

Four entirely new two-coach push-and-pull sets were built at Lancing during the half-year ending December 1911 and sent into traffic on Brighton to West

Worthing services to supplement the 'Balloon' trailers. They were a mixture of the archaic, with their narrow width, low height and arc roofs, and the innovative, with their side corridors that lacked partitions, and the gangways that connected the two coaches. The corridors and gangways were more for the benefit of the guard, who sold tickets to passengers joining at the halts, than for the benefit of the passengers; there were no lavatories but at least passengers could search for seats while the train was in motion. Smoking and non-smoking compartments for both classes were divided by sliding doors in the side corridors. At the driving end was a large compartment occupied by driver, guard and luggage; access was by means of a sliding door each side, as on the earlier motor cars.

Electric lighting was provided, with batteries and dynamo on the 3rd Brake only, supplying both cars. Spencer-Moulton heavy self-contained buffers were fitted. Although the sets were semi-permanently coupled, and because of the lighting arrangements could not be divided when in traffic, no set numbers were carried in LB&SC days.

All four units remained on Brighton-West Worthing services until about 1918. By 1921 Nos. 1343/640 and 1345/642 only were still performing these duties, whilst Nos. 1344/641 and 1346/643 had been transferred to West Croydon for Sutton/Epsom Downs and Wimbledon services respectively.

From 1924 the Southern Railway numbered the sets 995 to 998, in numerical order, the carriage numbers being altered at overhaul to 3825-28 for Third Brakes and 6201-04 for Composites. Westinghouse air brakes were replaced by automatic vacuum brakes (the air-control system being retained) on Sets 995/97 in February 1930, 998 in March 1930 and 996 in April 1930. Set 998 was still working the West Croydon to Wimbledon backwater in June 1929, and Sets 995/97 were still based at Brighton in August 1930. After electrification of the West Croydon to Wimbledon line in July 1930 Set 998 was transferred back to Brighton, where it continued to be based until about 1936; Set 996 was at Eastbourne by September 1931 but had gone to Brighton by 1935, replacing Set 997 which was now to be found at Littlehampton. Set 995 was allocated to Brighton throughout this whole period.

In 1936/7 Sets 995 to 998 were renumbered 728 to 731; this was to clear the higher steam set numbers for additional electric trailer sets and it also grouped all the ex-LB&SC push-and-pull sets in a range now running from 714 to 759.

Set 731 did not bear this number for very long. In April 1938 it was adapted for use in the Isle of Wight and renumbered 503; the Third Brake was renumbered from 3828 to 4169 and the Composite from 6204 to 6367. The sliding doors were replaced by a pair of swing doors each side, and the driver was provided with a droplight at each corner. Westinghouse braking was reinstated and the set was shipped across in May 1938, being put to work on the Ventnor West branch. In May 1947 Set 728 was similarly adapted, being renumbered 505, with Third Brake No. 3825 altered to 4167 and Composite No. 6201 altered to 6366. This set was sent over to work the Brading to Bembridge branch line.

After the closure of the Merstone to Ventnor West line in September 1952, and of the Bembridge branch in September 1953, there was very little work for these two Island push-and-pull sets and so both were withdrawn in May 1954. It does not appear that either was sent back to the mainland for further use and presumably both were broken up on the Isle of Wight.

Meanwhile the two sets that remained on the mainland outlasted their Island fellows by some years. The 1939 allocations were: 729 - Relief on Eastern Section. 730 - Eastbourne. From 1941 until withdrawal both sets were allocated continuously to the Central Section, as was Set 728 until its transfer to the Isle of Wight; it had worked the Hayling Island branch during 1939. On 29th June, 1946, Set 730 was on the 2.02 pm Tunbridge Wells West to Lewes, hauled by 'J1' class 4-6-2 tank locomotive No 2325. In the 1950s Set 730 wore BR's red livery, with coach numbers on the waist at the left-hand end of the body.

TRAILER THIRD BRAKES (DIAGRAM No. 182)

No.	Built	SR No.	Re-No.	Set No.	IOW No.	Set No.	Wdn
1343	12.11	3825	9.26	995, 728	4167	505	5.54
1344	12.11	3826	1.26	996, 729	-		6.60
1345	12.11	3827	9.24	997, 730	-		9.59
1346	12.11	3828	11.27	998, 731	4169	503	5.54

TRAILER COMPOSITES (DIAGRAM No. 110)

No.	Built	SR No.	Re-No.	Set No.	IOW No.	Set No.	Wdn
640	12.11	6201	9.26	995, 728	6366	505	5.54
641	12.11	6202	1.26	996, 729	-		6.60
642	12.11	6203	9.24	997, 730	-		9.59
643	12.11	6204	11.27	998, 731	6367	503	5.54

Sets 729 and 730 were both cut up at Newhaven.

TRAILER THIRD BRAKES

Nos. 1325, 1347-50 (SR Nos. 3820 to 3824)

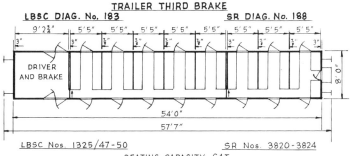

Body length: 54 ft Body width: 8 ft. Bogie centres: 37 ft.
Compartments: Eight (5 ft 5 in. between partitions). Driver and brake compartment.
Seats: 64. Tare weight: 25 tons approximately.
Diagram No. 183 (SR No. 188). Built 1912 and 1914.

TRAILER COMPOSITE

No. 644 (SR No. 6236)

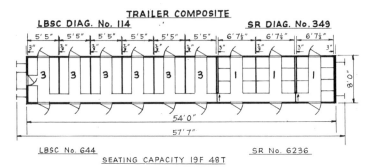

SEATING CAPACITY 19F 48T

Body length: 54 ft. Body width: 8 ft. Bogie centres: 37 ft.
Compartments: Three 1st class (6 ft 7½ in. between partitions) and six 3rd class (5 ft 5 in. between partitions). Seats: 19 1st and 48 3rd class. Tare weight: 25 tons approximately. Gangway at 3rd-class end only.
Diagram No. 114 (SR No. 349). Built 1914.

In 1912 the two steamcars were withdrawn from the Eastbourne-Hastings line and replaced by four new push-and-pull Third Brakes, Nos. 1347 to 1350, which ran either singly or coupled in pairs.

These Third Brakes differed from the previous ones in having eight compartments instead of seven, and ordinary swing doors on each side of the guard's compartment instead of sliding doors. Like them, they had 'open' side corridors without partitions, and a sliding door in the corridor separated the inner three compartments from the five nearest the driving end. Originally the driving end had two small windows, one at each corner. Sometime after 1924 these were replaced by the standard four-window layout. The driver also had the use of a droplight each side, right by the body corner.

Two years later another push-and-pull set, this time with first-class accommodation, was built to supplement the Chichester to Portsmouth local service. This unit was formed with Third Brake No. 1325, to the same design as the 1912 vehicles, and Composite No. 644, which had a similar layout to Nos. 640-43 of 1911 but with larger first-class compartments and all the 'Thirds' the same width. This coach had three sliding doors in the 'open' corridor, dividing the third class into groups of three and the first class into groups of one and two compartments. The position of these sliding doors could be judged from the outside as the partitions at these points were three inches thick, resulting in the quarter-lights being spaced slightly further apart. The trailer Composite was wired for electric lighting, the current being supplied from the dynamo of the adjacent Third Brake.

Nos. 1347-50 were still allocated to Eastbourne-St Leonards duties and Nos. 1325/644 to Chichester-Portsmouth workings in 1921. A year later ten trailer

Composites were constructed (Diagram No. 120, see later) and, of these, four - Nos. 652-55 - were formed with the four Third Brakes of 1912 to make semi-permanent two-car sets.

The new Composites were not paired in numerical order with the Third Brakes, and when the Southern came to number the sets 991 to 994 these numbers were not in order either. Repainting in green livery was carried out at Lancing between 1925 and 1927. The 1914-built set took the number 999 and acquired SR colours in December 1924.

Vacuum braking replaced air on Sets 994 in December 1929, 993/99 in February 1930, 992 in March 1930 and 991 in May 1930. Air-control was retained, a pump on the locomotive supplying the compressed air.

Allocations of sets in 1930/1 were: 991 - Chichester, for Portsmouth local services. 992 - Hastings. 993 - Horsham. 994 - Eastbourne. 999 - Portsmouth & Southsea. In August 1932 Set 993 was observed working the Hastings to Rye local service.

By 1935 Set 992 had moved to Seaford, for local working in the Lewes area; 993 was a relief set allocated to the Eastern Section; Set 994 had moved to Littlehampton; 991 and 999 were unchanged.

Sets 991-94 were renumbered 724-27 in 1937, while No. 999, which for a time had been given the number 980 as its old number was required for an electric trailer set, became Set 504. This was well away from the normal sequence, and it is thought the set may have been intended for transfer to the Isle of Wight along with No. 503 in 1938; but it never went.

From 1939 the allocations of Sets 724 to 727 were shown as: 724 - Relief set, Eastern Section. 725 - St Leonards. 726 - Hastings. 727 - Hayling Island branch. Push-and-pull working on this line seems to have been fairly short-lived. From about 1944 the nominal allocations of Nos. 724-26 to the Eastern and No. 727 to the Central Sections never changed until the sets were withdrawn. Set 504 was nominally Eastern Section but appeared on the Central from time to time.

First set to be withdrawn was No. 724, in April 1953. The Third Brake, No. 3823, lost its gangway connection and became a loose coach on the Midhurst branch until closure in February 1955; the vehicle then went to the Eastern Section, then the Central in 1957 until its withdrawal in 1960. It was cut up at Newhaven. Set 725 was withdrawn complete in December 1956. Set 726 was withdrawn in July 1957, but its Third Brake, No. 3821, also survived as a loose coach, first on the Eastern Section then on the Western until withdrawal in October 1959. Set 504 went in September 1958 and finally Set 727 was taken out of service at the beginning of 1959.

No. 3820, from Set 504, was temporarily reinstated for crew training on the Kent Coast line until June 1959.

TRAILER THIRD BRAKES (DIAGRAM No. 183)

No.	Built	SR No.	Re-No.	Set No.	Wdn
1325	12.14	3820	12.24	999, 980, 504	10.58
1347	12.12	3821	6.26	993, 726, L	10.59
1348	12.12	3822	4.26	992, 725	12.56
1349	12.12	3823	2.27	991, 724, L	12.60
1350	12.12	3824	4.25	994, 727	1.59

TRAILER COMPOSITE (DIAGRAM No. 114)

No.	Built	SR No.	Re-No.	Set No.	Wdn
644	12.14	6236	12.24	999, 980, 504	9.58

TRAILER THIRD BRAKES

Nos. 1401 to 1404 (SR Nos. 3846 to 3849)

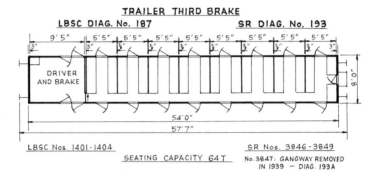

Body length: 54 ft. Body width: 8 ft. Bogie centres: 37 ft.
Compartments: Eight (5 ft 5 in. between partitions). Driver and brake compartment.
Seats: 64. Tare weight: 24 tons approximately. Gangway at non-driving end.
Diagram No. 187 (SR No. 193). Built 1921.

TRAILER COMPOSITES

Nos. 645 to 648 (SR Nos. 6237 to 6240)

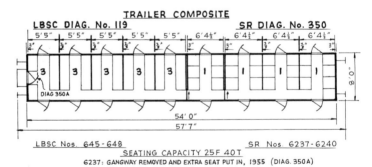

Body length: 54 ft. Body width: 8 ft. Bogie centres: 37 ft. Compartments: Four 1st class
(6 ft 4½ in. between partitions) and five 3rd class (5 ft 5 in. between partitions).
Seats: 25 1st and 40 3rd class. Tare weight: 25 tons approximately. Gangway at 3rd-
class end only.
Diagram No. 119 (SR No. 350). Built 1921.

In 1921, after a seven-year hiatus, four more bogie Composite trailer cars and four bogie Third Brake trailer cars were authorised to be built at Lancing Works and these - Nos. 645-48 and 1401-04 - were duly turned out by December of that year. They showed no advance in design over the pre-War cars: still with the same overall dimensions, still the same arc roof, still the same 'open' side corridors. The chief difference was in the proportion of 1st-class accommodation, there now being four such compartments, of which the one nearest the centre was for non-smokers and was protected from both the adjacent 1st- and 3rd-class compartments by two sliding doors in the corridor. The eight-compartment Third Brakes were not quite the same as the 1912-built ones for there was no sliding door in the corridor and therefore no extra-thick partition. The drive-end had the now-standard window arrangement with four windows grouped in twos, each one being 3 ft high by 1 ft 4 in. wide. The driver had the use of a droplight each side, and entry to the combined guard's/luggage/driver's compartment was by double doors (one of which opened inwards) each side. Spencer-Moulton self-contained buffers were fitted as standard. Electric lighting was supplied by a dynamo and batteries on the Third Brake, the Composite being electric-wired only; the sets were thus indivisible in traffic, but there were no set numbers until about 1924.

The four units, whose coaches were paired in numerical order, were given the numbers 981 to 984 by the SR and repainted in sage green at Lancing during 1927/8. The driving ends were given flush steel panels.

Vacuum braking replaced air braking on Sets 981/83 in January 1930, 984 in March and 982 in May 1930.

The 1928 allocations of Sets 981-84 are stated to have been Cranleigh, Seaford, Eastbourne and Tunbridge Wells West. Set 982 briefly worked on the West Croydon to Wimbledon line, but was back at Seaford by August 1930. At that time Set 981 was still working from Cranleigh and Set 983 from Eastbourne. By September 1931 Set 981 had moved to Brighton, Sets 982/83 were still at Seaford and Eastbourne, and Set 984 remained at Tunbridge Wells.

The January 1935 Carriage Working Notice indicated that Set 984 was still working from Tunbridge Wells West and Set 983 from Eastbourne, but Set 982 had now moved to join its fellow at the Sussex resort whilst No. 981 was now a relief set on the Eastern Section.

In the 1937 renumbering scheme Sets 981-984 became Nos. 714-717. A year later Composite No. 6238 was removed from Set 715 and replaced by a non-corridor ex-SE&C 50 ft Composite, No. 5298. The original Composite was rebuilt into a driving Brake Composite for use in the Isle of Wight. The two 1st-class compartments nearest the end were stripped, their place being taken by a driver's compartment with brake and luggage space; the usual arrangement of four windows was incorporated in the body end. The carriage was renumbered 6987 in the Island Composite Brake series and sent across in May 1938; a new diagram had to be issued, No. 439. It seems this coach was a spare, either working as a temporary replacement for the driving Third Brake in Set 503 or working as an extra coach in times of heavy traffic, or even working singly during the winter season. No. 6987, which seated 12 1st and 40 3rd class passengers in two 1st and five 3rd-class compartments, lasted in the Isle of

Wight until December 1955.

The reformed Set 715 worked briefly on Horsham to Dorking local trains until electrification in July 1938; later it was allocated to the Hawkhurst branch. Sets 714/16 also were on the Eastern Section by July 1939, based at New Romney and Hythe respectively, but Set 717 was still at Tunbridge Wells. However, by 1941 it too had moved to the Eastern Section and the allocation was now: 714 - Ashford and Hastings. 715 - St Leonards and Rye. 716 and 717 - Bexhill West branch. From then until withdrawal all four sets remained on the Eastern Section, at least nominally; temporary exchanges no doubt occurred from time to time.

In 1944 Third Brake No. 3846 was removed from Set 714, its place being taken by ex-SE&C Third Brake No. 3467. No. 3846 ran as a single coach on the Pulborough-Midhurst-Petersfield service until final withdrawal in May 1948. In 1952 Set 715 also lost its 'Brighton' Third Brake, No. 3847, which was replaced by another ex-SE&C Third Brake, No. 3475; consequently this set now had two ex-SE&C vehicles, which it retained until February 1961. No. 3847 worked on the Midhurst branch between 1952 and February 1955, then went to the Eastern Section and, in 1957, the Central Section. Its gangway connection had been removed in 1939. Until March 1958, No. 3847 was the regular coach on the four-trains-a-day Lewes and East Grinstead service. Even when this ceased the coach was not finished, being retained as a spare until August 1960.

Another trailer to have its gangway removed was Composite No. 6237, in about 1955; an extra 3rd-class seat was built across the aisle. During October 1957 Set 716 worked on the Brighton to Horsham line, but Set 717 had strayed even further afield in July 1949 when it was observed on the Bisley branch.

Sets 716 and 717 were withdrawn intact in September 1960 and July 1959 respectively. The very last ex-LB&SC push-and-pull trailer in traffic, No. 6237, was withdrawn in July 1961 along with its partner, the ex-SE&C Third Brake in Set 714. After withdrawal No. 6237 was sent in spring 1962 to join the long line of condemned carriages standing on one road of the Ardingly branch, and came within an ace of being preserved by the nearby Bluebell Railway, having actually been promised by BR. However in October 1962 it was sent to Newhaven, supposedly to be prepared for the Bluebell but actually for breaking up. It was still in the red livery employed by BR for local trains between 1949 and 1956.

Because of its association with the Lewes-East Grinstead line, Third Brake No. 3847 was considered for purchase by the newly-opened Bluebell Railway in the summer of 1960, but unfortunately before anything could be done the coach was sent from Lancing to Newhaven for scrapping, which occurred in September 1960.

TRAILER THIRD BRAKES (DIAGRAM No. 187)

No.	Built	SR No.	Re-No.	Set No.	IOW No.	Wdn
1401	12.21	3846	7.27	981, 714, L		5.48
1402	12.21	3847	2.27	982, 715, L		8.60
1403	12.21	3848	2.28	983, 716		9.60
1404	12.21	3849	5.27	984, 717		7.59

TRAILER COMPOSITES (DIAGRAM No. 119)

No.	Built	SR No.	Re-No.	Set No.	IOW No.	Wdn
645	12.21	6237	7.27	981, 714		7.61
646	12.21	6238	2.27	982, 715	6987, 5.38	9.55
647	12.21	6239	2.28	983, 716		10.60
648	12.21	6240	5.27	984, 717		7.59

Set 716 was cut up at Newhaven.

TRAILER THIRD BRAKES

Nos. 1405 to 1410 (SR Nos. 3850 to 3855)

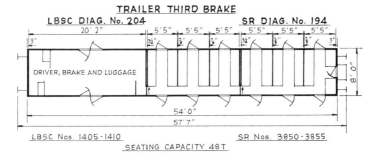

TRAILER THIRD BRAKE
LBSC DIAG. No. 204   SR DIAG. No. 194
LBSC Nos. 1405-1410   SR Nos. 3850-3855
SEATING CAPACITY 48 T

Body length: 54 ft. Body width: 8 ft. Bogie centres: 37 ft.
Compartments: Six (5 ft 5 in. between partitions). Driver and brake compartment.
Seats: 48. Tare weight: 24 or 25 tons. Gangway at non-driving end.
Diagram No. 204 (SR No. 194). Built 1922.

TRAILER COMPOSITES

Nos. 649 to 658 (SR Nos. 6241 to 6250)

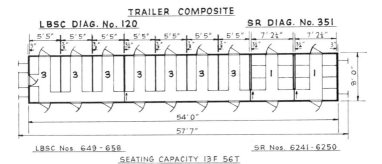

TRAILER COMPOSITE
LBSC DIAG. No. 120   SR DIAG. No. 351
LBSC Nos. 649 - 658   SR Nos. 6241- 6250
SEATING CAPACITY 13 F 56 T

Body length: 54 ft. Body width: 8 ft. Bogie centres: 37 ft.
Compartments: Two 1st class (7 ft 2½ in. between partitions) and seven 3rd class (5 ft 5 in. between partitions). Seats: 13 1st and 56 3rd class. Tare weight: 25 or 26 tons. Gangway at 3rd-class end only.
Diagram No. 120 (SR No. 351). Built 1922.

These push-and-pull trailers were the last to be built by the LB&SCR and comprised six sets plus four additional Composites to go with the Third Brakes built in 1912. Like the earlier ones these coaches had 'open' side corridors to enable the guard to sell tickets, and the Composites were electrically wired for lighting, only the Third Brakes having a dynamo and batteries. In these vehicles the number of passenger compartments was reduced to six to allow for a larger luggage compartment, and in the Composites only two 1st-class compartments were provided, although they were much wider than those in the earlier vehicles.

Three sets were built at Lancing on capital account in the first half of 1922; the underframes were second-hand, having been taken from Ambulance Train carriages, and did not have Spencer-Moulton self-contained buffers. The sets comprised Third Brakes 1405-07 and Composites 649-51. Three more sets, plus four Composites, were ordered in July 1922 and built at Lancing on renewals account; all these had new underframes with self-contained buffers. Composites 652-55 were paired, not in numerical order, with Third Brakes 1347-50 (Diagram No. 183 of 1912), and the final three sets comprised Third Brakes 1408-10 and Composites 656-58, all completed during the second half of 1922.

A sliding door in the corridor of the Third Brakes marked the point of division of the compartments into non-smoking and smoking (three each), and three sliding doors in the Composites divided the accommodation into three 3rd-class non-smoking, four 3rd-class smoking, one 1st-class non-smoking and one 1st-class smoking. Until external doors started to be swapped around in later years one could identify the respective accommodation by the style of door ventilator, which was either ribbed or flat steel.

On 5th July, 1923, the push-and-pull set comprising Third Brake No. 1410 and Composite No. 658 was derailed between Culver Junction (near Lewes) and Barcombe Mills station because of track distortion caused by the intense heat on that summer's day. The train, worked by 'D1' class 0-4-2 tank locomotive No. 253, was the 4.27 pm Brighton to Tunbridge Wells and it was entirely derailed. Only minor injuries were caused, and passengers were soon able to continue their northward journeys by using the stock of the 3.45 pm from Victoria, which was turned short at Barcombe Mills. The push-and-pull set was not badly damaged.

The six sets were numbered 985-90 from about 1924; No. 985 was repainted in SR livery in 1925, and the other five in 1927. Westinghouse brake gear was replaced by vacuum on Set 989 in November 1929, Sets 985/87 in March 1930, 986/88 in May 1930 and Set 990 in June 1930.

During August 1930 Set 985 was working from Bognor, 986 from Tunbridge Wells West, 987 from Horsham, 989 from Brighton and 990 from Eastbourne. The September 1931 allocations were similar except that Set 986 was now at Brighton; in addition, Set 988 was based at Littlehampton. By late 1934 Set 985 had moved to Horsham, 986 to Hastings, 987 to Tunbridge Wells West, 989 to Haywards Heath and 990 to Hastings. Set 988 was still working from Littlehampton.

Some of the ex-Ambulance underframes must have been getting a bit tired, for in October 1931 that of No. 6243 was replaced by a frame taken from

Composite No. 6184, and in December 1936 that of No. 6241 was replaced by the frame of Third No. 2183. It is stated that the Third Brake of Set 985 also received a replacement underframe.

In 1936/7 the six sets were renumbered 718 to 723 in the same order as the old numbers. In mid July 1939 they were berthed at a wide range of places: Ashford (Set 719), Brighton (Set 718), Tunbridge Wells West (Set 720) and Seaton (Set 723). Sets 721/22 were kept on the Eastern Section as reliefs to others working there. Set 723 was scheduled to work the Seaton branch in Devon, many miles from home, for over a decade from about 1938 until April or May 1949. Nominal allocations in May 1941 were: 718/20, Central Section and 719/21/22, Eastern Section.

Set No. 718, working the Horsham-Guildford line on 16th December, 1942, was shot up by an enemy aircraft and very badly damaged near Bramley & Wonersh. Seven passengers were killed. It was the corridor side of the train that received most damage, which was sufficiently severe to cause the withdrawal of the whole set. After this, the allocations of Sets 719-22 remained fairly constant: the first three being on the Central and Set 722 on the Eastern. Set 720, which had ex-Ambulance underframes, was withdrawn in 1948, and the other set with old frames, No. 719, managed to remain in traffic until late 1957.

Set 723 finished its exile on the Seaton branch in 1949 and was transferred to Eastern Section workings until 1959, when it officially returned to the Central. By the mid-1950s the bodywork of both Sets 721 and 722 had been covered with steel sheets in an attempt to 'modernise' them, but it seems doubtful that any passengers were fooled. Set 719 appeared in BR's red livery, lined yellow and black along the waist mouldings, and with coach numbers in the left-hand position, in 1950. Set 721 still had left-hand numerals in 1957, although revarnished green by then.

TRAILER THIRD BRAKES (DIAGRAM No. 204)

No.	Built	SR No.	Re-No.	Set No.	Wdn
1405	6.22	3850	2.25	985, 718	12.42
1406	6.22	3851	12.27	986, 719	11.57
1407	6.22	3852	1.27	987, 720	4.48
1408	12.22	3853	3.27	988, 721	5.58
1409	12.22	3854	7.27	989, 722	1.59
1410	12.22	3855	1.27	990, 723	10.60

TRAILER COMPOSITES (DIAGRAM No. 120)

No.	Built	SR No.	Re-No.	Set No.	Wdn
649	6.22	6241	2.25	985, 718	12.42
650	6.22	6242	12.27	986, 719	11.57
651	6.22	6243	1.27	987, 720	4.48
652	12.22	6244	4.26	992, 725	12.56
653	12.22	6245	6.26	993, 726	6.57
654	12.22	6246	4.25	994, 727	1.59
655	12.22	6247	2.27	991, 724	4.53
656	12.22	6248	3.27	988, 721	5.58
657	12.22	6249	7.27	989, 722	1.59
658	12.22	6250	1.27	990, 723	9.60

Sets 721 and 723 were cut up at Newhaven.

Chapter Ten

Electrification

In July 1903 the LB&SCR obtained an Act of Parliament that gave powers to electrify parts of its system. Electrification was seen as a way of working the traffic more efficiently, and of arresting a decline in the number of passengers. This decline was a result of a depressed economy, movement of the population, and bad weather; later, tramway competition also began to eat into the receipts.

After careful consideration a single-phase alternating current system of 6,700 volts using overhead wire contact was chosen. After Philip Dawson, the consulting electrical engineer, had presented his report recommending this system in July 1904, tenders were invited for electrification of the South London line between Battersea Park and Peckham Rye. Later this was altered to take in the whole route between Victoria and London Bridge. The Allgemeine Elektricitäts Gesellschaft of Berlin contracted to electrify the line, and sub-contracted R.W. Blackwell & Co. of Westminster to supply the lineside gantries and wiring. The Metropolitan Amalgamated Railway Carriage & Wagon Co. of Birmingham was contracted to build the rolling stock.

Power was supplied from a substation at Peckham Rye to the contact lines, which were supported by twin catenaries slung from gantries spanning both tracks. Whilst the overhead equipment was not exactly elegant it did at least mean that the railway track was kept clear of live rails, always a danger to men working there. The contact line was suspended at a normal height of 16 ft above rail level, at 19 ft 6 in. at Victoria and London Bridge stations, and at 13 ft 9 in. under low bridges; at these points there were 'dead' sections. New car sheds and repair shops were built at Peckham Rye in the 'vee' where the line from Streatham and Tulse Hill joined the South London line.

On 17th January, 1909, an electric train gave a first demonstration run between Battersea Park and East Brixton. Public services between Victoria and London Bridge began on 1st December, 1909; there were about four trains per hour, the through journey time being 24 minutes, each train doing the round trip once an hour.

Of the South London line stations, only Wandsworth Road, Clapham, Denmark Hill and Queens Road Peckham were adjacent to tram routes that gave direct communication to Victoria in competition with the LB&SCR trains. Battersea Park, East Brixton, Peckham Rye and South Bermondsey stations were not served by tram routes to Victoria and no station on the line was anywhere near a tram route serving London Bridge. Clearly in this area the South London line had a virtual monopoly. Electrification was a success, and the number of passengers rose from four million in 1909 to 7,500,000 in 1910.

Encouraged by the results of electrification, the 'Brighton' in July 1910 decided to electrify the lines from Victoria to Crystal Palace and from Peckham Rye to Crystal Palace, using the same contractors for the works (AEG). The overhead equipment was of lighter construction than that used on the pioneer scheme. Victoria to Crystal Palace electric services began on 12th May, 1911 (full services from 1st June), the wiring being carried on to Selhurst via

168

Norwood Junction. On 3rd March, 1912, partial services began running between Peckham Rye and Tulse Hill (prematurely because of a coalminers' strike) and the full service London Bridge-Crystal Palace, plus the spur connecting Tulse Hill with Streatham Hill on the Victoria-Crystal Palace route, began on 1st June, 1912. There was no regular electric service between Crystal Palace and Selhurst, where an electrical depot was set up, but trains running into service from the depot and out of service to the depot were advertised between Crystal Palace and Norwood Junction. Victoria-Crystal Palace trains ran about every 15 minutes, and London Bridge-Crystal Palace trains about every 20 minutes, with extras at odd intervals. London Bridge to Victoria trains via Tulse Hill and Streatham Hill ran about hourly in slack times and about twice-hourly at other times. The LB&SCR was not a great believer in strict regular-interval timetables, though the Sunday services came very close to the principle. On Sundays Victoria-Crystal Palace trains ran every 30 minutes, London Bridge-Crystal Palace was every hour, Victoria-Streatham Hill-Tulse Hill-London Bridge about every two hours, and the South London line every 30 minutes.

In 1913 a decision was made to electrify several more suburban lines and contracts were placed for overhead equipment and rolling stock. Unfortunately World War I prevented much work from being completed, and AEG could no longer be used to supply electrical equipment. However, by 1914 the overhead had been erected from Balham to Selhurst and West Croydon and from Tulse Hill to Streatham Common. The contracts later had to be cancelled, although Lancing Works did continue construction of trailers against the day when work on electrification could be resumed. It was now planned to extend the wiring from West Croydon to Wallington (and later to Sutton) and from Selhurst through East Croydon to Coulsdon & Smitham Downs. In February 1922 the tender of the General Electric Co. for traction equipment was accepted and in July Blackwell & Co. were ordered to start work on the overhead equipment for the extensions.

With Grouping imminent the Brighton Board decided not to proceed with any further electrification schemes; it was merely a matter of completing the ones that had been started before the War. New stock for the 'Coulsdon/Wallington' extensions was ordered, and this was delivered in late 1923/early 1924. Trial runs began on 11th March, 1925, and public services were inaugurated between Victoria and Coulsdon North (formerly Coulsdon & Smitham Downs), and Victoria and Sutton (both via Streatham Common), on 1st April, 1925.

The Southern Railway Board, although keen on extending electrification, was determined to use the low-voltage direct current third-rail system by which much of the London & South Western suburban network had already been electrified, and it was not going to tolerate two different systems on its railway. The third rail apparently could be installed much more quickly than could overhead equipment, and the A.C. motors then in use were less powerful than, and gave inferior acceleration to, the D.C. motors. Even so, many people must have been shocked when, in August 1926, the Southern announced its intention of dismantling all the A.C. equipment and replacing it with third rail. The overhead between Tulse Hill and Streatham Junction (apparently never used for regular services) was dismantled in 1927. From 17th June, 1928, the South London line, the London Bridge-Streatham Hill and the London Bridge-Crystal Palace services went over to D.C. operation. From 3rd March, 1929, the Victoria-Crystal Palace and Victoria-Streatham Hill services were replaced by D.C. trains, and the Coulsdon/Sutton routes succumbed on 22nd September, 1929, the last A.C. train being the 12.10 am Victoria to Coulsdon North.

The lineside equipment was removed between 1930 and 1932, save for a few switchcabins used as platelayers' huts, and some gantries which were used to support signals. Noteworthy was a large cantilever gantry near Pouparts Junction (between Battersea Park and Clapham Junction) which was retained for many years.

SOUTH LONDON LINE STOCK 'SL'

MOTOR THIRD BRAKES

Nos. 3201/03/04/06/07/09/10/12/13/15/16/18/19/21/22/24 (SR Nos. 8601-16)

Body length : 60 ft. Body width: 9 ft. Bogie centres: 41 ft.
Compartments: Eight (6 ft between partitions). 'Open' side corridor. Driver and guard's compartment. Seats: 66, or 82 in 'crush' conditions. Tare weight: 54 tons.
Diagram No. 280 (SR No. 677). Built 1909.

TRAILER FIRSTS

Nos. 3202/05/08/11/14/17/20/23 (SR Nos. 7644-51)

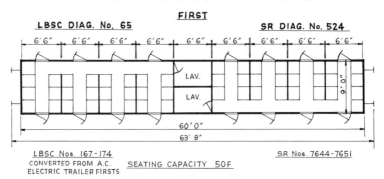

Body length: 60 ft. Body width: 9 ft. Bogie centres: 41 ft.
Compartments: Nine (6 ft 6 in. between partitions). 'Open' side corridor. Seats: 56, or 74 in 'crush' conditions. Tare weight: 30 tons.
Diagram No. (as Lavatory First) 65. SR Diagram No. 524. Built 1909.

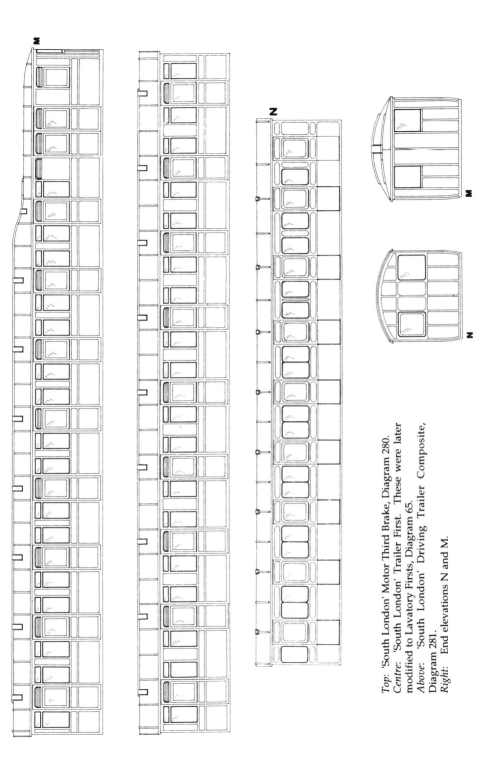

Top: 'South London' Motor Third Brake, Diagram 280.
Centre: 'South London' Trailer First. These were later modified to Lavatory Firsts, Diagram 65.
Above: 'South London' Driving Trailer Composite, Diagram 281.
Right: End elevations N and M.

DRIVING TRAILER COMPOSITES

Nos. 3225-30, 4057-60, 4065-68 (SR Nos. 9811-24)

Body length: 48 ft. Body width: 8 ft. Bogie centres : 32 ft.
Compartments: Two 1st class (6 ft between partitions) and six 3rd class (5 ft 2⅝ in.
between partitions). Driver's compartment. Seats: 16 1st, 60 3rd class.
Tare weight: 20 tons 8 cwt. Diagram No. 281 (SR No. 790). Rebuilt 1910, 1911 and 1912.

Designed jointly by Earle Marsh and Philip Dawson, the South London A.C.
electric stock, which was built by the Metropolitan Amalgamated Railway
Carriage & Wagon Co. of Saltley, Birmingham, was quite unlike any other
LB&SCR carriages in style. The bodies had square-cornered mouldings, and
above each quarter-light was a hinged, opening top-light. The bodies were
timber framed with side panels and roof coverings of aluminium; a feature of
the roofs of this and all subsequent A.C. stock was a series of transverse wood
strips, supposedly to protect the carriages in the event of the overhead
equipment collapsing. In each of the S.L. cars the 'open' side corridor changed
sides at the mid-point; it was thus possible to walk through from one end of a
car to the other, but there were no gangways between the cars. In the Trailer
Firsts the corridor had a swing door at the dividing point of the smoking and
non-smoking compartments. The carriages were much more luxuriously
appointed than most other suburban stock of the period, but there was no
heating. The drive-end was slightly bowed and originally there was no
headcode panel. Bodyside livery was brown with white upper panels, and
upholstery was blue in the first-class and red and black in the thirds.

Each motor coach was powered by four 115 hp Winter-Eichberg motors, one
on each axle. At the drive-end there were two bow collectors, one for each
direction of travel, to the design of Philip Dawson. They were raised and
lowered by compressed air, and interlocked with the control gear. As all the
electrical equipment on the roof was 'live' it was soon enclosed in a protective
wire-mesh 'basket'. The high-tension current passed through cables to the
transformers on the underframe and was stepped down to 750 volts before
passing to the motors.

The cars had 8 ft-wheelbase bogies and the underframes, on both motors and
trailers, were distinguished by immensely strong-looking plate-frame trusses.
Height of the trains from rail to roof was 12 ft 2⅝ in. and the extreme width was
9 ft 5 in. over cornices. These generous dimensions meant that 'SL' stock was
effectively restricted to its own line, being prohibited from passing through
Crystal Palace and Leigham tunnels.

The 'SL' stock was delivered as three-car units, formed motor-trailer-motor,
each with a total seating capacity of 56 1st class and 132 3rd class. When
passenger services began in December 1909 the trains carried unit numbers 1E
to 8E. Each drive-end was fitted with two lamps and occluders on a pivot, to
enable either a white headlight or a red tail-light to be displayed.

Regrettably, the 'SL' trains had a very short life in their original form. The
proportion of first-class was found to be too high and that of the third class too
low, so that there was considerable overcrowding. The obvious course would
have been to downgrade perhaps six of the compartments in the Trailer Firsts

and leave the three-sets intact, but the Brighton preferred to do things the hard way. The trailers were removed altogether and the three-sets were reduced to two cars each by substituting a Driving Trailer Composite for one of the Motor Third Brakes. These driving trailers all had to be rebuilt from seven-compartment 'Bogie Block' Third Brakes; in each reconstruction six compartments were retained, two first-class compartments were added, plus a driver's compartment at what had been the brake end. For details of which carriages were involved, see page 40. Six were converted in 1910, the first two-car train running in October; four in 1911 and four more in 1912. By June 1912 all South London line trains now ran as two-car, four-car or six-car, each formation including one original Motor Brake Third and one converted Driving Trailer Composite. Visually, it was an appalling mismatch; the conversions were shorter, narrower and lower than the original cars and were painted plain brown; the compartments were of very mean dimensions and lacked side corridors; and the first-class compartments were stuck inconveniently at one end. The majestic motor cars looked as though they had been saddled with poor relations.

Although there were 16 motor coaches, only 14 driving trailers were converted, on the theory that, because trailers were out of traffic for less time in shops for maintenance than motors, fewer trailers were required. Non-permanent formations were henceforth employed and the use of unit numbers was abandoned, never to reappear on any A.C. stock.

The Trailer Firsts were stored, then in 1913 emerged as steam Lavatory Firsts Nos. 167 to 174. In each one the centre compartment was rebuilt as two lavatories, each with access from four compartments. The Lavatory Firsts then ran in London-Brighton mainline services, sharing the same route restrictions as the 'City Limited' stock. By 1921 Nos. 170/73 had been formed in Set 17 and Nos. 167/72 in Set 47.

South London line trains carried no route headcode until 1925, when the code 'SL' appeared in the centre panel between the driver's nearside and offside windows. SR numbers began to be applied in 1924 as each car visited Lancing Works, and all were renumbered there except Motor Third Brake No. 3204. All were withdrawn from service on 17th June, 1928, when the South London line began to be worked by three-car D.C. trains until May 1929. During April and May 1929 the 16 motor coaches were adapted and rebuilt as eight two-car D.C. units, Nos. 1901-08, for further service on the South London line. Half the motor coaches were retained as such, with one less compartment each and correspondingly larger luggage compartment, and were renumbered 8723-30. The other eight motor coaches were altered to Driving Trailer Composite Brakes, retaining eight compartments of which two were now 1st class. These vehicles were renumbered 9751-58. The drive-ends were altered to be more in line with standard SR electric ends, but the heavy plate-trussed underframes and the depressed areas on the roofs where the electrical equipment had been were retained. Only eight units were required because the South London service had suffered a reduction to three trains per hour in the peaks and only two per hour off-peak. Hence only six units were in traffic, leaving two spare. Headcode '2' was initiated for the South London line trains, the unit numbers of which became 1801-08 in April 1934.

Except for Unit 1807, which was destroyed by enemy action at Peckham Rye in 1940, the South London units continued to run on their old route until the early 1950s, when they were withdrawn, being replaced by British Railways standard 2-EPB units.

The 'SL' driving trailers that had been converted in 1910-12 from Third Brakes were all rebuilt by the SR in 1929 into Motor Third Brakes, on 62 ft underframes, with new cabs and luggage compartments grafted on to the original eight compartments. Eleven were renumbered 8686-96 at Ashford and formed, one per unit, into Units 1717-27. Three were rebuilt at Eastleigh for Units 1737-39: vehicle numbers 8706-08. All survived until the 1950s, three lasting until late 1959.

The original South London Trailer Firsts, running as steam Lavatory Firsts, received SR numbers 7644-51 in 1927/8 at Lancing, but were taken out of service about 1930. In June 1930 they were extensively rebuilt at Lancing. The lavatories were replaced by ordinary compartments. Four of the Firsts became Motor Composite Brakes with two 1st-class and four 3rd-class compartments, a driver's and guard's compartment replacing three compartments at one end. The other four Firsts became Driving Trailer Third Brakes with seven compartments, a driver's and luggage compartment replacing two compartments at the other end. These rebuilds were paired as four units, Nos. 1909-12, for working the Wimbledon-West Croydon line, three being needed for the maximum 20-minute service. Renumbered 1809-12 in April 1934, all continued in use until 1953/4, when they were replaced by BR 2-EPB units.

'SL' MOTOR THIRD BRAKES (DIAGRAM No. 280)

No.	Built	SR No.	Re-No.	DC No.	Re-No.	Unit Nos.		Wdn
3201	Metro 1909	8601	2.25	9751	5.29	1901	1801	10.54
3203	Metro 1909	8602	9.24	9752	4.29	1902	1802	6.51
3204	Metro 1909	-	-	9758	4.29	1908	1808	9.54
3206	Metro 1909	8604	4.24	8723	5.29	1901	1801	10.54
3207	Metro 1909	8605	12.25	9753	4.29	1903	1803	9.54
3209	Metro 1909	8606	8.27	8724	4.29	1902	1802	6.51
3210	Metro 1909	8607	10.25	9754	4.29	1904	1804	9.54
3212	Metro 1909	8608	6.25	8725	4.29	1903	1803	9.54
3213	Metro 1909	8609	3.26	9755	5.29	1905	1805	10.54
3215	Metro 1909	8610	6.26	8726	4.29	1904	1804	9.54
3216	Metro 1909	8611	1.27	9756	5.29	1906	1806	9.54
3218	Metro 1909	8612	11.24	9757	5.29	1907	1807	.40
3219	Metro 1909	8613	1.24	8727	5.29	1905	1805	10.54
3221	Metro 1909	8614	5.27	8728	5.29	1906	1806	9.54
3222	Metro 1909	8615	4.25	8729	5.29	1907	1807	.40
3224	Metro 1909	8616	7.24	8730	4.29	1908	1808	9.54

'SL' TRAILER FIRSTS

No.	Built	Re-No.	SR No.	Re-No.	DC No.	Re-No.	Unit Nos.		Wdn.
3202	Metro 6.09	167	7644	11.27	9819	6.30	1910	1810	10.54
3205	Metro 6.09	168	7645	3.28	9951	6.30	1909	1809	12.53
3208	Metro 6.09	169	7646	6.27	9952	6.30	1910	1810	10.54
3211	Metro 6.09	170	7647	2.28	9821	6.30	1912	1812	8.54
3214	Metro 6.09	171	7648	7.27	9953	6.30	1911	1811	10.54
3217	Metro 6.09	172	7649	11.27	9820	6.30	1911	1811	10.54
3220	Metro 12.09	173	7650	2.28	9954	6.30	1912	1812	8.54
3223	Metro 12.09	174	7651	8.27	9818	6.30	1909	1809	12.53

'SL' DRIVING TRAILER COMPOSITES (DIAGRAM No. 281)

No.	Built	SR No.	Re-No.	DC No.	Re-No.	Unit Nos.	Wdn
3225	Lancing 6.10	9811	12.25	8686	1.29	1717, 4566	7.55
3226	Lancing 6.10	9812	5.24	8696	6.29	1727, 4530	9.56
3227	Lancing 6.10	9813	10.25	8695	6.29	1726, 4529	8.56
3228	Lancing 6.10	9814	5.27	8691	2.29	1722, 4520	5.54
3229	Lancing 6.10	9815	1.27	8694	5.29	1725, 4528, 4515	11.59
3230	Lancing 6.10	9816	7.24	8688	2.29	1719, 4568	6.52
4057	Lancing 6.11	9817	8.27	8706	6.29	1737, 4537	8.55
4058	Lancing 6.11	9818	10.24	8707	6.29	1738, 4538, 4508	12.59
4059	Lancing 6.11	9819	1.24	8708	6.29	1739, 4539, 4512	11.59
4060	Lancing 6.11	9820	3.25	8689	2.29	1720, 4569, 4573	2.56
4065	Lancing 12.12	9821	12.24	8690	2.29	1721, 4570	8.51
4066	Lancing 12.12	9822	5.25	8692	2.29	1723, 4571	3.56
4067	Lancing 12.12	9823	3.26	8693	5.29	1724, 4527	7.56
4068	Lancing 12.12	9824	7.26	8687	1.29	1718, 4567	2.56

SR Alterations or Conversions: 'SL' Motor Third Brakes (SR Diagram No. 677) became Motor Third Brakes Nos. 8723-30 (Diagram No. 681) or Driving Trailer Composite Brakes Nos. 9751-58 (Diagram No. 793) at Lancing. Former 'SL' Trailer Firsts, running as steam Lavatory Firsts, were rebuilt to Motor Composite Brakes Nos. 9818-21 (Diagram No. 696) or Driving Trailer Third Brakes Nos. 9951-54 (Diagram No. 794) at Lancing and Brighton. 'SL' Driving Trailer Composites (SR Diagram No. 790) became Motor Third Brakes Nos. 8686-96 and 8706-08 (Diagram No. 675) at Ashford (first 11) and Eastleigh (last three).

CRYSTAL PALACE STOCK 'CP'

MOTOR THIRD BRAKES

Nos. 3231-3264 (SR Nos. 8567-8600)

Body length: 54 ft. Body width: 8 ft. Bogie centres: 37 ft.
Compartments: Seven (5 ft 11 in. between partitions).   Driver and guard's compartment. Seats: 70. Tare weight: 51 tons 6 cwt.
Diagram No. 282 (SR No. 676). Built 1911/2.

DRIVING TRAILER COMPOSITES

Nos. 4001-4056, 4061-64, 4069-76 (SR Nos. 9825-9892)

Body length: 54 ft. Body width: 8 ft. Bogie centres: 37 ft.
Compartments: Three 1st class (6 ft 6⅝ in. between partitions) and five 3rd class (5 ft 10¼ in. between partitions). Driver's compartment. Seats: 24 1st, 50 3rd class. Tare weight: 24 tons.
Diagram No. 283 (SR No. 791). Built 1911-13.

For the Crystal Palace electrification the Metropolitan Amalgamated Railway Carriage & Wagon Co. constructed in 1911 thirty motor coaches (Nos. 3231-60) and thirty driving trailers (Nos. 4001-30). Lancing Works built an additional 26 driving trailers (Nos. 4031-56) during 1911.

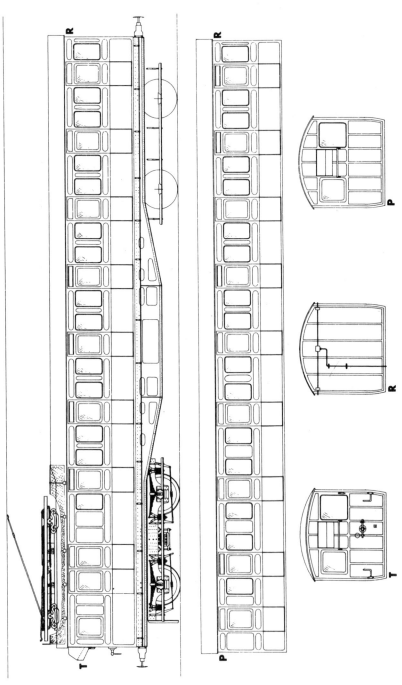

Top: 'Crystal Palace' Motor Third Brake, Diagram 282. This drawing also shows the motor bogie, the underframe and bow collector. This underframe was on the 'SL' Motor Brake Third, 'SL' Trailer First and 'CP' Motor Third Brake only.

Centre: 'Crystal Palace' Trailer Composite, Diagram 283

Above: End elevations T, R and P.

Body styling of these cars was entirely 'Brighton Standard', as were the overall dimensions; the Crystal Palace and Leigham tunnels did not in those days permit the passage of 9 ft-wide carriages. Compartments were full-width without side corridors. The 'CP' motor vehicles were more powerful than the 'SL' ones, each being equipped with four Winter-Eichberg 150 hp A.C. traction motors, and they were also not as heavy as the 'SL' motor cars. One 'CP' motor car, therefore, was quite capable of working with two driving trailers, and the normal formation was a three-car train consisting of trailer-motor-trailer. Still working on the principle that trailers spent less time in shops for maintenance than did motor cars, the LB&SC did not build sufficient to make up 30 permanent three-coach trains, with the result that formations changed constantly. Having a driver's compartment in every vehicle also ensured maximum flexibility of operation, and trains could vary in length from two to six cars. The carriages were all long-buffered, automatically classifying them as 'mainline' and not 'suburban' stock.

In 1912 four additional Motor Brake Thirds (Nos. 3261-64) and four Driving Trailer Composites (Nos. 4061-64) were delivered by the Metropolitan Carriage Wagon & Finance Co., as MARC&W Co. had become. To alleviate a shortage of trailers Lancing constructed eight more in 1913 - Nos. 4069-76.

Livery of the 'CP' stock was all-over brown from the start, with yellow and black lining. Upholstery in the 1st class was blue cloth and in the 3rd class the seats were covered with red and black tapestry. Total seating capacity of a three-car unit was 48 first class and 170 third class. The Motor Thirds had similar underframes to those of the 'SL' motors, and the electrical equipment was arranged in the same way, there being two bow collectors (one for each direction of travel) and a flattened portion of roof over the luggage compartment with the equipment surrounded by protective wire-mesh. Trailers had normal rod-trussed underframes. No attempt was made to design an attractive drive-end for the Crystal Palace trains; it was merely a standard coach-end with two windows either side of a central headcode indicator. There was also an electric headlamp which could become a tail light when a pivotted red glass was moved in front of it.

All the 'CP' carriages entered Southern Railway stock and most of them were repainted green and renumbered into the SR series at Lancing between 1924 and 1927. Between late 1928 and mid-1929 they were all withdrawn for conversion to D.C. electric stock.

The 'CP' Motor Third Brakes were converted to nine-compartment Trailer Thirds, retaining their original girder-trussed frames; the two new compartments were built in the space formerly occupied by the driver's and guard's compartments. The vehicles were formed into two-coach trailer sets Nos. 1168-87 between July 1929 and July 1930. Most lasted in this form until 1948. One coach in Set 1170 and one in Set 1184 were destroyed by enemy action on 20th November, 1940; the survivor in Set 1170 was then transferred to Set 1184 and Set 1170 was deleted.

Of the 'CP' driving trailers, two were altered to Trailer Thirds, the former driving compartment becoming a five-seat coupé (that is to say, each car had eight-and-a-half compartments seating 85 passengers). These two vehicles were formed into Sets 1182 and 1183. All the other 'CP' trailers were altered to Trailer Composites or converted to Motor Brake Composites, one each in the three-car D.C. trains.

Fourteen 'CP' Driving Trailer Composites were converted to Motor Brake Composites Nos. 8852-62/72-74 and formed in Units 1717-27/37-39 between January and June 1929. The underframes were lengthened to 62 ft but were not returned to their original bodies. A new cab and guard's compartment were grafted on to the third-class end of each body, one compartment being 'lost' in the process, and the original three 1st-class compartments were retained at the inner end of the vehicle. Seating capacity was now 24 1st, 40 3rd.

The remaining 52 Driving Trailer Composites were altered to Trailer Composites; the bodies were remounted on lengthened 'CP' frames, one additional 1st-class compartment being built at one end and an additional 3rd-class compartment at the other. The new numbers were 9717-49 in Units 1717-49 (altered between January and August 1929), and 9461-79 in Units 1750-68 (altered between December 1929 and April 1930). Seating capacity was now 32 1st, 60 3rd.

After World War II most of these three-car units were augmented to four cars by the addition of a steel trailer, running in this form until the mid 1950s. A few units were prolonged by being reformed with two ex-LB&SC trailers; these units lasted until late 1959.

'CP' MOTOR THIRD BRAKES (DIAGRAM No. 282)

No.	Built	SR No.	Re-No.	DC No.	Re-No.	Unit Nos.	Wdn
3231	Metro 1911	8567	7.24	9294	7.30	1187	4.48
3232	Metro 1911	8568	9.26	9265	8.29	1172	.47
3233	Metro 1911	8569	12.25	9280	1.30	1180	.47
3234	Metro 1911	8570	5.26	9267	8.29	1173	.45
3235	Metro 1911	8571	1.28	9291	3.30	1185, 1054	.41
3236	Metro 1911	8572	1.27	9259	7.29	1169	5.48
3237	Metro 1911	8573	12.24	9262	7.29	1171	.47
3238	Metro 1911	8574	3.25	9295	7.30	1187	4.48
3239	Metro 1911	8575	3.27	9269	8.29	1174	.47
3240	Metro 1911	8576	9.26	9275	9.29	1177	.47
3241	Metro 1911	8577	12.24	9271	8.29	1175	7.48
3242	Metro 1911	8578	5.24	9287	2.30	1183	.45
3243	Metro 1911	8579	12.25	9278	1.30	1179	10.48
3244	Metro 1911	8580	5.26	9260	7.29	1170, 1184	.47
3245	Metro 1911	8581	6.27	9263	7.29	1171	.47
3246	Metro 1911	-	-	9256	7.29	1168	.47
3247	Metro 1911	8583	9.25	9285	2.30	1182	.47
3248	Metro 1911	8584	6.27	9266	8.29	1173	.45
3249	Metro 1911	8585	9.27	9261	7.29	1170	11.40
3250	Metro 1911	8586	10.24	9272	9.29	1176	.47
3251	Metro 1911	8587	9.27	9289	2.30	1184	11.40
3252	Metro 1911	8588	5.24	9270	8.29	1175	7.48
3253	Metro 1911	8589	10.24	9273	9.29	1176	.47
3254	Metro 1911	8590	1.27	9276	9.29	1178	8.48
3255	Metro 1911	8591	6.25	9277	9.29	1178	8.48
3256	Metro 1911	8592	1.24	9268	8.29	1174	.47

No.	Built	SR No.	Re-No.	DC No.	Re-No.	Unit Nos.	Wdn
3257	Metro 1911	8593	6.25	9264	8.29	1172	.47
3258	Metro 1911	8594	10.25	9258	7.29	1169	5.48
3259	Metro 1911	8595	7.24	9274	9.29	1177	.47
3260	Metro 1911	-	-	9281	1.30	1180	.47
3261	Metro 1912	8597	4.27	9257	7.29	1168	.47
3262	Metro 1912	8598	1.24	9279	1.30	1179	10.48
3263	Metro 1912	8599	1.28	9283	2.30	1181	5.48
3264	Metro 1912	8600	3.25	9293	3.30	1186	.47

SR Conversions: All 'CP' Motor Third Brakes (SR Diagram No. 676) became Trailer Thirds Nos. 9256-81/83/85/87/89/91/93-95 (Diagram No 728) at Lancing, formed in two-coach trailer sets Nos. 1168-87.

'CP' DRIVING TRAILER COMPOSITES (DIAGRAM No. 283)

No.	Built	SR No.	Re-No.	DC No.	Re-No.	Unit Nos.	Wdn
4001	Metro 1911	9825	9.25	9749	8.29	1749, 4546	9.56
4002	Metro 1911	9826	9.25	9732	7.29	1732, 4533, 4514	10.59
4003	Metro 1911	9827	2.25	9476	3.30	1765, 4558, 4517	10.59
4004	Metro 1911	9828	4.25	9742	6.29	1742	12.41
4005	Metro 1911	9829	9.26	8874	6.29	1739, 4539, 4512	11.59
4006	Metro 1911	9830	5.24	9719	2.29	1719, 4568, 4133, 4506	12.59
4007	Metro 1911	9831	7.24	9468	2.30	1757, 4554, 4516	10.59
4008	Metro 1911	9832	1.24	9717	1.29	1717, 4566, 4133	9.56
4009	Metro 1911	9833	10.25	9726	6.29	1726, 4529, 4509	11.59
4010	Metro 1911	9834	6.27	9730	9.29	1730, 4254, 4501	12.59
4011	Metro 1911	9835	1 24	9720	2.29	1720, 4569, 4571, 4502	11.59
4012	Metro 1911	9836	9.26	8873	6.29	1738, 4538, 4508	12.59
4013	Metro 1911	9837	9.26	8859	5.29	1724, 4527, 4504	10.59
4014	Metro 1911	9838	12.24	9462	1.30	1751, 4548, 4515	11.59
4015	Metro 1911	9839	9.26	9738	6.29	1738, 4538, 4508	12.59
4016	Metro 1911	9840	6.27	9478	4.30	1767, 4559, 4503	9.59
4017	Metro 1911	9841	4.27	9284	2.30	1182	.47
4018	Metro 1911	9842	3.25	9725	5.29	1725, 4528, 4510	12.59
4019	Metro 1911	9843	9.24	9736	8.29	1736, 4251, 4518	11.58
4020	Metro 1911	9844	12.24	9463	2.30	1752, 4549, 4504	10.59
4021	Metro 1911	9845	9.27	9737	6.29	1737, 4537, 4511	12.59
4022	Metro 1911	-	-	8856	2.29	1721, 4570	8.51
4023	Metro 1911	9847	4.27	8862	6.29	1727, 4530	9.56
4024	Metro 1911	9848	6.27	9724	5.29	1724, 4527, 4504	10.59
4025	Metro 1911	9849	10.27	8861	6.29	1726, 4529	8.56
4026	Metro 1911	9850	9.27	9743	7.29	1743, 4541, 4509	11.59
4027	Metro 1911	9851	10.27	9727	6.29	1727, 4530, 4517	10.59
4028	Metro 1911	9852	1.28	9470	2.30	1759, 4556, 4505	7.59
4029	Metro 1911	9853	4.26	9728	6.29	1728, 4252, 4134, 4507	10.59
4030	Metro 1911	9854	1.24	8854	2.29	1719, 4568	6.52
4031	Lancing 1911	9855	12.25	9734	8.29	1734, 4535, 4516	10.59
4032	Lancing 1911	9856	1.28	9286	2.30	1183	.45
4033	Lancing 1911	9857	1.27	8860	5.29	1725, 4528?, 4510	12.59
4034	Lancing 1911	-	-	9721	2.29	1721, 4570	8.51
4035	Lancing 1911	9859	1.28	9467	1.30	1756, 4553, 4502	11.59
4036	Lancing 1911	9860	1.24	8853	1.29	1718, 4567	2.56

No.	Built	SR No.	Re-No.	DC No.	Re-No.	Unit Nos.	Wdn
4037	Lancing 1911	9861	2 25	9729	6.29	1729, 4531, 4512	11.59
4038	Lancing 1911	9862	7.24	9469	2.30	1758	3.48
4039	Lancing 1911	9863	1.27	9461	1.30	1750, 4547	7.59
4040	Lancing 1911	9864	12.24	9466	1.30	1755, 4552	9.56
4041	Lancing 1911	9865	1.24	9723	2.29	1723, 4571	9.56
4042	Lancing 1911	9866	2.25	9731	9.29	1731, 4532, 4507	10.59
4043	Lancing 1911	9867	7.24	9741	6.29	1741, 4251, 4518	11.58
4044	Lancing 1911	9868	12.24	9464	2.30	1753, 4550, 4513	11.59
4045	Lancing 1911	9869	9.25	9465	1.30	1754, 4551	10.51
4046	Lancing 1911	9870	6.27	9473	3.30	1762, 4555, 4515	11.59
4047	Lancing 1911	9871	6.25	9747	8.29	1747, 4544, 4514	10.59
4048	Lancing 1911	9872	5.24	9718	1.29	1718, 4567	11.56
4049	Lancing 1911	9873	6.25	9479	4.30	1768, 4560	11.56
4050	Lancing 1911	9874	1.24	8855	2.29	1720, 4569	5.52
4051	Lancing 1911	9875	1.27	9474	3.30	1763	5.48
4052	Lancing 1911	9876	6.25	9477	3.30	1766, 4561	8.56
4053	Lancing 1911	9877	4.26	9748	8.29	1748, 4545, 4506	12.59
4054	Lancing 1911	9878	1.27	9733	7.29	1733, 4534, 4503	9.59
4055	Lancing 1911	-	-	9722	2 29	1722, 4250	11.47
4056	Lancing 1911	-	-	8858	2.29	1723, 4571	3.56
4061	Metro 1912	9881	10.24	8872	6.29	1737, 4537	8.55
4062	Metro 1912	9882	7.24	9735	8.29	1735, 4536,4572	10.59
4063	Metro 1912	9883	5.24	8857	2.29	1722	4.41
4064	Metro 1912	9884	10.24	9739	6.29	1739, 4539, 4512	11.59
4069	Lancing 6.13	9885	1.26	9471	2.30	1760	11.40
4070	Lancing 6.13	9886	12.25	9472	2.30	1761, 4252, 4134,4508	12.59
4071	Lancing 6.13	9887	5.26	9744	7.29	1744, 4542	9.56
4072	Lancing 6.13	9888	10.25	9475	3.30	1764, 4557, 4513	11.59
4073	Lancing 12.13	9889	12.25	9746	8.29	1746, 4543, 4510	12.59
4074	Lancing 12.13	9890	1.28	9745	8.29	1745	11.40
4075	Lancing 12.13	9891	4.26	9740	6.29	1740, 4540	7.56
4076	Lancing 12.13	9892	5.24	8852	1.29	1717, 4566	7.55

SR Conversions: 'CP' Driving Trailer Composites (SR Diagram No. 791) became Motor Composite Brakes Nos. 8852-62 at Ashford, 8872-74 at Eastleigh (Diagram No. 693); or Trailer Composites Nos. 9717-36 at Ashford, 9737-49 at Eastleigh, 9461-79 at Ashford (Diagram No. 761). Two 'CP' Driving Trailer Composites were rebuilt as Trailer Thirds Nos. 9284/86 at Lancing (Diagram No. 729).

DRIVING TRAILER COMPOSITES

Nos. 4077-4106, 4113-18 (SR Nos. 9895-9901, 9893/94, 9902-14, 6251-64)

Body length: 54 ft. Body width: 8 ft. Bogie centres: 37 ft.
Compartments: Four 1st class (6 ft 6⅝ in. between partitions) and four 3rd class (5 ft 8 in. between partitions). Driver's compartment. Seats: 32 1st, 40 3rd class.
Tare weight 24 tons. Diagram No. 284 (electric), 118 (steam).
SR Diagram No. 792 (electric), 352 (steam). Built 1914-21.

DRIVING TRAILER COMPOSITES

Nos. 4107-4112 (SR Nos. 6265-6270)

Body length: 54 ft. Body width: 8 ft. Bogie centres: 37 ft.
Compartments: Three 1st class (6 ft 6⅝ in. between partitions) and five 3rd class (5 ft 10¼
in. between partitions). Driver's compartment. Seats: 24 1st, 50 3rd class.
Tare weight: 24 tons. Diagram No. 285 (electric), 100 (steam).
SR Diagram No. 353 (steam). Built 1921.

In 1913 work started on erecting the overhead for further extensions to the
LB&SCR's A.C. electrified network, and Lancing Works was ordered to
construct 60 Driving Trailer Composites, their intended numbers to be 4077-
4136. By 1914, 12 of these had been built, Nos. 4077-88. They differed from the
'Crystal Palace' driving trailers in having four 1st-class and four 3rd-class
compartments instead of three 1st class and five 3rd class. Only two of these
cars actually entered service, Nos. 4084/85, on the Crystal Palace lines, to which
they were always allocated until the end of A.C. operation. The other ten cars
were stored, minus control equipment. During 1915 a further 15 driving trailers
were built by Lancing, Nos. 4089-4103, before work ground to a halt, partly
because of the shortage of craftsmen caused by the War, and partly because of
uncertainty as to the future extent of the electrified services. All these cars were
stored, some partly finished, all minus electrical equipment. Work restarted
late in December 1919; there was still a shortage of craftsmen at Lancing and
progress was slow. Nos. 4104-12 were more or less completed in 1919/20; of
these, the last six were to the 'Crystal Palace' design, with three 1st class and five
3rd class compartments, but none ever entered service on those routes. Finally,
in August 1920, construction was authorised of six more trailers, Nos. 4113-18,
and these were completed during the first half of 1921.

Of the 42 carriages actually built, Nos. 4077-83/86-98 were eventually to see
service as A.C. driving trailers on the Coulsdon/Wallington extension.
However, before that happened, they were fitted with steam heaters, between
September 1920 and April 1921, and went into service as steam-hauled carriages
until about 1924. The other trailers, Nos. 4099-4118, were finished off in 1921,
also being adapted to run in steam-hauled services, but these never reverted to
A.C. stock.

When the Coulsdon/Wallington extensions were opened in April 1925, the
trains operating them included the 20 Driving Trailer Composites that had run
temporarily as steam stock (Nos. 4077-83/86-98) and which were now classed
'CW' stock. Nine of them were given new SR numbers in May 1924, but the
remainder kept their LB&SC numbers until withdrawal in 1929. The two
trailers running in 'CP' services, Nos. 4084/85, were renumbered 9893/94 in
1927.

Of the 'CW' Driving Trailer Composites, 18 were converted to D.C. Motor
Brake Composites Nos. 8885-88/90-8900, 9801-03 between January and April
1930; these ran, one per unit, in three-car units 1750-53/55-68. In each
conversion a lengthened 'CW' underframe was used and a new driver's cab and
guard's compartment were built at one end. The original four 3rd class
compartments and three of the original four 1st-class compartments were

retained, and the former driver's compartment and the 1st-class compartment next to it were scrapped.

The remaining two 'CW' Driving Trailer Composites, plus the two 'CP' examples to the same design, were altered to D.C. Trailer Thirds, all eight compartments being retained, with the erstwhile driver's compartment becoming a coupé compartment with five seats. The new numbers were 9282, 9288, 9290 and 9292, and the cars were formed one per unit in Sets 1181, 1184, 1185 and 1186 in February and March 1930.

Units 1758 and 1763 were withdrawn early in 1948. The other three-car units were augmented with an additional steel trailer between September 1947 and August 1949 and renumbered between 4547 and 4560; in 1956 seven of these were again re-formed, each now comprising four cars with ex-LB&SC bodywork, and these lasted until late 1959.

We now need to go back to 1924 in order to consider the 20 driving trailers running as steam stock and which were never used as A.C. stock. These, Nos. 4099-4118, had their driver's cabs sealed, the windows being obscured so that they looked like lavatory windows: 'a singularly thoughtless decoration', in C. Hamilton Ellis's opinion. Nos. 4099-4106/13-18 were renumbered 6251-64 and Nos. 4107-12 (the ones with three firsts and five thirds) became SR Nos. 6265-70, all at Lancing between 1924 and 1927. Most were dual braked. They ran thus, some formed in sets, until 1930, when eight were withdrawn for conversion into D.C. electric stock. Four were converted to Motor Brake Composites Nos. 9804-07 in the same way as the earlier ones. Four were altered to Trailer Composites, the redundant driver's cabs being done away with and an extra 1st-class compartment built on at one end and an extra 3rd-class compartment built on at the other end. The new numbers were 9480-83, each with four 1st-class and six 3rd-class compartments; these vehicles were formed with the Motor Brake Composites into Units 1769-72 in June 1930.

On 24th October, 1947, Unit 1770 ran into the back of a train standing near South Croydon and was very severely damaged. Trailer Composite No. 9481 was cut up on site and the other two cars, Nos. 8747 and 9805, were withdrawn as beyond economic repair. The other three units were subsequently 'augmented' and renumbered: Nos. 1769/72 became 4564/65 and Unit 1771 became 4590, lasting until the mid 1950s.

After 1930 there were 12 steam Composites remaining. In March 1931 three of these, Nos. 6257, 6261 and 6263, were rebuilt into push-and-pull driving trailer Composite Brakes. In each of these, all four 3rd-class compartments were retained, as well as three of the four 1st class; the space formerly occupied by one first-class compartment and the intended driver's compartment was made into a combined driver's and guard's compartment, 10 ft 8 in. long. Up to a ton of luggage was permitted to be carried. The three rebuilds were numbered 6939-41 and formed into push-and-pull sets 649 to 651 with eight-compartment Thirds: in Sets 649/50 the Thirds were originally ex-L&SW, that in Set 650 later being replaced by ex-LB&SC Third No. 2087; in Set 651 the Third was always an ex-LB&SC one, No. 1960. The driving trailer Composite Brakes were easily distinguishable from other ex-LB&SC push-and-pulls in that they had only two windows in the drive-end instead of four, betraying their A.C. origins. The luggage compartment was provided with double doors each side, the guard's door opening inwards.

The three sets were allocated to the Eastern Section, as reliefs, in 1931. They could be seen on the Allhallows and Westerham branches; later they sometimes worked in the Horsham area on Brighton or Guildford services. Set 649 was withdrawn after a fairly short life, in August 1937, but the other two lasted well into BR days and went in the late 1950s. Set 650 was scrapped at Newhaven in 1959, still wearing the red livery applied about 1950.

Allocations in 1934/5 were: Set 649 - Hythe; Set 650 - Westerham; Set 651 - Relief, Eastern Section. In 1939 both Sets 650 and 651 were allocated to the Bexhill West branch.

The nine steam Composites remaining in 1931, Nos. 6252-55/58/62/64/68/69, were altered to Thirds and adapted to run as trailers in push-and-pull sets 751 to 759. The vehicles were renumbered 2186-92 (Diagram No. 79, formerly Composites with four 1st- and four 3rd-class compartments) and 2193/94 (Diagram No. 80, formerly Composites with three 1st- and five 3rd-class compartments). The disused driver's compartment in each carriage became a luggage compartment, with a single inward-opening door each side, and the two windows in the end were retained so that the luggage could see where it was going. The conversions were carried out between October 1931 and May 1932. In most of the sets the luggage compartment was at the end next to the locomotive, but in some it was at the end adjacent to the driving trailer. These push-and-pull sets are described more fully on pages 155/6.

Nos. 2192/94 after withdrawal were converted to Mess and Tool Vans Nos. 1546S and 1548S in May 1940 for the Locomotive Running Department at Bournemouth and St Leonards respectively. No. 2193, the last to be withdrawn, was sent from Lancing in November 1960 to Newhaven for scrap, but was still there in August 1961.

DRIVING TRAILER COMPOSITES (DIAGRAM No. 284)

Stored and converted to run in steam services, 20 being reconverted to A.C. for 'Coulsdon/Wallington' scheme. Two were always used in 'CP' services.

No.	Built	SR No.	Re-No.	Set	DC No.	Re-No.	Unit Nos.	Wdn
4077	Lancing 1914	-	-		9292	3.30	1186	.47
4078	Lancing 1914	9896	5.24		8886	1.30	1751, 4548, 4507	10.59
4079	Lancing 1914	-	-		9803	4.30	1768, 4560	12.56
4080	Lancing 1914	-	-		9801	3.30	1766, 4561	8.56
4081	Lancing 1914	-	-		8898	3.30	1763	5.48
4082	Lancing 1914	9900	5.24		8891	1.30	1756, 4553, 4502	11.59
4083	Lancing 1914	-	-		8899	3.30	1764, 4557	11.56
4084*	Lancing 1914	9893	4.27		9288	2.30	1184	.47
4085*	Lancing 1914	9894	3.27		9290	3.30	1185	10.40
4086	Lancing 1914	9902	5.24		8887	1.30	1752, 4549	5.56
4087	Lancing 1914	9903	5.24		9802	4.30	1767, 4559	10.54
4088	Lancing 1914	-	-		8900	3.30	1765, 4558, 4517	10.59
4089	Lancing 1915	-	-		8888	2.30	1753, 4550, 4513	11.59
4090	Lancing 1915	-	-		8896	2.30	1761, 4252	5.53
4091	Lancing 1915	-	-		8895	2.30	1760, 1785, 4526, 4501	12.59
4092	Lancing 1915	9908	5.24		9282	2.30	1181	5.48
4093	Lancing 1915	9909	5.24		8897	2.30	1762, 4555, 4515	11.59
4094	Lancing 1915	-	-		8893	2.30	1758	2.48

No.	Built	SR No.	Re-No.	Set	DC No.	Re-No.	Unit Nos.	Wdn
4095	Lancing 1915	-	-		8885	1.30	1750, 4547	8.56
4096	Lancing 1915	9912	5.24		8894	2.30	1759, 4556, 4505	7.59
4097	Lancing 1915	9913	5 24		8890	1.30	1755, 4552	9.56
4098	Lancing 1915	9914	5.24		8892	2.30	1757, 4554, 4516	10.59
4099	Lancing 1915	6251	10.24		9806	6.30	1771, 4590	3.56
4100	Lancing 1915	6252	11.24		2186	4.32	756	7.44
4101	Lancing 1915	6253	6.25	923	2187	5.32	758	8.58
4102	Lancing 1915	6254	11.26		2188	3.32	755	12.58
4103	Lancing 1915	6255	4.27		2189	10.31	754	1.38
4104	Lancing 12.19	6256	9.24		9805	6.30	1770	10.47
4105	Lancing 12.19	6257	10.27		6939	3.31	649	8.37
4106	Lancing 12.19	6258	10.26?	735	2190	4.32	757	8.59
4113	Lancing 6.21	6259	12.24		9807	6.30	1772, 4565	7.55
4114	Lancing 6.21	6260	5.25		9804	6.30	1769, 4564	2.56
4115	Lancing 6.21	6261	7.27		6940	3.31	650	10.59
4116	Lancing 6.21	6262	8.25	890	2191	4.32	753	4.59
4117	Lancing 6.21	6263	8.26	936	6941	3.31	651	10.58
4118	Lancing 6.21	6264	6.27		2192	1.32	752	12.39

* 'CP' Stock.

DRIVING TRAILER COMPOSITES (DIAGRAM No. 285)

Stored, then converted to run in steam services. Similar design to 'CP' Trailer Composites, but never used as AC stock.

No.	Built	SR No.	Re-No.	DC No.	Re-No.	Unit Nos.	Wdn
4107	Lancing 12.19	6265	11.25	9480	4.30	1769, 4564	11.56
4108	Lancing 12.19	6266	4.25	9481	6.30	1770	10.47
4109	Lancing 12.19	6267	10.27	9483	6.30	1772, 4565	7.55
4110	Lancing 12.19	6268	7.27	2193	1.32	759, 37	12.60
4111	Lancing 12.19	6269	10.26	2194	1.32	751	12.39
4112	Lancing 12.19	6270	10.26	9482	6.30	1771, 4590	3.56

SR Conversions: 22 'CW' Trailer Composites (SR Diagram No. 792) became Motor Composite Brakes Nos. 8885-88/90-8900, 9801-07 (Diagram No. 695) at Ashford. Four 'CW' vehicles became Trailer Thirds Nos. 9282/88/90/92 (Diagram No. 730) at Lancing. Four 'CP' vehicles became Trailer Composites Nos. 9480-83 (Diagram No. 768) at Ashford. Remaining twelve vehicles were converted to steam pull-and-push trailers.

COULSDON/WALLINGTON STOCK 'CW'

DRIVING TRAILER THIRDS

Nos. 3268-3287 (LB&SC) and 9169-9188 (SR)

Body length: 48 ft. Body width: 8 ft.
Compartments: Eight (5 ft 2⅝ in. between partitions). Driver's compartment. Seats: 80.
Tare weight: 24 tons. SR Diagram No. 738. Built 1923/4.

TRAILER COMPOSITES

Nos. 4119-4128 (LB&SC) and 9655-58/61-63/72-74 (SR)

Body length: 48 ft. Body width: 8 ft
Compartments: Four 1st class (6 ft 6⅜ in. between partitions) and four 3rd class (5 ft 8 in. between partitions). No driver's compartment. Seats: 32 1st, 40 3rd class. Tare weight: 24 tons. SR Diagram No. 768. Built 1923/4.

MOTOR LUGGAGE VANS

SR Nos. 10101-10121

Body length: 38 ft 5 in. Body width: 8 ft. Bogie centres: 21 ft 5 in.
Compartments: Driver at each end, guard/luggage in centre, two equipment compartments. Tare weight: 62 tons. SR Diagram No. 830. Built 1923/4.

Now that the completion of the Coulsdon/Wallington (and Sutton) A.C. extensions was in sight, the LB&SC in December 1922 ordered the necessary rolling stock to work it. The Metropolitan Carriage Wagon & Finance Co. was contracted to build 21 motor coaches (in fact, motor luggage vans), three Driving Trailer Thirds and three non-driving Trailer Composites. Lancing Works was ordered to build the balance of 37 Driving Trailer Thirds (Nos. 3268-3304) and 17 non-driving Trailer Composites (Nos. 4119-35), These, together with the Driving Trailer Composites already built (Nos. 4077-83/86-98), would run as 20 five-coach trains, each formed with the motor luggage van in the centre, flanked by a 48 ft non-driving Composite and a 54 ft driving Composite, with a driving Third at each end of the formation.

The motor luggage vans were the most interesting and unusual feature of the whole scheme. Many people regarded them as electric locomotives pure and simple; however, they were classed as carriage stock, presumably because they included a guard's and luggage compartment. The staff dubbed them 'milk vans'. They were built by MCW&F Co. at Saltley Works, Birmingham, with electrical equipment by the General Electric Co. Completion dates were December 1923, Nos. 10101-08; January 1924, Nos. 10109-16; March 1924, Nos. 10117/18; and April 1924 10119-21. The bodywork was painted SR green.

Bogie wheelbase was 8 ft 9 in. and wheel diameter 3 ft 7 in. There were four 250 hp traction motors, each driving one axle. The underframe carried an air compressor and air blower. The body comprised a driver's compartment at each end, as it was intended that the 'locomotives' be used for shunting; in practice these cabs were seldom used. Adjacent to each cab was an equipment room, 10 ft 3¾ in. long, with side corridor communication. The main transformer, high-tension equipment, control contactors and air blower motor were housed within each of the two compartments. In the centre of the body was the guard's and luggage compartment, 9 ft 9 in. long. Width over stepboards was 8 ft 9 in. Height from rail to roof was 11 ft 5 in. and the roof itself was covered with aluminium sheet. On the roof, mounted centrally, were the main and auxiliary air reservoirs, and for current collection from the overhead wire there were four bows, of which two were in use at one time for each direction of travel; they were raised and lowered by compressed air.

The six carriages built by MCW&F Co. were completed in Southern Railway green, with new SR numbers; their intended LB&SC numbers would have been 3265-67 and 4136-38.

The Lancing-built carriages should also have appeared in SR livery with SR numbers, but somewhere there seems to have been a lack of communication between Head Office and the Works for in fact all Lancing's quota emerged in brown livery, lettered 'L.B.S.C.' and carrying LB&SC numbers 3268-87 and 4119-28. All were to have such a short life as AC. stock that none was ever repainted in SR colours before conversion to D.C. Lancing also built the underframes intended for Nos. 3288-3304 and 4129-35 but not the bodywork; the 24 frames were dispatched to Eastleigh Works, ex-L&SWR, where the bodies were built. The Eastleigh carriages duly emerged in SR sage green with Southern numbers 9172-88 and 9655-58/61-63. The Eastleigh bodies did not go on to the Lancing frames in strict numerical order, but each frame could be identified by the LB&SC number impressed on the headstock.

All the 'CW' stock, which was classed as 'Renewals' for accountancy purposes, was ready for service by about April 1924, but unfortunately there were problems with the supply of electrical equipment for the route extensions and another year was lost, during which time the travelling public became more and more disgruntled with the SR and its seeming inertia. At long last, trial running on the Coulsdon and Sutton routes began on 11th March, 1925, and public services between Victoria and Coulsdon North and Sutton on 1st April. The new stock ran very smoothly. Five-vehicle trains ran at slack times and 10-vehicle formations in the peaks; because each train included three 48 ft carriages and only one 54 ft one the overall length of the five-vehicle train was no greater than a four-car unit of 54 ft stock would have been. From the passenger's point of view, however, the presence of a 'locomotive' in the middle of the train was a minor irritation; but after four years this arrangement was seen no more, for all the 'CW' stock, including the motor luggage vans, was withdrawn between March and September 1929.

Between June 1929 and June 1930 all 40 'CW' Driving Trailer Thirds were rebuilt into D.C. Motor Third Brakes, using all eight compartments in each, with new driving cabs and luggage compartments being built on; the 'CW' underframes were lengthened to 62 ft, but not reunited with their original bodies. The new numbers were 8697-8705, 8709-22, 8731-46 and 8749, each Motor Third Brake being formed, one per unit, in three-car units 1728-36/40-53, 1754-69/72. Exceptionally, No. 8749 received a completely new underframe.

Between June 1929 and September 1929 the 'CW' Trailer Composites were converted to D.C. Motor Brake Composites Nos. 8863-71/75-84 (Units 1728-36/40-49), the last one, No. 9663, becoming Motor Brake Composite No. 8889 in Unit 1754 in January 1930. Lengthened 'CW' underframes were used and new motorman's and guard's compartments were added to the original four third-class compartments and three of the four first-class compartments. No unit numbers had been allocated to the 'CW' stock as the individual carriages making up the trains had been exchanged frequently, as required by the demands of maintenance.

So it will be seen that all the A.C. stock was given a further lease of life as D.C. stock, and the waste of money involved in the conversion was not as great as it might have been. A total of 68 D.C. units was made up of former A.C. stock: three-car Nos. 1717-72 (except for the Motor Third Brakes of Units 1770/71, which were former steam 'Bogie Block' vehicles) and two-car Nos. 1901-12. There were also 20 trailer sets, Nos. 1168-87.

The motor luggage vans came off worst, however. All were officially withdrawn at the end of 1929, and stood for some years at Streatham Hill while the Southern pondered what to do with them. In 1934 they were converted to goods brake vans, retaining their frames and bogies (demotored) and central guard's compartments but losing their cabs and equipment compartments, which were replaced by open verandahs. They were renumbered 56261-81, not in the same order as the original numbers. It seems likely that all the bodywork was new; the guard's compartment was 9 ft 6 in. long, as opposed to that originally provided, which was 9 ft 9 in. One seat each side was placed to give the guard a view through a ducket, and there was a stove. Width of the body was 9 ft over duckets. There was gravity sanding, a handbrake, and the vans were fully fitted with automatic vacuum brakes as they were intended for running in fast freight trains on the Western Section. Their riding at high speed was vastly superior to that of four-wheeled goods brake vans!

Former No.	New No.	Rebuilt	Former No.	New No.	Rebuilt
10106	56261	3.34	10101	56272	8.34
10107	56262	5.34	10102	56273	7.34
10108	56263	9.33	10103	56274	12.34
10109	56264	6.34	10104	56275	7.34
10112	56265	3.34	10105	56276	10.34
10113	56266	4.34	10110	56277	8.34
10114	56267	3.34	10111	56278	1.35
10115	56268	4.34	10116	56279	7.34
10117	56269	5.34	10119	56280	10 .34
10118	56270	9.34	10121	56281	8.34
10120	56271	3.34			

Units 1717-71 kept their formations until the 1940s, when wartime damage and the plan to abolish trailer sets and augment the three-coach motor units to four cars caused some alterations. The following three-car units were deleted:

1722	8691 to Unit 4520, 9.47. 9722 to Unit 4250, 6.43. 8857 wdn 4.41.
1728	8697 to Unit 4520, 9.47. 9728 to Unit 4252, 8.44. 8863 wdn 6.44.
1730	8699 wdn? 9730 and 8865 to Unit 4254, 3.47.
1736	8705, 9736 and 8871 to Unit 4251, 3.44.
1741	8710 to Unit 4483 , 3.49. 9741 to Unit 4251, 3.44. 8876 wdn 2.44.
1742	8711 and 9742 wdn 12.41. 8877 to Unit 1771, 1948; to 4590 2.49.
1745	8714, 9745 and 8880 wdn 11.40. (Enemy action.)
1758	8735, 9469 and 8893 wdn 3.48.
1760	8737 and 9471 wdn 11.40. 8895 to Unit 1785; to 4526 7.48.
1761	8738, 9472 and 8896 to Unit 4252, 8.44.
1763	8740, 9474 and 8898 wdn 5.48. (South Bermondsey accident.)
1770	8747, 9481 and 9805 wdn 10.47. (South Croydon accident.)
1771	8748 wdn 1948, repl. by 8877 ex-1742. This and 9482, 9806 to 4590, 2.49.

All remaining units made from ex-A.C. stock were augmented by steel trailers and renumbered 4527-61/64-71 at various dates between September 1947 and August 1949. Most were withdrawn in the mid-1950s, but between June 1956 and January 1957 18 units were reformed and renumbered 4501-18, most of them being formed with three ex-LBSC vehicles from one unit and an extra trailer from another unit, the rest of which was scrapped. Unit 4501 included two ex-L&SW vehicles and two ex-LB&SC, and Unit 4518 was a straight renumbering of Unit 4251.

The last D.C. units made from ex-LB&SC A.C. electric bodywork were withdrawn in December 1959.

'CW' DRIVING TRAILER THIRDS (SR DIAGRAM No. 738)

No.	Built	DC No.	Re-No.	Unit Nos.	Wdn
3268	Lancing 12.23	8735	2.30	1758	2.48
3269	Lancing 12.23	8731	1.30	1754, 4551, 4511	12.59
3270	Lancing 12.23	8702	7.29	1733, 4534	7.56
3271	Lancing 12.23	8714	8.29	1745	11.40
3272	Lancing 12.23	8743	3.30	1766, 4561	8.56
3273	Lancing 12.23	8711	6.29	1742	12.41
3274	Lancing 12.23	8717	8.29	1748, 4545, 4506	12.59
3275	Lancing 12.23	8738	3.30	1761, 4252	5.53
3276	Lancing 12.23	8712	7.29	1743, 4541, 4509	11.59
3277	Lancing 12.23	8720	1.30	1751, 4548	3.50
3278	Lancing 12.23	8698	6.29	1729, 4531	12.56
3279	Lancing 12.23	8715	8.29	1746, 4543	10.56
3280	Lancing 12.23	8749	6.30	1772, 4565	7.55
3281	Lancing 12.23	8733	1.30	1756, 4553, 4502	11.59
3282	Lancing 12.23	8697	6.29	1728, 4520	9.56
3283	Lancing 12.23	8746	6.30	1769, 4564	2.56
3284	Lancing 6.24	8736	2.30	1759, 4556, 4505	7.59
3285	Lancing 6.24	8722	1.30	1753, 4550, 4513	11.59
3286	Lancing 6.24	8737	2.30	1760	11.40
3287	Lancing 6.24	8701	7.29	1732, 4533, 4514	10.59
9169	Metro 12.23	8713	7.29	1744, 4542	4.56
9170	Metro 12.23	8718	8.29	1749, 4546, 4503	9.59
9171	Metro 12.23	8700	9.29	1731, 4532	10.56
9172	Eastleigh 11.23	8734	1.30	1757, 4554, 4516	10.59
9173	Eastleigh 11.23	8721	1.30	1752, 4549, 4504	10.59
9174	Eastleigh 11.23	8703	8.29	1734, 4535, 4507	10.59
9175	Eastleigh 11.23	8745	4.30	1768, 4560	12.56
9176	Eastleigh 12.23	8719	1.30	1750, 4547	12.59
9177	Eastleigh 12.23	8709	6.29	1740, 4540	7.56
9178	Eastleigh 12.23	8705	8.29	1736, 4251, 4518	11.58
9179	Eastleigh 12.23	8704	8.29	1735, 4536	?
9180	Eastleigh 2.24	8699	9.29	1730	?
9181	Eastleigh 2.24	8744	4.30	1767, 4559	10.54
9182	Eastleigh 2.24	8716	8.29	1747, 4544	11.56
9183	Eastleigh 2.24	8740	3.30	1763	5.48
9184	Eastleigh 2.24	8741	3.30	1764, 4557	11.56
9185	Eastleigh 2.24	8739	3.30	1762, 4555, 4510	10.59
9186	Eastleigh 2.24	8710	6.29	1741, 4483	8.51
9187	Eastleigh 2.24	8742	3.30	1765, 4558, 4517	10.59
9188	Eastleigh 2.24	8732	1 30	1755, 4552	9.56

All the 'CW' Driving Trailer Thirds (Diagram No. 738) were converted to Motor Third Brakes Nos. 8697-8705 at Ashford, 8709-18 at Eastleigh, and 8719-22/31-46/49 at Ashford (Diagram No. 678).

'CW' TRAILER COMPOSITES (SR DIAGRAM No. 768)

No.	Built	DC No.	Re-No.	Unit Nos.	Wdn
4119	Lancing 12.23	8863	6.29	1728	6.44
4120	Lancing 12.23	8875	6.29	1740, 4540	7.56
4121	Lancing 12.23	8879	7.29	1744, 4542	4.56
4122	Lancing 12.23	8866	9.29	1731, 4532	12.59
4123	Lancing 12.23	8867	7.29	1732, 4533, 4514	10.59
4124	Lancing 12.23	8870	8.29	1735, 4536	7.53
4125	Lancing 12.23	8882	8.29	1747, 4544	?
4126	Lancing 12.23	8881	8.29	1746, 4543	10.56
4127	Lancing 1.24	8868	7.29	1733, 4534, 4503	9.59
4128	Lancing 6.24	8884	8.29	1749, 4546	9.53
9655	Eastleigh 11.23	8880	8.29	1745	11.40
9656	Eastleigh 11.23	8865	9.29	1730, 4254	9.56
9657	Eastleigh 12.23	8878	7.29	1743, 4541, 4509	11.59
9658	Eastleigh 12.23	8864	6.29	1729, 4531	12.56
9661	Eastleigh 2.24	8871	8.29	1736, 4251, 4518	11.58
9662	Eastleigh 2.24	8877	6.29	1742, 1771, 4590	9 56
9663	Eastleigh 2.24	8889	1.30	1754, 4551, 4511	12.59
9672	Metro 12.23	8869	8.29	1734, 4535	10.56
9673	Metro 12.23	8883	8.29	1748, 4545, 4506	4.58
9674	Metro 12.23	8876	6.29	1741	2.44

All 20 'CW' Trailer Composites (Diagram No. 768) were converted to Motor Composite Brakes Nos. 8863-71 at Ashford, 8875-84 at Eastleigh, and 8889 at Ashford (Diagram No. 694).

MISHAPS

The following were withdrawn after damage caused by accidents or enemy action.

Motor 3rd Bke	8711 (Unit 1742)	Accident damage, Dorking, 12.41
Motor 3rd Bke	8714 (Unit 1745)	Enemy Action, 20.11.40
Motor 3rd Bke	8729 (Unit 1807)	Enemy Action, Peckham Rye, 1940
Motor 3rd Bke	8737 (Unit 1760)	Enemy Action, 6.11.40
Motor 3rd Bke	8740 (Unit 1763)	Accident damage, S. Bermondsey, 5.48
Motor Cpo Bke	8857 (Unit 1722)	Enemy Action, Charing Cross, 4.41
Motor Cpo Bke	8863 (Unit 1728)	Enemy Action, Walworth, 28.6.44
Motor Cpo Bke	8876 (Unit 1741)	Enemy Action, Slades Gn, 2.44
Motor Cpo Bke	8880 (Unit 1745)	Enemy Action, 20.11.40
Motor Cpo Bke	8898 (Unit 1763)	Accident damage, S. Bermondsey, 5.48
Trailer Third	9261 (Unit 1170)	Enemy Action, 20.11.40
Trailer Third	9289 (Unit 1184)	Enemy Action, 20.11.40
Trailer Third	9290 (Unit 1185)	Accident damage, Effingham Jn, 9.10.40
Trailer Compo	9471 (Unit 1760)	Enemy Action, 6.11.40
Trailer Compo	9474 (Unit 1763)	Accident damage, S. Bermondsey, 5.48
Trailer Compo	9481 (Unit 1770)	Accident damage, South Croydon, 24.10.47

Trailer Compo	9722 (Unit 4250)	Accident damage, Herne Hill, 6.11.47
Trailer Compo	9742 (Unit 1742)	Accident damage, Dorking, 12.41
Trailer Compo	9745 (Unit 1745)	Enemy Action, 20.11.40
Tlr Compo Bke	9757 (Unit 1807)	Enemy Action, Peckham Rye, 1940
Motor Cpo Bke	9805 (Unit 1770)	Accident damage, South Croydon, 24.10.47

Four Motor Brakes entered the service vehicles list early in 1957 as two-car 'tractor units'. These were:

DS 347, from Motor Third Brake 8741	(Unit 4557)
DS 348, from Motor Compo Brake 8899	(Unit 4557)
DS 349, from Motor Third Brake 8698	(Unit 4531)
DS 350, from Motor Compo Brake 8864	(Unit 4531)

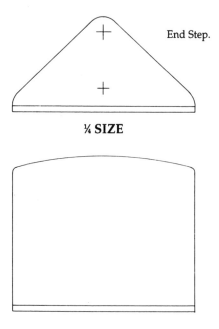

End Step.

¼ SIZE

Chapter Eleven

Non-Passenger Carrying Stock

BOGIE BRAKE VANS

The LB&SCR constructed 19 bogie brake vans of three different types between 1899 and 1907, and converted a further two from Mail Vans in 1921. All types were 48 ft long over body, including a solitary specimen with 'balloon' roof, designed for working in the Newhaven Boat Train. The types are summarised below:

Nos. 154/55/59/60, built 1899, SR Nos. 910-13; Nos. 433-442, built 1900, SR Nos. 914-923.
Body length: 48 ft. Body width: 8 ft. Bogie centres: 32 ft. Tare weight: 18 tons. Diagram No. 226 (SR No. 905).

Nos. 472-475, built 1905, SR Nos. 924-927.
Body length: 48 ft. Body width : 8 ft. Bogie centres: 32 ft.
Tare weight: 18 tons 9 cwt. Maximum load 10 tons of luggage.
Diagram No. 231 (SR No. 906).

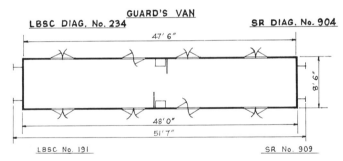

GUARD'S VAN
LBSC DIAG. No. 234   **SR DIAG. No. 904**

No. 191, built 1907, SR No. 909.
Body length: 48 ft. Body width: 8 ft 6 in. Bogie centres : 33 ft 6 in.
Tare weight: 19 tons 12 cwt. Maximum load 10 tons of luggage. Diagram No. 234 (SR No. 904).

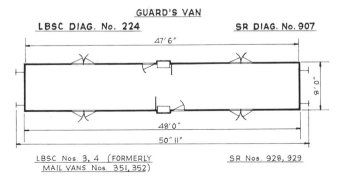

GUARD'S VAN
LBSC DIAG. No. 224   **SR DIAG. No. 907**

Nos. 3 and 4, converted 1921, SR Nos. 928, 929.
Body length: 48 ft. Body width: 8 ft. Bogie centres: 32 ft.
Tare weight: 19 tons approximately.
Diagram No. 224 (SR No. 907).

The vans built in 1899 and 1900 each had two sets of double doors each side, giving access to two luggage compartments, and there was a central guard's compartment complete with side duckets. Originally, oil lighting was fitted, but this was later replaced by gas illumination. The 1905-built vans differed in having four sets of double doors each side.

The high-roofed van, No. 191, had eight doors each side, grouped in pairs and including an inward-opening door for the use of the guard. Livery when new was umber with white upper panels, and the van, which carried enormous roof destination boards, was formed as part of Boat Train No. 87. It was gas lighted.

By 1917 six examples of Diagram 226 and two of Diagram 231 had been formed into four Brighton-Portsmouth sets, two per set. Presumably these five-vehicle sets (Nos. 5, 26, 31 and 32) required high-capacity luggage space because of the amount of fruit that often needed to be carried. These sets were disbanded after 1921 and none of the bogie brakes appeared in a set in Southern days, except No. 909 in Set 927.

No. 434 was withdrawn in 1924 without ever receiving its SR number. The others received vacuum brake equipment in addition to their air brakes, and a start was made to remove Westinghouse equipment in 1929. Nos. 909 and 924-927 were given electric lighting in place of gas during 1929/30, but withdrawal of the vans was begun in earnest in 1931 and completed in 1933.

BRAKE VANS (DIAGRAM No. 226)

LBSC No.	Built	Set No.	SR No.	Re-No.	Wdn	LBSC No.	Built	Set	SR No.	Re-No.	Wdn
154	1899	26	910	3.28	1.33	436	1900		917	2.27	6.31
155	1899	31	911	4.26	5.31	437	1900		918	3.28	1.31
159	1899		912	4.25	1.32	438	1900		919	8.26	2.32
160	1899		913	.26	12.32	439	1900		920	8.26	11.32
433	1900		914	8.27	4.31	440	1900	32	921	12.25	5.32
434	1900	26	-	-	8.24	441	1900	5	922	2.26	3.31
435	1900		916	11.27	6.31	442	1900	31	923	4.26	1.33

BRAKE VANS (DIAGRAM No. 231)

LBSC No.	Built	Set No.	SR No.	Re-No.	Wdn	LBSC No.	Built	Set No.	SR No.	Re-No.	Wdn
472	1905		924	2.27	4.32	474	1905	5	926	8.24	1.33
473	1905		925	11.25	3.31	475	1905	32	927	3.25	6.33

BRAKE VAN (DIAGRAM No. 234)

LBSC No.	Built	Set No.	SR No.	Re-No.	Set No.	Wdn
191	1907	87	909	4.25	927	11.33

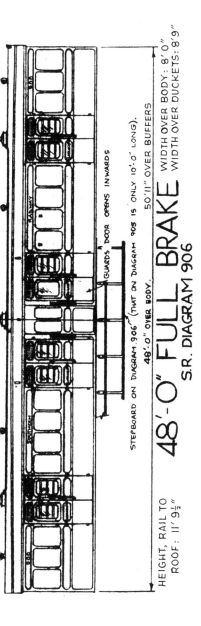

STEPBOARD ON DIAGRAM 906 (THAT ON DIAGRAM 905 IS ONLY 10'-0" LONG).

GUARDS DOOR OPENS INWARDS

48'-0" OVER BODY.

50'11" OVER BUFFERS

48'-0" FULL BRAKE
S.R. DIAGRAM 906

WIDTH OVER BODY: 8'0"
WIDTH OVER DUCKETS: 8'9"

HEIGHT, RAIL TO
ROOF: 11'9½"

DRAWN BY M. S. KING

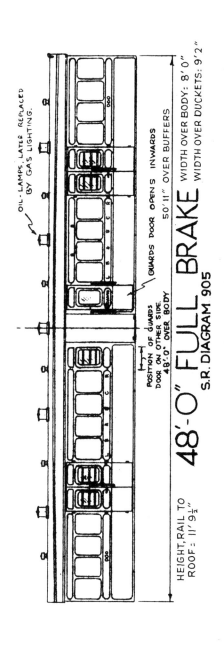

OIL LAMPS, LATER REPLACED
BY GAS LIGHTING.

GUARDS DOOR OPENS INWARDS

POSITION OF GUARDS
DOOR ON OTHER SIDE.
48'-0" OVER BODY

50'11" OVER BUFFERS

48'-0" FULL BRAKE
S.R. DIAGRAM 905

WIDTH OVER BODY: 8'0"
WIDTH OVER DUCKETS: 9'2"

HEIGHT, RAIL TO
ROOF: 11'9½"

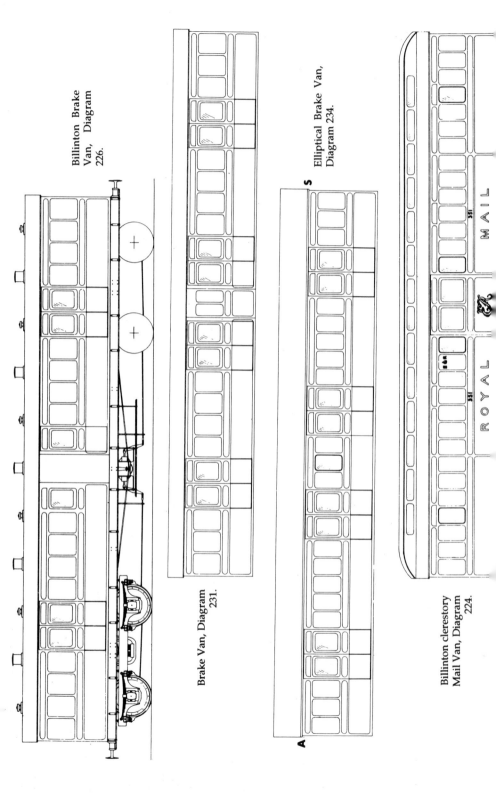

Billinton Brake
Van, Diagram
226.

Brake Van, Diagram
231.

Elliptical Brake Van,
Diagram 234.

Billinton clerestory
Mail Van, Diagram 224.

ROYAL MAIL VANS

Only two bogie mail vans were constructed, both in 1897. Each was 48 ft over body and sported a clerestory roof. Sole access to the van was by means of a large sliding door each side; there were no end gangways.

Both vans were converted to brake vans in 1921, retaining gas lighting, and ran in this form until the early 1930s. Conversion included the removal of the sliding doors and the fitting of two sets of swing doors plus a single inward-opening guard's door in each bodyside.

Nos. 351/52, built 1897.
Body length: 48 ft. Body width: 8 ft.
Tare weight: 20 tons.

LBSC No.	Built	Conv.	Re-No.	SR No.	Re-No.	Wdn
351	1897	1921	3	928	1.26	5.31
352	1897	1921	4	929	4.26	2.33

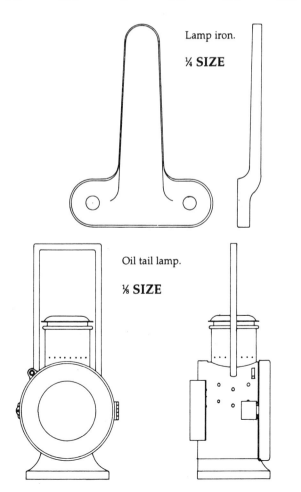

Lamp iron.

¼ SIZE

Oil tail lamp.

⅛ SIZE

Tailpiece

Carriage stock was not perhaps the LB&SCR's strongest point. It has been said of Stroudley that he designed carriages merely as loads for his engines to haul about, and even the best ordinary carriages, apart from the magnificent 'City Limited', were suburban stock basically, with their 'isolated' compartments and paucity of lavatory accommodation. In these days of open-plan seating in coaches it is hard to realise that people actually preferred the closed-in compartment, and accepted the fact that each compartment was usually without any communication with its neighbours. Both the London & South Western and the South Eastern & Chatham Railways were building side-corridor stock after World War I, but the Brighton (which still possessed only one proper side-corridor carriage) had no plans to do the same. Similarly, the other two railways had for many years standardised on the semi-elliptical roof for all new construction, but the Brighton persisted with its decidedly old-fashioned plain arc roofs.

And so, while examples of LSW and SEC carriages lasted well into the 1950s, all the LB&SC's carriages disappeared in the early 1940s, except for push-and-pull sets and the Isle of Wight transfers. By the time the preservation era got going, there was practically nothing left to save. In 1961 Trailer Second No. 2193 was offered to the Bluebell Railway for £225, but this was deemed too expensive. The railway nearly had Trailer Composite No. 6237, which was at the Ardingly 'dump' in March 1962; it was promised by BR as soon as it could be cleared from the branch line, but in October 1962 it was quite unaccountably sent to Newhaven and scrapped there. The Directors' Saloon, No. 60, *was* saved, and on the Isle of Wight three examples of ordinary carriages are running at Haven Street. Of recent years the Bluebell has been forced to purchase near-wrecks, in the hope of restoring them to working order; had it adopted this policy earlier it might have saved one of the last 'Balloon' trailers that was quietly rotting at Lancing Carriage Works in 1963. Anyway, the body of a Billinton six-compartment First was acquired in 1989, and work on its restoration has been proceeding steadily ever since.

One day, perhaps, one will be able to ride in this remarkable survivor - when its restoration has been completed and it has been placed on a bogie underframe - over a line that it may well have passed over in the early part of the century. That day will be well worth waiting for, if and when it comes.

Appendix One

A Selection of LB&SCR Bogie Set Trains

As running between 1917 and 1921 without changes in formation

	Train 5			Train 19			Train 31
474	Bke Van		1178	3rd Bke		442	Bke Van
435	Compo.		244	Compo.		660	Third
265	Compo.		1181	3rd Bke		99	Compo.
1230	Third					208	Compo.
441	Bke Van			Train 21		155	Bke Van
			423	6-wh. Bke Van			
	Train 7		1174	Third			Train 32
479	3rd Bke		100	First		475	Bke Van
436	Compo.		460	Third		488	Third
298	Compo.		357	6-wh. Bke Van		426	Compo.
376	3rd Bke					52	Compo.
				Train 24		440	Bke Van
	Train 9		16	6-wh. Bke Van			
342	6-wh. Bke Van		546	Compo.			Train 34
444	Compo.		462	Lav. Compo.		1147	3rd Bke
521	Compo.		447	6-wh. Bke Van		213	Compo.
612	Third					510	Compo.
19	6-wh. Bke Van			Train 25		440	3rd Bke
			109	6-wh. Bke Van			
	Train 10		537	Compo.			Train 35
1153	3rd Bke		64	Lav. Compo.		851	3rd Bke
257	Compo.		542	Compo.		59	Compo.
375	3rd Bke		169	6-wh. Bke Van		3	First
						241	Compo.
	Train 11			Train 26			
478	3rd Bke		154	Bke Van			Train 45
446	Compo.		425	Compo.		497	3rd Slip Bke
549	3rd Bke		36	Compo.		591	Lav. Compo.
			501	Third		270	Compo.
	Train 15		434	Bke Van		458	3rd Bke.
389	6-wh. Bke Van						
880	Third			Train 28			Train 46
299	Compo.		1294	3rd Bke			Elliptical Stock
1592	Third		1400	Third		829	Lav. 3rd Bke
48	6-wh. Bke Van		568	Compo.		110	Compo.
			569	Compo.		154	Lav. First
	Train 16					156	Lav. First
514	3rd Slip Bke			Train 30		416	Lav. Compo.
149	Lav. 1st		852	3rd Bke		624	Lav. 3rd Bke
59	3rd Slip Bke		58	First		158	Lav. First
			282	Compo.			
	Train 18						
1275	3rd Bke						
201	First						
549	Compo.						
548	Compo.						

	Train 53			*Train 82*			*Train 92*
	Dual braked			Two half-trains	483	3rd Bke
452	3rd Bke	382	3rd Bke	468	Compo.
489	Lav. Compo.	209	Compo.	-	Compo.
550	Lav. 3rd Bke			1243	3rd Bke
412	3rd Bke	288	Compo.		
79	Compo.	491	3rd Bke		*Train 93*
417	3rd Bke			1154	3rd Bke
			Train 83	276	Compo.
	Train 63	896	3rd Bke	-	Compo.
372	3rd Bke	595	Lav. Compo.	1191	3rd Bke
246	Compo.	593	Lav. Compo.		
378	3rd Bke	887	3rd Bke		*Train 94*
				474	3rd Bke
	Train 64		*Train 84*	132	Lav. First
337	3rd Bke	1183	3rd Bke	504	3rd Bke
470	Compo.	101	Compo.		
473	3rd Bke	427	Compo.		*Train 95*
		464	Lav. Compo.		Dual braked
	Train 70	482	3rd Bke	468	Lav. 3rd Bke
355	3rd Bke			255	Lav. Compo.
433	Compo.		*Train 85*	450	Compo.
592	Lav. Compo.	516	3rd Bke	550	Lav. 3rd Bke
449	Compo.	134	Lav. First		
46	3rd Bke	591	3rd Bke		*Train 96*
				407	3rd Bke
	Train 72		*Train 86*	289	Compo.
425	3rd Bke	434	3rd Bke	476	3rd Bke
454	Compo.	140	Lav. First		
368	3rd Bke	512	3rd Bke		*Train 97*
				564	3rd Bke
	Train 73		*Train 88*	240	Compo.
593	3rd Slip Bke	-	3rd Slip Bke	389	3rd Bke
181	Compo.	139	Lav. First		
12	Lav. Compo.	398	3rd Bke		*Train 98*
1244	3rd Bke			1151	3rd Bke
			Train 89	281	Compo.
	Train 79	446	3rd Bke	369	3rd Bke
869	3rd Bke	296	Compo.		
401	Compo.	1140	3rd Bke		*Train 100*
597	Lav. Compo.			472	3rd Bke
871	3rd Bke		*Train 90*	447	Compo.
		435	3rd Bke	441	3rd Bke
	Train 80	264	Compo.		
444	3rd Bke	445	3rd Bke		*Train 101*
452	Compo.			363	3rd Bke
490	3rd Bke		*Train 91*	460	Compo.
		401	3rd Bke	1185	3rd Bke
	Train 81	249	Compo.		
367	3rd Slip Bke	-	Compo.		
150	Lav. First	1165	3rd Bke		
475	3rd Slip Bke				

	Train 102				Train 117
582	3rd Bke	147	6-wh. Slip Bke V.	366	3rd Bke
258	Compo.	239	Compo.	126	Lav. Compo.
496	3rd Bke	530	Lav. Compo.	525	3rd Bke
	Train 103		Train 109		Train 118
1172	3rd Bke	421	6-wh. Bke Van	245	3rd Bke
252	Compo.	855	Third	155	Lav. Compo.
397	3rd Bke	85	First	364	3rd Bke
		874	Third		
	Train 104	463	6-wh. Bke Van		Train 119
442	3rd Bke			493	3rd Bke
247	Compo.		Train 110	160	Lav. Compo.
492	3rd Bke	1269	3rd Bke	645	3rd Slip Bke
		558	Compo.		
	Train 105	1285	3rd Bke		Train 120
390	3rd Bke			97	3rd Bke
78	Compo.		Train 111	152	Lav. Compo.
140	Lav. Compo.	422	3rd Bke	547	3rd Bke
565	3rd Bke	461	Compo.		
		1252	3rd Bke		Train 121
	Train 106			1248	3rd Bke
370	3rd Bke		Train 112	588	Lav. Compo.
291	Compo.	470	3rd Bke	1249	3rd Bke
391	3rd Bke	448	Compo.		
		1159	3rd Bke		Train 122
	Train 107			895	3rd Bke
568	3rd Bke		Train 113	589	Lav. Compo.
292	Compo.	477	3rd Bke	556	3rd Bke
1155	3rd Bke	295	Compo.		
		1179	3rd Bke		Train 123
	Train 108			333	3rd Bke
	Three portions		Train 114	590	Lav. Compo.
532	Lav. Compo.	365	3rd Bke	457	3rd Bke
54	Compo.	128	Lav. Compo.		
11	Third	386	3rd Bke		Train 124
20	6 wh. Bke Van			888	3rd Bke
			Train 116	594	Lav. Compo.
174	6-wh. Bke Van	500	3rd Bke	890	3rd Bke
8	Lav. Compo.	125	Lav. Compo.		
423	Compo.	402	3rd Bke		

Based on information contained in Programme of the Formation of Main Line and Suburban Line Trains issued in October 1917 and February 1921. Lavatory Third Brake No. 550 was shown in the lists of both these books as being formed in Sets 53 *and* 95.

Ten Set Trains Running in 1908

	Train 78			Train 82			Train 86
1243	3rd Bke		376	3rd Bke		473	3rd Bke
497	Lav. Compo.		62	Compo.		431	Compo.
41	Compo.		183	Compo.		430	Compo.
1178	3rd Bke		-	3rd Bke		1145	3rd Bke
	Train 79			Train 83			Train 87
407	3rd Bke		1245	3rd Bke			Elliptical Stock
118	Tri-Compo.		1214	Third		91	2nd Bke
429	Compo.		57	Lav. 2nd		145	Lav. Compo.
1172	3rd Bke		138	Lav. First		151	Lav. Compo.
			444	3rd Bke		526	Compo.
	Train 80					527	Compo.
445	3rd Bke			Train 84		130	Lav. Compo.
38	Compo.		1183	3rd Bke		146	Lav. Compo.
43	Compo.		101	Compo.		191	Bke Van
368	3rd Bke		427	Compo.			
			482	3rd Bke			
	Train 81						
1182	3rd Bke			Train 85			
432	Compo.		446	3rd Bke			
486	Lav. Compo.		481	Compo.			
493	3rd Bke		505	Compo.			
210	Lav. Compo.		483	3rd Bke			
-	3rd Bke						

Formations of Sets of Ex-LB&SCR Carriages

As shown in the SR Carriage Working Notice, Eastern Area
for 6th January, 1935

Set 761

4011	3rd Bke	
6233	Lav. Cpo.	C
6167	Compo.	

Set 762

4016	3rd Bke	
6227	Lav. Cpo.	R
4030	3rd Bke	

Set 763

4027	3rd Bke	
6228	Lav. Cpo.	R
4022	3rd Bke	

Set 764

4024	3rd Bke	
6166	Compo.	E

Set 765

3856	3rd Bke	
6110	Compo.	E

Set 767

4021	3rd Bke	
6226	Compo. Lav.	R
4035	3rd Bke	

Set 768

3886	3rd Bke	
6220	Lav. Cpo.	R
3896	3rd Bke	

Set 769

3912	3rd Bke	
6211	Lav. Cpo.	R
3947	3rd Bke	

Set 770

3904	3rd Bke	
6218	Lav. Cpo.	R
3948	3rd Bke	

Set 772

3878	3rd Bke	
6223	Lav. Cpo.	R
3885	3rd Bke	

Set 773

4014	3rd Bke	
6224	Lav. Cpo.	R
4023	3rd Bke	

Set 775

4002	3rd Bke	
6205	Lav. Cpo.	R
4003	3rd Bke	

Set 776

3893	3rd Bke	
6206	Lav. Cpo.	R
3975	3rd Bke	

Set 777

3879	3rd Bke	
6207	Lav. Cpo.	R
3924	3rd Bke	

Set 778

3803	3rd Bke	
-	Lav. Cpo.	R
-	3rd Bke	

Set 780

3857	3rd Bke	
6126	Compo.	E

Set 782

3858	3rd Bke	
6107	Compo.	E

Set 783

3992	3rd Bke	
6103	Compo.	E

Set 784

3891	3rd Bke	
6112	Compo.	E

Set 785

3957	3rd Bke	
6141	Compo.	E

Set 786

3994	3rd Bke	
6109	Compo.	E

Set 787

3981	3rd Bke	
6137	Compo.	E

Set 788

3877	3rd Bke	
6119	Compo.	W
3991	3rd Bke	

Set 789

3980	3rd Bke	
6152	Compo.	W
3990	3rd Bke	

Set 790

3900	3rd Bke	
6115	Compo.	E

Set 791

3905	3rd Bke	
6118	Compo.	C

Set 792

3908	3rd Bke	
-	Compo.	
3909	3rd Bke	

Set 793

3907	3rd Bke	
6146	Compo.	E
3910	3rd Bke	

Set 794

3959	3rd Bke	
6158	Compo.	
3999	3rd Bke	

Set 795

3862	3rd Bke	
6225	Lav. Cpo.	R
3926	3rd Bke	

Set 796

3936	3rd Bke	
6127	Compo.	E
3944	3rd Bke	

Set 797			Set 808			Set 823	
3890	3rd Bke		3897	3rd Bke		3872	3rd Bke	
6105	Compo.	W	6099	Compo.	W	6234	Lav. Cpo.	R
3989	3rd Bke		3960	3rd Bke		3874	3rd Bke	

Set 798			Set 809			Set 824	
3880	3rd Bke		3888	3rd Bke		3869	3rd Bke	
6159	Compo.		6121	Compo.	W	6171	Compo.	W
3931	3rd Bke		3983	3rd Bke		3871	3rd Bke	

Set 799			Set 810			Set 825	
3940	3rd Bke		3982	3rd Bke		3868	3rd Bke	
6124	Compo.	W	6140	Compo.	W	6168	Compo.	E
3950	3rd Bke		3995	3rd Bke				

Set 801			Set 813			Set 826	
4040	3rd Bke		3901	3rd Bke		3968	3rd Bke	
6149	Compo.	W	6162	Compo.	W	6232	Lav. Cpo.	R
4041	3rd Bke		3911	3rd Bke		4025	3rd Bke	

Set 802			Set 814			Set 828	
4006	3rd Bke		3917	3rd Bke		3864	3rd Bke	
6125	Compo.		6106	Compo.		6213	Lav. Cpo.	R
						4038	3rd Bke	

Set 803			Set 815			Set 829	
3941	3rd Bke		3943	3rd Bke		4026	3rd Bke	
6175	Lav. Cpo.	E	6235	Compo.		6157	Compo.	E
6147	Compo.							
3918	3rd Bke		Set 816			Set 840	
			3962	3rd Bke			Restr. 5	
Set 804			6132	Compo.	W	3818	Lav. 3rd Bke	
3932	3rd Bke		3986	3rd Bke		2184	Third	
6179	Lav. Cpo.	E				6277	Lav. Cpo.	C
6136	Compo.		Set 818			2338	Lav. 3rd	
3978	3rd Bke		3937	3rd Bke		3805	Lav. 3rd Bke	
			6156	Compo.				
Set 805			4004	3rd Bke		Set 847	
3914	3rd Bke					3865	3rd Bke	
6153	Compo.	W	Set 819			6209	Lav. Cpo.	R
3919	3rd Bke		3870	3rd Bke		3882	3rd Bke	
			6222	Lav. Cpo.	R			
			3987	3rd Bke				
Set 806			Set 820			Set 849	
3903	3rd Bke		3934	3rd Bke		3966	3rd Bke	
6108	Compo.		6210	Lav. Cpo.	R	6096	Compo.	
3988	3rd Bke		3993	3rd Bke		6176	Lav. Cpo.	
						6177	Lav. Cpo.	
Set 807			Set 821			6097	Compo.	C
3906	3rd Bke		4028	3rd Bke		6155	Compo.	
6129	Compo.	W	6230	Lav. Cpo.	R	6231	Lav. Cpo.	
3933	3rd Bke		4039	3rd Bke		6142	Compo.	
						4031	3rd Bke	

	Set 850			Set 875			Set 890	
4015	3rd Bke		3985	3rd Bke		3967	3rd Bke	
6216	Lav. Cpo.	R	6117	Compo.	W	6182	Lav. Cpo.	
4018	3rd Bke		3998	3rd Bke		5973	Compo.	C
						6111	Compo.	
	Set 851			Set 876		6165	Compo.	
3861	3rd Bke		3963	3rd Bke		3969	3rd Bke	
6217	Lav. Cpo.	R	6160	Compo.	E			
3929	3rd Bke						Set 891	
				Set 879		3996	3rd Bke	
	Set 852			Restr. 5		6122	Compo.	
3976	3rd Bke		7774	1st Bke		6101	Compo.	C
6187	Lav. Cpo.		2185	Third		6151	Compo.	
6134	Compo.	C	6272	Lav. Cpo.	C	6185	Lav. Cpo.	
5942	Compo.		6276	Lav. Cpo.		3938	3rd Bke	
6169	Compo.		3808	Lav. 3rd Bke				
3971	3rd Bke						Set 893	
				Set 880			Restr. 5	
	Set 853			Restr. 5		3812	Lav. 3rd Bke	
3952	3rd Bke		3809	Lav. 3rd Bke		6274	Lav. Cpo.	
6180	Lav. Cpo.		6197	Lav. Cpo.	C	6199	Lav. Cpo.	C
7596	First	E	3817	Lav. 3rd Bke		2182	Third	
2177	Lav. 3rd					3815	Lav. 3rd Bke	
3953	3rd Bke			Set 881				
				Restr. 5			Set 911	
	Set 857		3806	Lav. 3rd Bke		3921	3rd Bke	
3945	3rd Bke		2183	Third	C	6102	Compo.	C
6113	Compo.	E	6196	Lav. Cpo.				
			3807	Lav. 3rd Bke			Set 915	
	Set 859						9 Bogies.	C
3972	3rd Bke			Set 882				
6212	Lav. Cpo.	R		Restr. 5			Set 927	
3973	3rd Bke		3810	Lav. 3rd Bke			Restr. 5	
			2181	Third		3801	3rd Bke	
	Set 861		6195	Lav. Cpo.	C	2342	Lav. Third	
4019	3rd Bke		6198	Lav. Cpo.		6200	Lav. Cpo.	C
6229	Lav. Cpo.	R	4054	Lav. 3rd Bke		2333	Lav. Third	
4037	3rd Bke					4045	Lav. 3rd Bke	
				Set 883				
	Set 873			Restr. 5			Set 929	
3942	3rd Bke		3811	Lav. 3rd Bke			Restr. 5	
2032	Third		6281	Lav. Cpo.		7768	Lav. 1st Bke	
6183	Lav. Cpo.	C	6193	Lav. Cpo.	C	7629	Lav. 1st	
6173	Lav. Cpo.		2340	Lav. 3rd		7621	Lav. 1st	
2084	Third		3814	Lav. 3rd Bke		7637	Lav. 1st	
3895	3rd Bke					7630	Lav. 1st	W
				Set 885		7632	Lav. 1st	
	Set 874		3970	3rd Bke		7634	Lav. 1st	
3939	3rd Bke		6120	Compo.	W	7627	Lav. 1st	
6208	Lav. Cpo.	R	3977	3rd Bke		7771	1st Bke	
4000	3rd Bke							

Set 933			Set 934		
Restr. 5			Restr. 5		
7770	Lav.1st Bke		7772	1st Bke	
7638	Lav. 1st		7619	Lav. 1st	
7639	Lav. 1st		7633	Lav. 1st	
7641	Cor. 1st		7635	Lav. 1st	
7642	Cor. 1st	C	7628	Lav. 1st	W
7643	Lav. 1st		7620	Lav. 1st	
7640	Lav. 1st		7622	Lav. 1st	
7631?	Lav. 1st		7636	Lav. 1st	
7775	1st Bke		7773	1st Bke	

C - Allocated to Central Section. E - Allocated to Eastern Section. R - Rover Set. W - Allocated to Western Section.

Route Restriction 5 - Prohibited between Gipsy Hill and Crystal Palace (Low Level) and on former L&SW and SE&C (except Sets 929 and 934). Set 933 was additionally prohibited between Cooksbridge and Lewes.

Bibliography

This makes no claim for completeness, but the undermentioned books and articles may be found useful, if they can be obtained:

C. Hamilton Ellis, *The London, Brighton and South Coast Railway*, Ian Allan, 1960.
K. Marx and J. Minnis, *London, Brighton & South Coast Railway Album,* Ian Allan, 1982.
Ernest Protheroe, *Railways of the World*, Routledge, *c*.1911. Description of the 'City Limited', p. 430.
R.C. Riley, *Brighton Line Album*. Ian Allan, 1967.

Bluebell News
'Balloon' trailers. Vol. 14 No. 2 (1972), p. 53.
Directors' Saloon. Vol. 7 No. 4 (1965), p. 13; Vol. 7 No. 7 (1965) p.5; Vol. 8 No. 5 (1966), p. 70.
Barcombe Mills derailment. Vol. 11 (1969), p. 40.

Electric Railway Society Journal
S.C.W.S. [i.e. L.A. Mack] *The A.C. Stock of the LB&SCR and SR.* Series of articles between Sep. 1972 and Mar. 1974.

Model Railway News
'Balloon' trailers. Vol. 27 (1951), p.136.
Motor Luggage Vans. Vol. 40 (1964), p. 431.

Railway Magazine
Conversion of Motor Luggage Vans to Goods Brakes. Vol. 75 (1934) p. 144.
H.C. Hughes, *Southern Electric Coaching Stock.* Vol. 96 (1950), p. 507.
C.E. Lee, *London's Elevated Electric.* Vol. 105 (1959), p. 813.

Model Railway Constructor
Ellipt. 3rds, Lav. Tri-Compos, 3rd Brakes, 1st Brakes. Vol. 38 (1971) pp. 388, 389.
Ellipt. Compos, Lav. 2nds. Vol. 38 (1971) p. 422.
Rebuilt 3rd Brakes. Vol. 39 (1972) p. 268.
48 ft 1sts, Lav. Compos, 3rd Brakes, 3rds. Vol. 39 (1972) pp. 305-8.
Ellipt. Lav. Compos, Lav. 3rd Brakes. Vol. 40 (1973) pp 22, 23.
Royal Saloons. Vol. 42 (1975) pp. 233-5.
Rebuilt Compos and 3rd Brakes. Vol. 43 (1976) p. 308.
Push-and-pull sets. Vol. 47 (1980) pp. 32, 96, 544, 608. Vol. 49 (1982) pp. 96, 224.
Isle of Wight coaches. Vol. 30 (1963) pp. 178, 182.
Isle of Wight rebuilt Third. Vol. 35 (1966) p. 166.

Index

INDEX TO DRAWINGS

All drawings of carriage side and end elevations are reproduced to a scale of 3 mm to one foot. Details such as grab-handles, door handles, lamp tops, etc. are omitted from most of the drawings.